Going Through Hell
to Get to Heaven

— • • —

Dr. Scot Hodkiewicz

Published by KiCam Projects
109 N. Main St.
Georgetown, OH 45121

KiCamProjects.com

ISBN (paperback): 978-0-9991581-6-6
e-ISBN: 978-0-9991581-7-3

Library of Congress Control Number: 2018947932

Cover and book design by Mark Sullivan
Printed in the United States of America

DEDICATION

There are a lot of people who are the reason I wrote this story. Certainly those most important in my life are my wife, Mona, and my three kids, Alexa, Victoria, and Chase. They are the inspiration for everything I do and this book is no different. We, as the story will demonstrate, have been through great pain, fear, and doubt. But those same experiences have brought us great joy and strength. To them, I dedicate this book. I really wrote it to tell *our* story, not mine.

Yet, there are many others to whom I owe a great debt. Many of them I either never met or never knew by their names. They are the "angels" I mention throughout the story, the men and women who stepped forward when they were needed to do what was good and right. Whether it was Dr. Lang, who was so pivotal in the events of my life, or the unknown people who seemingly appeared, did what God had put them in place to do, and then just as quickly vanished, never to be seen again. These were all angels in our lives, and it is to them that I also dedicate this book; the people who took action, who refused to sit by and do nothing, the ones who needed no recognition, no glory. In fact, many probably never got anything for their services other than the joy of knowing they made a difference—that one day, they were in the right spot at the right time and jumped in to help someone else. These are the angels in our lives whom I now strive to emulate. These people, placed so carefully in our lives at just the right time and in just the right circumstance, I will never be able to repay. It is to the angels here on earth that I dedicate this book.

But in keeping with this effort to repay what is owed, a portion of all proceeds from this book will go to various charities whose purposes are to be angels to others in need.

CONTENTS

FOREWORD

On a fall day in 2006, we received an emergency call informing us that Dr. Scot and his family had been in a horrific automobile crash. While everyone in the family sustained injuries, Scot's were so extensive that the staff confided in us it would take nothing short of a miracle for him to survive. Those words proved to be prophetic.

What you are about to read is the unfolding story of many miracles that would ultimately bless the Hodkiewicz family, our church, the community, and every reader.

This book is so gripping, we guarantee you won't be able to put it down and will want to give a copy to everyone you know. Scot humbly tells his story with raw honesty, searing personal insights, and a degree of vulnerability rarely put in print.

Skating so close to death and being utterly helpless opened Scot's mind to the deeper meaning of life. Where was God in the midst of his extensive, life-threatening injuries?

The Bible says, "Suffering produces endurance" (Romans 5:3).

We have never seen anyone work harder than Scot did at enduring multiple surgeries and torturous physical therapy. But those challenges were so agonizing, they kindled a rage that Scot admits was far more destructive than his physical injuries.

Scot's fury at the drunk driver who caused the crash consumed him. As you read this book, you'll discover the personal revelation that caused Scot to examine his own culpability, birthing in him what he calls a much-needed humility.

"Endurance produces character," Scripture continues (Romans 5:4). A humbled Scot was transformed as he changed his focus to what he describes as his own shortcomings. God was doing great work recreating Scot's heart as he endured the demands of his recovery.

Scot diligently studied God's Word, facilitated Bible studies at church, helped lead numerous mission trips, and served as our congregational president.

In addition to being Scot's personal account, this book has a wider reach, pressing us all to examine what we most value: our priorities, our relationship with God, and how we might use our lives to better serve others.

There is nothing theoretical about this book. It's the real deal. Scot takes the reader on a roller coaster of emotions, with agonizing valleys of despair, the tenacity to endure seemingly impossible challenges, and stunning small victories that restored not only his body but also his spirit.

This book is a testament to courage, perseverance, the power of the human spirit, and the ways God is able to do immeasurably more than all we could ask or imagine.

—*Pastors Mary Ann and Mark Moller-Gunderson*

CHAPTER 1

MY GREAT PLAN

I thought I had a great plan.

I had always done well in school. I was valedictorian at my high school graduation and ranked second in my undergraduate class in college, although I never received my undergraduate degree. Because I had been accepted into veterinary school, I left a year early to fulfill my dream of working in medicine. Why veterinary school? In spite of my academic accomplishments, I was shy as an adolescent, with a bit of an inferiority complex; becoming a top-notch physician and taking on the responsibility of treating people seemed too much for me to handle. When you're lacking in confidence, putting another human being's life in your hands is way too risky. So instead, I became a veterinarian.

Of course, I still have to cope with a great deal of pressure as a vet because my patients are often regarded as members of the family. Yet it pales in comparison to what physicians face every day. Even now, losing someone's beloved pet rattles me, but losing someone's child or spouse would haunt me forever. During my training, I discovered that veterinary medicine fit my personality perfectly; I absolutely *loved* it. I enjoyed the challenge of medicine and the freedom that working with animals affords. Because I was in my element, I developed confidence, lost my shyness, and blossomed. This career just made sense to me; I had found my calling. Four years later, I graduated at the top of my veterinary class with job offers everywhere I applied.

My great plan.

Step One: Become a vet. Step Two: Get a good job. Step Three: Get married and start a family.

Right out of vet school I married Mona—a beautiful, intelligent woman from the veterinary class behind me. Because she had her pick of guys, I felt incredibly lucky to have won her over. Mona and I began working at a mixed animal practice where we treated dogs and cats as well as farm animals. Here, I perfected my craft and honed my skills by developing a specialty in surgery. I became especially adept at orthopedics—fixing broken bones.

Soon after, we started our family. With the birth of our first child, Alexa, we took yet another step on my carefully laid-out plan.

The last step? Open our own veterinary hospital.

Five years after graduation, Mona and I got our chance and moved to a beautiful area in Lake Geneva, Wisconsin. Home to about ten thousand residents, this Midwestern town boasts a gorgeous lake and constant activity, in addition to safe neighborhoods and great schools—the perfect place for us to raise our family. We spent the next eight years building a successful veterinary practice and expanding our family to include another daughter, Victoria, and a son, Chase.

Life was good. I truly believed the hard part was over—the sixty-hour workweeks spent building a new business and the constant reading and studying to sharpen my skills in surgery and medicine. All of this was winding down and life was getting progressively easier. We'd survived the baby stages and the terrible twos, having changed countless diapers and dealt with constantly interrupted sleep, courtesy of either crying kids or emergency calls.

The rest of my plan was simple. We'd already put in the hard work building a practice and raising the kids so we could coast by the time they grew into teenagers. At that time, we would hire more staff, work fewer hours, and play more. With our eyes on retirement at sixty, we'd practice veterinary medicine for another twenty years, then sell the business for a bunch of money. Thereafter, we would travel. Yes, sir. We had it all figured out. By sticking to our great plan, we were now in complete control of our lives as successful business owners, parents, and pet owners (even our dogs listened well). Not only were we making good money, we were the toast of the town—regular invitees to the best parties and events hosted by the wealthiest people in Lake Geneva, most of whom were also our clients.

Was it any wonder Mona and I were absolutely convinced we could handle anything life threw at us?

We'd built it all ourselves without any help from anyone else. I figured now I could sit down and write a self-help book about my great plan, in which I'd tell others how to build the perfect life. People would rush to read all about it. It would be a bestseller and elevate me to a whole new level of success, with Oprah and Dr. Phil calling to interview the young veterinarian who had achieved it all by his late thirties.

Yeah, great plan.

Then came that fateful October. We were returning home from our cabin in northern Wisconsin following our "get ready for winter" weekend. The boat needed to be winterized and the dealer up north had offered a special deal: "Saturday only, winterization for $65." Since the winterization down where I lived often cost over $200, this was a bargain I couldn't resist. (Boy, was I smart!)

Of course, the cabin required some maintenance too. The gutters were full of pine needles, and a few windows were in desperate need of caulking. Soon snow would be piling up two feet high on the roof (and in the driveway, on the roads, and everywhere else). Although there were also some dead trees around the property in need of cutting, I figured that task could wait until the next time we were up. No rush, plenty of time.

The weekend had been productive but still fun. Our cabin had no TV—just the way we like it—so we spent most of our time outside fishing (or at least *trying*, since we've never had much luck on the lake) and hiking with our two dogs (a Golden Retriever named Annabelle and a little Yorkie-poo named Olivia). We made "pudgie pies," a family tradition of meat, spaghetti sauce, and cheese cooked in a sandwich iron over a fire. We talked and ate s'mores around the bonfire until either the weather or the mosquitoes chased us inside, where we then played Clue and Battleship. Often the night ended with blackjack, which is a pretty easy game to understand for three little kids. In fact, at the last parent-teacher conference prior to this October weekend, Chase's teacher had commented on my son's remarkable addition abilities as a pre-K student. When I replied that Chase was really good at adding to twenty-one, I got the "bad parent" look and a kick from Mona under the table. At the ripe old age of four, Chase already was becoming quite a little card shark!

I love fall in Wisconsin. Actually, I enjoy all the seasons here—hot summers, cold winters, and beautiful springs—but fall is by far my favorite. Wisconsin is known for long, frigid winters, Packers games at Lambeau Field, and brats on the grill. When most people think of Wisconsin, they automatically start to shiver. To me, there is nothing better than being in a warm sweatshirt next to a hot fire with a book in hand when the leaves are changing colors. During that October weekend, the temperature had ranged from high fifties during the day to low forties at night. Fall is the season when fishing picks up and we toss footballs in the driveway. It's the time of year when being at the cabin is all about campfires in the cool nights, countless twinkling stars, a crackling fireplace, and a thick, warm comforter.

By Sunday we'd completed our chores and playtime at the cabin; it was time to head home. To avoid traffic, we'd left early. There are typically a lot of cars heading back from northern Wisconsin on Sunday nights, so we got on the road around noon. Naturally, I timed the three-hour trip so I could listen to the Packers game on the way, having been a die-hard fan since I was a kid. My dad was at the famous Ice Bowl of 1963 (game-time temperature of minus-thirteen degrees), when the Packers beat the Cowboys on a last-second quarterback sneak by Bart Starr. Of course, half of Wisconsin claims to have been there!

Because Mona does not share my enthusiasm for the Green and Gold, she sleeps when we drive so I can listen to the game. Our minivan was also equipped with a DVD for the kids, who sat with their headphones on, watching a Scooby-Doo cartoon. Mona and the dogs, exhausted from the activity of the previous forty-eight hours, drifted off to sleep. As per her habit, Mona doesn't even try to stay awake and is usually asleep within a mile or two of leaving, feet propped up on the dash and seat set as far back as possible.

This was the very definition of peace and tranquility: wife asleep, kids watching a video, and a football game playing on the radio. It was *my* idea of heaven. The leaves were changing and the temperature was a pleasant fifty-five degrees. The Packers were having a good season, with a high probability of making the playoffs. All was right in my world.

Yes indeed, my plan had come together perfectly. What could possibly go wrong?

Although an avid fan, I was not really listening to the game that day because I was busy using the time to figure out ways to make the veterinary clinic more successful, i.e., more *profitable.*

What if I learned to do a different surgery or added another piece of equipment? How much money would that bring in? Could I raise my prices or cut back on staff? The business was booming and my focus had shifted. When I started, I wanted nothing to do with the business side; I just wanted to work on my patients. Now I'd set my sights on how much money I could make, doing what Americans naturally do—pursuing happiness through the accumulation of wealth. And why not? Our earnings were already paying for our cabin in the woods; what was wrong with wanting more?

Truth be told, I was losing my way by chasing other people's definition of the American dream. Although I did have some misgivings about my relatively new and nearly exclusive focus on income versus the care and healing of animals, I'd usually brush them off. After all, I was making good money, running with the wealthy in town, enjoying the respect of my community, and buying anything I wanted. And still, I wanted even more.

Oh yes, I had it all figured out. Life was perfect. We would miss church again this Sunday, but who cared? We hadn't really been going much anyway, because we were just too busy living the dream. At some later point, we'd start to attend more regularly. Plenty of time for that.

I don't remember the impact.

I heard and felt nothing. The only thing I know is what witnesses have told me. The other car was a 2005 Jeep, purchased from a dealer the day before by a drunk driver with a record of seven DUIs and a suspended driver's license (it is legal to sell a car to someone with no legal way to drive it in Wisconsin). Today would be his eighth offense. The driver, a man about my age whom I'll call Mike Jacobs (that's not his real name), had spent the morning driving around with a case of Miller High Life in the car. He had stopped by his mother's house that morning already drunk but had driven away (she had not even tried to stop him) and continued guzzling beer. He had already spent seven years in prison, three after his sixth DUI, and four after his seventh. As soon as he'd get out, he'd start drinking all over again.

Jacobs was out on parole the day of the accident, but like every other time prior to that, it mattered little to him. He'd violated the conditions of his parole numerous times since his last stint in prison. The pattern would go like this: His mother would call his parole officer to report he was drinking again; the parole officer would stop by his house, see beer in the fridge and empty cans all over the place (a condition of parole was that no alcohol could be on the premises); give Jacobs a warning; and leave. *Nothing* had been done. Jacobs had been caught driving drunk a month earlier in a hotel parking lot and once again let off with only a warning. In Wisconsin, DUI can be charged only if you are on a public road. On that particular day, he had been in violation of his parole since he wasn't supposed to drink in the first place. He was not allowed to be in possession of car keys—much less drive a car—after consuming alcohol. Although Jacobs could have been sent back to serve more prison time, instead he was given another meaningless warning. These warnings and threats of punishment carried no weight, and he knew it. By one o'clock on this particular Sunday afternoon, he was over halfway through another case of beer.

Our decision to leave early that day to avoid the worst traffic put us directly in his path. Mike Jacobs was going to change everything I knew, everything that was so right in my perfect world, and my perfect plan. Good thing I hadn't written my self-help book yet.

About halfway home, just outside of Madison, Wisconsin, the crash happened. Jacobs was heading north on I-94; we were heading south. The median at that point was about fifteen feet across, and there was no guardrail—only a shallow ditch to separate the north-bound and southbound lanes. I was probably going about seventy miles per hour, as was Jacobs. Though I don't remember anything about the collision, Mona does. She had drifted off to sleep but was awakened by my voice. I can't say I muttered anything too intelligent or profound as I realized there was a Jeep about to hit us. My words of wisdom after being the class valedictorian and becoming a doctor were, "Oh shit!"

That is about all I had time to say, and it pretty much summed up what was about to happen: Our lives were about to change forever, and we all were going to go through a lot of shit.

It is humbling to consider the force such a crash can generate. It spun a fifteen-hundred-pound vehicle one and a half times, moved the front end and engine by a foot and a half, and still had enough energy to smash bones and mangle bodies. The impact was simply incredible.

I always figured that in a crash I could "just hold on" and ride it out. I was in pretty good shape at thirty-eight and had never had any serious injuries. My job as a veterinarian kept me on my feet for eight hours straight and required lifting dogs weighing over one hundred pounds (the one-hundred-fifty-pounders I no longer lifted by myself like I used to). At the start of my veterinary career, I had done 50 percent dairy work, which meant dealing with very large and often stubborn animals, so I was in decent shape. I had kept my weight fairly well in check at about one hundred seventy-five pounds on a five-foot, ten-inch frame. Not bad for a guy pushing forty, but still no match for the pounding I was about to take from a half-ton vehicle hitting us at a combined closing speed of one hundred forty miles per hour.

The half-second I had to react gave me no time and no good options. They were basically limited to turn right, turn left, stop, or speed up. Actually, stopping was never an option, since I was going way too fast. I instinctively hit the brakes but had no way of avoiding a collision. Plus, Jacobs was drunk or passed out and not trying to stop anyway. Speeding up isn't an option either when a car is careening toward you in your lane while you're driving a minivan not known for its great acceleration. Turning left would have turned us into the Jeep coming across the median from the other direction; that didn't seem like a very smart choice. Turning right would have put Jacobs's front end into my door or, worse yet, into my son, Chase's, door (he was strapped into his car seat right behind me). That would have put three inches of door between us and the front of Jacobs's car as it sped right into us. There were no good choices: The crash was going to happen, and it was going to hurt. All that could save us was the car's engineering and God's help. As for me, the only thing I could do was hit the brakes and hold on for dear life.

"Oh shit!"

The front corner of Jacobs's Jeep hit the front driver's-side corner of our van. The engine was instantly pushed back, forcing the driver's compartment back into my legs. The van spun, coming to a rest on the exterior guardrail three lanes over facing the opposite direction. The impact smashed my body with such force that multiple bones shattered instantly. Bones in my arms, legs, pelvis, and nose were all broken. In spite of the airbag and seat belt, the impact to my chest and abdomen ruptured vessels, causing massive internal bleeding. Mona was thrown forward and to the right, her head impacting the car door, knocking her unconscious. The kids were whipped violently forward and sideways. For us to just survive this amount of impact would be a miracle.

There was nothing I could do. And in the end, I didn't do much. I simply hit the brakes. I didn't even swerve, because it happened too fast. I just braked and braced for impact, knowing our lives were about to change in a very bad way. The crash was completely out of my control. And it was definitely *not* part of my perfect plan.

For Reflection

The heart of man plans his way, but the Lord *establishes his steps. (Proverbs 16:9)*

1. Have you ever had a plan for your life that changed?
2. Have you ever been without a plan at all?
3. How often have your plans come to fruition?
4. Is planning for the future worthwhile?

CHAPTER 2

Is This How It Ends?

Some things went right. Because they'd been fastened correctly, the car seats and seat belts for the kids did their jobs. Though not a huge car, the minivan had some mass to it. A small, fuel-efficient car might be great when you fill up the tank, but not when you have to survive a head-on crash with a Jeep at seventy miles per hour. Here, size mattered.

Airbags cushioned the blow for Mona and me, but an impact was inevitable. There is no airbag in the world that can protect a body from this kind of hit. The injuries were going to be severe, and the pain was going to be intense—there was just no way around it.

Incredibly, nobody else was hit as our cars were spinning to a stop. The impact was head-on but mostly on my side. Although the driver's side was completely smashed in, our car was able to spin off, thereby dissipating a ton of energy that otherwise would have been transferred to us.

I had done what is natural during a crash; I locked my arms against the wheel, pushed both feet to the floor, and braced for impact. Though I don't think you can consciously change this kind of reaction, it is ultimately the worst thing to do because it results in what doctors later told me were "aviator injuries." These are the injuries typically seen in pilots after plane crashes in which you lock your elbows to hold the steering wheel, push one foot onto the brake and the other against the floor, while wedging your pelvis against the seat and locking your knees. Then on impact, your body continues forward at whatever speed you were traveling. The seat belt holds your body back, but the steering wheel, dash, and floorboards are now hurtling at you with your hands and feet pushed against them. With my elbows and knees locked like that, the bones had to give. The force was just too overwhelming.

When the cars collided, my heels were both firmly anchored against the floorboards, which now began moving at seventy miles per hour right back at me. The result was two smashed heels and a broken ankle—the first of my "aviator injuries."

Higher up, the steering wheel pushed into my now straightened arms and locked elbows. The elbows bent backward, shattering the bones. With bones no longer held in place and elbows dislocated, my hands fell to the side, the joint grotesquely bent beyond anything that could be normal.

Because of my elbows' locked position on impact, the force continued up my left arm. The bone broke just below the shoulder while simultaneously forcing the shoulder out of joint. I was left with the ball of the shoulder sitting behind my back and my arm twisted over ninety degrees past where it would normally go. If I could have looked, I would have seen the back of my elbow.

Though I hit the airbag and was seat-belted in, my upper body did not escape unharmed. Safety advances notwithstanding, your chest still hits the seat belt and airbag at seventy miles per hour, much like doing a belly flop off a three-story building onto a ten-inch pillow. The impact tore vessels in my lungs, liver, and spleen, initiating a gusher of blood. Bleeding in the lungs fills them up like a sponge absorbing water. As the blood saturates the little air sacs, it stops the lungs from getting oxygen. Once too much blood filled the air sacs, I would suffocate to death. Worse yet, there is no way to stop bleeding in the lungs once it starts. Even if medics got there in time, they could not apply pressure or a tourniquet. Either the bleeding would stop on its own or I would die. As I struggled to take in air, every breath became a bit shallower.

In my abdomen, the impact tore my spleen. The spleen is a highly vascular organ that sits just below the ribcage on the left side—which was where Jacobs slammed into us. The spleen's large blood supply practically guarantees it will bleed profusely when ruptured. My spleen tore in half, and its three large arteries began pumping blood into my abdomen.

Like the spleen, the liver is also very vascular because its job is to filter blood. On impact with the seat belt and airbag, my liver—a three-pound sack of potatoes—went from seventy miles per hour to zero. Its forward progress had been stopped only by my ribs, which already had been arrested by the airbag. Luckily, the tough outer capsule that encloses the liver did not tear through, which helped contain the bleeding. A large clot would inevitably develop, but a tear in the capsule would have been catastrophic. That capsule is less than a sixteenth of an inch thick. My survival—my entire life—hung on something that thin.

To stand a chance, I needed all these injuries to clot and the bleeding to stop or at the very least slow down until I could get to a hospital. In addition to the torn major vessels, thousands of smaller vessels tore as well. Their success in clotting would determine whether I lived or died.

It never occurred to me that someday my life would be saved by some nameless, faceless engineers in Detroit, but the van design had helped to lessen the blow. It had been engineered with "crumple zones" in the front that allow certain areas of the front end to accordion in or "crumple" while the areas around the passengers remained intact. The bending of the frame and metal exterior used up much of the energy without transferring it to the passenger compartment. The more solid areas resist crumpling while redirecting the big, heavy engine away from the "vital" areas. It moved toward us but in a downward direction, which saved Mona and me from enduring a thousand pounds of hot metal being pushed back into our laps, burning and crushing our chests and abdomens. This almost certainly would have been fatal for both of us.

Unfortunately, my legs were not in that vital area and were going to be crushed—the price that must be paid in order to protect the organs higher up in the body. An impact like this is simply too much for any engineering to absorb; it is just impossible to protect everything from this amount of force. The crush of metal and plastic had missed my chest and abdomen, giving my heart a place to beat and my lungs a place to expand but nowhere for my legs to go. On impact, the dash was pushed back and down, thus pinning my left knee against the front edge of the seat, while the rest of my body above the knee was still moving forward. Something had to give. Although the thighbone, the femur, is the biggest bone in the body, it had no chance of resisting this kind of force. It snapped instantly, shattering into multiple pieces. The jagged end was driven like a spear, cutting through the thick quad muscle on the outside of the thigh, the shards of bone exploding through the skin like shrapnel.

The impact traveling through my legs from the floor broke my pelvis. The pelvis is a "box of bone," multiple bones all fused together to make a solid "box." Any solid box must break in at least two spots (take a box and try it), and my pelvis was no exception to the rule. Add two more fractured bones to the list.

We didn't know it then, but this break in my thigh would nearly kill me more than once. It takes an awful lot of trauma to break a thighbone, and mine had shattered just above the knee. As the upper thighbone bone blew out the side, the lower part of the fractured bone cut in to the inside where the femoral artery and vein are located. Because the artery and vein are each about the size of an index finger, a tear in either will kill you very quickly. And since they run right next to each other, there is almost always damage to both in a case like this. A tear in the vein will result in a gusher of blood fast enough to cause death in five minutes, a tear in the artery two minutes, and a tear in both just one minute. My vein was sliced in half by a three-inch-thick piece of jagged bone, but somehow it missed the artery entirely. Another bit of luck that would give me a chance to survive.

As a result of the collision and the vehicle spinning, my nose had been broken, bent flat against my face as I hit the airbag. However, Mona got it the worst. First, her head hit the airbag before smashing against the side window. Then it impacted the door at whatever speed we were spinning in, while her brain hit the inside of her skull at the same velocity. Being pretty tough, the skull withstood the impact, but since the brain is soft and "floats" inside the skull in a very thin layer of fluid, it does not handle impact well. Consequently, we were both knocked unconscious.

On impact, the nerve impulses went haywire. There are literally billions of connections between the nerves in the brain; millions of them are firing off at any one time. All were shaken with such violent force that the signals—so very well organized a second ago—were now a jumbled mess. Like a computer with a frazzled hard drive, our brains shut down to protect themselves. Fortunately, the basic but essential functions like heartbeat and breathing continued working because they are controlled in the brain stem, buried deep away from the skull. However, the more complex functions of conscious thought, information-processing, logic, speech, and memory abruptly ceased. Mona and I had been completely knocked out until our brains could reboot—if they ever would.

As Mona spun, she was forced against the door. Attached to the seat by the seat belt, her butt moved with the car to the left, but her top half did not. The force of the twisting overwhelmed the three bones in the middle of her back, breaking them instantly. Exactly how they had fractured and whether they'd hit the vital spinal cord running through the middle of them would determine if she would ever feel her legs again. In that horrific moment, there was no way to tell; she was out cold.

Once the van stopped, debris had been thrown all over the road and the engine boiled steam. I sat pinned in with a torn femoral vein, ruptured spleen, and multiple other sources of bleeding, with the nearest ambulance fifteen minutes away and the nearest hospital another twenty minutes beyond that. All signs pointed to me being a dead man.

What saved me? A wild stroke of luck and those crumple zones. When the dashboard moved back and down, it pinned my leg, crushed the muscle, and locked me to the seat, but it also applied enough pressure to hold off the torn vein and limit the blood loss until the paramedics arrived. In fact, there was surprisingly little blood in the car when I was removed. Pictures of the car afterward showed hardly any blood on the seat. By the time the helicopter and paramedics arrived, twenty minutes had passed; I should have bled to death. But the crushing weight of the car held off the bleeding long enough for help to arrive.

Obviously, the impact and spin would have killed us all had we not been securely buckled. Wisconsin, like most states, has a mandatory seat belt law for adults, and all kids must be in child seats or boosters until seven years of age. I remember when the law passed I was completely against this invasion of my freedom because it was my choice whether or not to wear a seat belt. The government had no right to interfere in my life. Furthermore, I had grown up long before this law was passed and never used seat belts. Turned out, this invasion of privacy by the ever-intrusive government would ultimately save our lives. I had been wrong; thank God they had been smart enough to enact this law.

The kids were buckled in in the back, and because we hit head-on, they were mostly protected—at least physically. Chase, our four-year-old, was in a car seat with a five-point harness, but his little body was deeply bruised by the belts. Flying glass cut his face, chest, and hands. Today he will proudly show you the scars that signify his bravery, but at the time he just hurt all over. The glass sliced into his shirt so badly it looked like moths had eaten it.

Victoria, our seven-year-old, was in the far back and buckled with a shoulder strap and a booster seat. Although she was at an age when she'd soon be out of boosters, she was in one that day. Though severely shaken up and bruised by the straps, she was otherwise all right.

Alexa, our oldest, was in a seat belt but did not have a shoulder strap, so she was thrown around harder, especially during the spin. We had been traveling with an antique chicken coop Mona and the kids had found at a flea market that weekend. The kids had started raising chickens in the backyard and were a bit crazy about them. Alexa was excited to have found this coop and couldn't wait to bring it back for her birds. As the car spiraled out of control, the chicken coop smashed against her left arm, breaking it near the shoulder. As for the coop, it was so badly damaged, it had to be thrown out. Even the chickens were going to have a tough few months in the cold winter.

The only ones not buckled in—our family dogs—were tossed around like rag dolls. Having been sitting on Chase's lap when Jacobs slammed into our van, our eight-pound Yorkie, Olivia, endured the worst, having been ejected through the side window. Her head hit it with enough force to shatter the glass and hurl her body out of the car. Though the skull is a very hard bone, she was an eight-pound dog breaking quarter-inch-thick tempered glass. As with Mona's concussion, the dog's brain bounced off the inside of her skull as it hit the window. Olivia fractured her skull and immediately began to have a seizure as she landed outside of the van. Ultimately, the state patrol would cover her with a blanket, expecting her to die.

Annabelle, the Golden Retriever, was thrown against the vehicle door, bruised and terrified. As soon as she could get out, she fled, disappearing into the surrounding countryside. More concerned for the human family injured in the terrible accident than their dog, everyone let her go. Our beloved pet was on her own, beaten up, terrified, and lost in a cornfield sixty miles from home.

Within a few seconds, we had gone from a normal, healthy family traveling with hundreds of other cars down the highway to a mangled mess of broken and battered bodies. Our perfect plan was not to be; another plan was starting to unfold, one over which we had no control. The one that Mona and I had worked so hard to achieve was gone forever, and life would never be the same. I didn't know at that time just how much our lives were about to change. We hadn't considered or anticipated this unwelcome fork in the road. And where the road now led, nobody could predict. We had no plan now; we just were hoping to take another breath.

FOR REFLECTION

For everything there is a season, and a time for every matter under heaven. (Ecclesiastes 3:1)

1. Have you ever had a near-death experience? If so, how did it change you?

2. Have you ever had to help during an accident or emergency? Were you trained to help, or did you just do what you could?

3. Should the government implement safety laws, such as mandatory seat belts, or should we rely on God to protect us? I was initially against mandatory seat belt laws. Have you ever been saved or helped by something you were initially against?

CHAPTER 3

ANGELS APPEAR

In the aftermath of the accident, people stopped immediately and rushed to the van. They had no choice but to stop, since there was debris all over the road and two cars now blocking three lanes of traffic.

They hurried to open the doors in the hope of freeing us, but the van was locked. Since Mona and I were both unconscious and all three kids were in shock, we were oblivious to pounding fists on the windows. Some folks ran to get gloves to pull out the smashed glass and get inside. Steam billowed from the ruptured radiator while the smell of burning rubber permeated the air. The threat of fire was foremost on everyone's mind. With the doors locked, kids buckled in, and two unconscious people in the front, the flames would consume us all very quickly as the horrified crowd stood by, helplessly watching and listening to us burn to death. They had to get the doors open.

It was Alexa, our ten-year-old, who stepped up. She was belted in the back and unable to reach any door, broken left arm lying limply by her side. So she did the only thing she could: She yelled to her mother, "Mom, wake up, *wake up*! The doors are locked. *Mom, you need to unlock the doors*!" It took a minute of constant yelling for a seriously dazed Mona to comprehend the instructions, but Alexa didn't give up until she was heard. That's when Victoria and Chase began to cry while our would-be rescuers kept pounding on the glass.

Alexa looked at the people trying to get in and noticed one in particular, a man in his thirties with a small beard and mustache. He had blood running down his face from a cut on his nose. As she gazed at him, he gazed back at her before abruptly turning to leave. She would lay eyes on that face again sometime later in the newspaper. It was Mike Jacobs, the man who had just nearly killed us.

Mona started to come around and felt for the button to unlock the doors. She didn't know if the electric locks would work and wasn't aware enough to even realize what she was doing. She just obeyed Alexa's urgent commands to open the door locks. After trying every button, Mona finally hit the right one. She drifted back to unconsciousness while our Good Samaritans yanked open the doors and flooded in to help us.

Neither Mona nor I was in any shape to move; luckily, no one attempted to make us try. By now, the kids were more awake and able to get out of the crushed minivan. If the vehicle caught on fire, at least the kids would be safely out of harm's way. Onlookers dialed 911 from their cellphones, and traffic on the interstate came to a complete stop, creating a traffic jam that would stretch for twenty miles.

Within minutes of opening the doors, the kids were taken off to the side of the road as people wrapped them in blankets taken from their own vehicles. It was about fifty degrees outside, and none of the kids was wearing a coat. Three women appearing like angels held them close, comforting them. One held Victoria in a blanket and gently rocked her while she sang a hymn. I never did find out the names of these earth angels who appeared seemingly out of nowhere and took care of my children. They had been placed there at the right time to do what they could: hold each child in a warm embrace until the police and paramedics could take them to a hospital. The one thing they were powerless to do was tell them that their parents would be okay. I was still unconscious and starting to cough up blood. Mona was slowly coming around but had obviously taken a major impact to the head. It certainly did not look good. Then more angels started to appear.

Mona's angel was a large, bearded man who looked like he carried boulders for a living. He had yanked her door open and stayed with her, trying to calm her as her brain began to process what had happened. In spite of the horrific crash and a serious back injury, Mona kept fighting her way out. Her angel held her in her seat and told her to not move, to wait for the ambulance, and to keep talking to him. Mona kept repeating that her back hurt. He would repeat in response: "Don't move. Let the paramedics check you out. They are almost here; just don't move." Mona started to unfasten her seat belt in an effort to free herself from the van. Once again, this man stopped her. He soon realized she was oblivious to anything he said; she just kept repeating herself, unaware that she had just said the same thing ten seconds earlier. Most people would have become frustrated with this strange, crazy woman who refused to follow the simple instructions to sit still and wait, but this burly angel patiently talked to Mona, keeping her still and in place by holding one powerful hand on her shoulder. He never lost his cool or raised his voice. Mona might have been able to push past a smaller person, or one that was not so determined to keep her still, but she could not prevail against this unyielding force. Even with a scrambled brain, she eventually understood that trying to overcome him would be futile. By the grace of God, he'd been the first to arrive at Mona's side just when she needed a person with the calm understanding and the pure brute strength to keep her in place—an angel with muscle.

A man rushed to my aid also. It was obvious I'd sustained severe injuries: Blood was streaming down my face through my broken nose while I simultaneously coughed it up from my lungs. My rescuer could hear the gurgling as I struggled to take each successive breath with more and more blood in my throat. I was drifting in and out of consciousness with my right arm lying down by my side—bent backward and twisted, obviously broken. My twisted left arm was limp by my other side and the palm was turned thirty degrees beyond where I could have placed it normally. It was not only broken in three places but dislocated in two, with the elbow smashed and the ball of the shoulder joint now sitting four inches past where it should have been. All this man could say was, "The kids are okay and you are going to be all right."

A well-intentioned lie. The kids were anything *but* okay; they were terrified and hurt. And I looked far from all right.

Soon, I could hear sirens in the distance.

The state patrol arrived first. I never thought I'd feel this way, but their sirens and lights were soothing; this modern-day bugle cry signaled that our cavalry was here and that the paramedics would soon take over. Our angels at the scene were there to comfort us, but we needed much more than comfort.

The highway patrol took over the scene and ordered the paramedics to hurry. After one look at me, they called for a helicopter; I would need to be airlifted out. Although we were only about ten miles from the University of Wisconsin teaching hospital—a Level I Class-A trauma hospital—an ambulance would have been too slow. A winding path through city traffic guaranteed certain death, so a helicopter was my only hope.

The paramedics were arriving to deal with the injuries and the fire department was in charge of getting me out. The police started interviewing witnesses to determine what had happened. The Jeep that had hit us was now resting on the side of the highway, but its driver was long gone. No one had seen him leave, and no one could describe him with any more detail than that he was a white man sporting a goatee. While the witnesses had concentrated on helping us, the other driver had just slipped away. The police immediately called in the license plate to track down the owner. It came back registered to Mike Jacobs.

All things considered, it was a miracle that the kids were pretty well intact with no life-threatening injuries; the down side was that they remember it all. Oddly, the thing Alexa remembers most was the smell—the stench of burning rubber permeated us all, and even a week later, she could still smell it in her hair and on her skin. It just refused to wash off, a constant reminder that her life was now completely changed. The kids also remember the noises—tires screeching, glass shattering, and metal bending.

Worst were the voices: mine yelling out and Mona's screaming. Then the unforgettable sounds of wailing police cars and fire truck sirens, Mona's shrieks of pain, police converging upon the scene. After my initial "Oh shit!" I was quiet, save for the gurgling sounds I made as I struggled to breathe past the blood.

Victoria was the most shaken. She had been farthest in the back and the most protected during the crash, enabling her to hear and see it all. Now she was on the outside sitting with her angels on the guardrail as the paramedics began to extricate me from the van just a few feet away. One of the paramedics hung a blanket between me and the open side door, blocking the kids' view but not muffling his voice. Another paramedic asked why he was doing this and his answer was simple: "I don't want the kids to see their dad die." Although he tried to speak quietly, he was just loud enough for Victoria to hear. She is a stoic child—our thinker—but it was starting to sink in: Mom and Dad were really hurt badly. For the first time in her young life, she began to contemplate life without parents. *Would she and her siblings be orphans?*

Her mind raced to the movie *Annie* and the orphanage. Would they be sent there to live with the mean lady who ran the place? Or would they be shipped off to live in another town with their aunt or grandparents? At best, they would no longer have a dad, and Mom was going to be on her own. The shock started to fade and the reality began to sink in. Fear paralyzed her; she was too scared to even cry.

Paramedics were beginning the long process of extricating us from the car. Since Mona's side of the vehicle was not crumpled like mine, getting to her was relatively easy; her back was the problem. They would treat her as a possible spinal fracture and let the doctors determine the extent of the damage. While they noticed she was moving her arms but not her legs, they remained quiet, fully aware that crash victims tend to panic and lose the will to fight once they realize they can't feel their lower extremities. Watching for any signs of motion, the paramedics removed Mona from the van, each saying a silent prayer.

Next came the backboard and stretcher. A brace was carefully placed around Mona's neck to prevent any movement, and then multiple paramedics and policemen jockeyed into position to slide Mona out of the van and onto the board. Because spinal fractures are inherently unstable, the major concern was the transition from sitting in the van to lying on the board. The vertebrae of the spinal column form a tunnel called the spinal canal, within which runs the spinal cord. About an inch thick, the cord is composed of all the nerves that carry messages from your brain to various body parts. Spinal fractures can move bone into the canal or on to the nerves as they exit, resulting in severe damage. Any damage to the nerves will stop the messages from getting through, which leads to numbness and paralysis from the site of the injury on down.

Paralysis might not be a consequence of the actual crash but from the movement of an injured body afterward, so paramedics are trained to be extremely careful when transporting anyone with a back or neck injury.

With the backboard in place and multiple hands around her, Mona was lifted out of the car and onto a stretcher. As they slid her into the ambulance, she continued to repeat her complaints of a sore back and requests for a pillow. By this time, her burly angel had disappeared. We never knew his name and would never see him again. He appeared when he was needed most and disappeared just as quickly.

The kids were now crying again as they watched their mother being carted away, unable to signal them that she was all right. They'd seen paralysis before. We have a family friend who has been paralyzed for the last eighteen years after also being hit by a drunk driver. Staring at their immobile mother, the tears flowed quickly while the angels continued to hold the kids close. The angels could not promise that their mom would walk again; they could only say they were praying for her. It was in God's hands now.

The paramedics came and loaded the kids into a second ambulance to get them to the hospital while their comforters vanished without a word and returned to their lives. I would meet one of these angels later; she lived only one town over and knew us as the local veterinarians. She'd been two cars behind us when the Jeep crashed into our van. Another fifty yards—a second or two—and she would have been hit. Instead, her role that day was to be an earth angel caring for a child she didn't even know.

With Mona and the kids off to the hospital, the paramedics focused on me. First, the door and roof had to be cut away. They covered me with a blanket to protect me from glass and metal and keep me warm as the car was disassembled. The roof was cut off and peeled back. The windshield, shattered but designed to stay in one piece and minimize flying glass, was pulled away. Now they could see that my left leg was crushed between the seat and the dash. The dash would have to be lifted to get my leg out. The Jaws of Life were brought in, but it was difficult to find a good spot to place them. My leg had moved to the left during the crash, so it was now on the left edge of the seat. Unfortunately, the seat did not have a solid place to put the bottom jaw to enable them to lift the dash. The fireman tried again and again, but the jaws kept slipping out. Finally, they managed to wedge it between the dash and the van's frame, which was bent in from the impact. By this time, the helicopter had arrived ready to transport me to the hospital. The order was given, "Lift the dash and get him out!"

The diesel engine powering the Jaws of Life roared while thick smoke belched forth. Although the diesel fuel had a terrible odor, for me it was the smell of salvation. The fireman gunned the engine and the dash started to rise. My leg was freed.

Paramedics rushed in to get me out, unable to see that my leg, now relieved from the crush of the dash, had started to bleed profusely. With this rate of blood loss, I would have only minutes to live. The bleeding from my leg was increasing as the clots that had been formed by the pressure of the dashboard now succumbed to the incredibly large volume of blood rushing out from the torn femoral vein. My team moved fast, but if they couldn't stop or at least slow the bleeding, my fight would be over quickly.

These angels among us knew what they were doing, having seen plenty of these crashes before. They did not pry up the dash and remove me from the van until the helicopter had landed and the gurney transporting me to it had been set in place.

As they placed me gently onto the gurney, they noticed the sheets turning red. My leg flopped lazily from side to side, an obvious indication that the bone was completely broken. The helicopter was about fifty yards away on the highway. Once securely loaded into the helicopter, I met my next angel—the flight nurse named Robert.

FOR REFLECTION

But if anyone has the world's goods and sees his brother in need, yet closes his heart against him, how does God's love abide in him? (1 John 3:17)

1. Have you ever encountered everyday angels in your life? How did they affect you?

2. Is survival a result of one's own actions or a result of something beyond our control? Is it simply luck?

3. How can we help children deal with major trauma?

CHAPTER 4

LESSONS FROM A WAR ZONE

Robert was in his early thirties and just what you would expect from a guy working on a rescue helicopter. He was lean and muscular, having been trained as a search-and-rescue medic in the U.S. Army. He'd spent two tours in Afghanistan pulling wounded soldiers out of hellholes and patching up injuries much worse than mine; he'd also been a star athlete in high school. As a result, he was extremely competitive and hated to lose. This was now his battle—Robert versus death—and he wasn't going to let death win.

When he set his eyes on me, his adrenaline started pumping. For a paramedic, it is always a very personal fight to save someone. Robert viewed each lost victim as his own personal failure—no matter how badly they'd been torn up, he considered it *his* fault if they died during transport. And he wasn't about to let that happen to me.

He spoke loudly over the noise of the helicopter, hurrying the paramedics to get me inside, wanting me transferred to his care ASAP because he thought of himself as the best at what he did. Once I was securely in the chopper, he took over. Robert had the attitude all the great ones display—he believed that only *he* could save me; he just needed the others to get out of his way and let him work. The paramedics quickly retreated, allowing the transport to throttle up and begin to lift off. I was in Robert's care now. He was in charge.

Afghanistan had been his hell, but it had trained him well for this role. His job was to stabilize me and get me to the hospital. In order to accomplish this, he went through the ABCs of trauma:

A. Airway: I was spitting blood but had started to talk in spite of my injuries. Even though he couldn't hear what I was saying, my talking told him my airway was clear enough—at least for now.

B. Breathing: I was breathing. He checked my lips and saw they were red, not blue. If the lips turn blue, it means there is not enough oxygen getting into the blood. Mine were still red, but Robert made sure to watch me breathe; he'd seen enough soldiers wounded by roadside bombs to know what an impact to the chest can do. Witnessing my fast and shallow breathing confirmed his suspicions, even though the roar of the helicopter made it impossible to listen with a stethoscope. My lungs were bruised and possibly punctured.

Though the airbag and the seat belt prevented my body from hitting the steering wheel, my lungs were still going seventy miles per hour inside my ribcage when the rest of me stopped. Thus, my lungs and heart hit my ribcage, tearing things apart. Even worse? Because I saw it coming, my reflex was to suck in a breath and hold it during impact. That *Oh shit!* response shut off the only escape route for the air when my lungs were violently compressed. The impact pressed on the fully inflated lungs like a balloon and, just like a balloon, they popped, shredding the tissue and blood vessels. Consequently, air leaked out into my chest while blood seeped into the airways. Both created a deadly scenario.

Each breath filled my chest with more air and further compressed my lungs, making breathing more difficult and less effective. My lungs were progressively collapsing.

Robert had placed an oxygen monitor on my finger and noticed that my levels were starting to drop. Despite the oxygen mask he placed over my mouth, the levels continued to decrease; I had started at 90 percent oxygen and was now at 85 percent. Alarms would blare on the monitor if I fell below 80 percent, and I was perilously close.

C. Circulation: Robert checked my circulation. Seeing the blood pooling under my leg, he cut my jeans to better determine the source. The extent of the injury became apparent: Blood was welling up through a gaping hole in the outside muscle of my thigh, just above my knee. A jagged piece of bone protruded through the skin, surrounded by a huge blood clot. Purple-red muscle pushed out from the hole like raw hamburger. Blood was flowing out of the hole at a rapid rate that indicated a major vessel had been torn somewhere within all that mess. Robert grabbed some gauze and pressed it into the hole. I moaned from the pain. After a few seconds, he pulled the gauze out again and watched for the wound to refill with blood. At this point, the goal was not to stop the bleeding but to ascertain how quickly the wound refilled. Because the blood returned instantly to fill the hole, Robert surmised that the femoral vessel—the main supply of blood running down my leg—must have been torn in the accident. He should be able to stop it with a pressure bandage.

Robert had missed this once before and had long ago vowed, *Never again*. In Afghanistan, he'd been deployed to rescue a soldier whose convoy had been attacked with an I.E.D. The lead Humvee had been destroyed, and numerous soldiers had been wounded. Robert had been the first to get to them and ran to the one with the worst injuries: His name tag read "Bennett," and he looked about eighteen years old. Robert quickly bandaged wounds on both arms and his abdomen, but Bennett continued to fade. Robert guessed that there was internal bleeding and removed the abdominal bandage to check. Although there was a gaping hole, there wasn't that much blood, indicating there had to be another source. Robert assumed it must be in the chest and had no way to stop it. He further surmised that there had been a tear in one of the major arteries coming out of the heart; therefore, there was nothing he could do except start an IV and pump fluids into the young soldier. Robert had been in the country just a month and was not yet proficient at starting IVs, but this soldier was surely going to die if he didn't do so ASAP. While he desperately tried, the young man's veins had collapsed, preventing a catheter feed. Robert blew through catheter after catheter as Bennett bled to death. He watched Bennett die.

Soon, Robert was ordered to stop and attend to the rest of the wounded while other soldiers came to move the dead man away. Robert then noticed a huge pool of blood where Bennett's leg had been lying. He had bled out from a punctured artery in his leg that had been bleeding into his fatigues. The blood was soaking quickly into the sand and was obscured by the ever-present dust of Afghanistan. Robert had never checked. He was horrified. He'd made a terrible mistake by assuming the bleeding originated in Bennett's chest. That miss had haunted him ever since, nearly causing him to quit being a medic. The nightmares he experienced after the tragic incident were always the same; he would be trying to save a soldier who would not stop bleeding. The soldier would yell repeatedly, "Why can't you save me?!" Robert would shoot up in bed, startled awake after seeing a huge pool of blood and Bennett lying dead in his nightmare.

Consequently, Robert requested to be reassigned, but there was another plan. His superiors turned him down; there was no one to take his place. With no other choice, Robert decided to refocus and make himself better at his job. He recruited fellow medics to act as guinea pigs and would practice setting catheters on them. Soon, the other medics started to avoid him, so he went to the soldiers. Since they had a vested interest in helping Robert improve his skills—after all, it was their lives he was entrusted to save—they willingly volunteered to have catheters placed. At first, Robert was terrible, struggling to hit even the biggest vein and causing even the toughest soldier to fight to stay still. But memories of Bennett forced him to improve, and within weeks Robert was the best in the division at setting catheters. No other soldier would die because of a faulty IV placement; Robert would make sure of that. Thanks to his Afghanistan experience, I had a chance; Robert could set an IV into a dying man in a moving helicopter. He would not allow me to be another Bennett, the angel who in spite of never knowing me, died for me on that battle-field years before.

Robert immediately stuffed another wad of gauze back into the torn skin and flesh to plug the hole in my leg. Although the bleeding slowed, it did not stop completely. It was flowing from so many places in my leg—the vein, the torn quad muscle, and the bone itself—that the gauze couldn't possibly put an end to it. Additionally, blood oozed from a multitude of other places on my body; this site had been the biggest one he could identify. By hampering the blood flow here, he could buy me a few more minutes. Thus the race was on to get to the hospital before I bled out. Robert shoved more gauze into the leg wound and wrapped it in place.

However, I was still bleeding internally and going into shock. "Shock" is defined as the loss of consciousness and eventual death that occurs when blood pressure drops, depriving organs of the perfusion they need to function properly. When your brain doesn't get enough blood, you pass out; when your vital organs don't get the oxygen and energy they need, they fail. The kidneys are especially vulnerable; in fact, kidney failure is often the cause of death for people who endure this kind of trauma.

Robert began to place an intravenous catheter into my arm as he talked to me in an effort to keep me awake. I needed more blood in my system to replace what I had lost. It wasn't easy in the bouncing helicopter, but on his second try, Robert set the catheter and breathed a huge sigh of relief. He knew this was my lifeline. He also knew that only a select few could have done what he had done. His hell of Afghanistan had saved my life.

That one was for you, Bennett.

Next, he hung a bag of O-negative blood, the blood type anyone can receive regardless of their own blood type. All Robert could do was impede the blood flow and transfuse the new blood as fast as possible. Placing the IV meant he had won this round. The fight was far from over, but I at least had a chance.

Although I'd been talking the entire time, Robert started listening to what I was saying. At first, he'd assumed I was just babbling because my eyes were closed, but I had reverted to my veterinary training and began to describe my injuries.

"I have an open comminuted femoral fracture, a fractured humerus (the upper arm bone), and a dislocated shoulder. My other arm hurts (the elbow was smashed), and I probably have a ruptured spleen since I hit the airbag so hard."

In spite of all my injuries, I was not complaining about the pain. My body had released its own painkillers, called endorphins (the body's morphine), to block it.

Robert looked at me a bit perplexed as I explained my injuries and asked, "Are you a doctor?" I told him I was a veterinarian and started mumbling about dogs and cats I had worked on that had been hit by cars. But as I did, my voice got softer and my eyes closed. I continued to speak, but my words came slower and I started to slur. Soon I wasn't making any sense, and Robert could no longer hear me over the noise of the helicopter. My eyes were closed and my skin was a ghostly white; I was fading in spite of Robert's stellar efforts. He tried to keep me talking for a while but soon realized I was no longer conscious. His goal now was to keep me alive until we reached the hospital. He was losing the race to save me.

My oxygen level had dropped to 75 percent, setting off the alarms. Robert reached for a large needle and syringe he had pulled out previously. He cut my shirt back, exposing a terribly bruised chest. He splashed some iodine on my ribs on my left side. My oxygen level was continuing to drop. He pushed the needle in between the ribs hoping not to hit a lung. He felt it "pop" through and immediately pulled back on the syringe. It pulled easily, confirming that he was in the chest and the chest was filled with air (if he'd been in a lung, it would've pulled out air very slowly, if at all). He emptied the syringe and pulled again, sucking out more air. As he repeated the process, my oxygen levels started to rise. Soon I was up to 90 percent again and breathing more slowly. He pulled out the needle. Robert had won once more.

He did not take time to celebrate; I was getting paler and paler, indicating that my blood loss was unabated.

Recalling Bennett, Robert checked my leg again. The bandage he had stuffed into my leg wound was soaked and the blood was dripping through onto the helicopter floor. He reached for a tourniquet, knowing he had to get the bleeding to stop. He lifted my leg near the wound to get the tourniquet around it. I hadn't screamed in pain before, but even semi-conscious, I screamed now. He had to get the tourniquet around the thigh above the break, so he was working it under my leg trying to get it past. As hard as he tried to keep from moving my leg, it had to move some. He pushed his hand into the mattress, trying to get the tourniquet past while the exposed nerves sent out waves of pain signals. I hadn't torn the major nerve running down the leg, the sciatic, so I wasn't numb. Any movement of the leg sent a flood of intense pain through me.

Robert saw this as a bit of a good sign—at least I was feeling things. He'd been watching for signs that I could feel my legs but dared not ask, as the thought of being paralyzed would sap my will to fight to stay alive. Robert had seen that before with some of the soldiers he had treated. When I screamed as he tightened the tourniquet, he smiled for knowing that at least I wasn't paralyzed. If I could survive, I probably would walk again.

I was done talking as the helicopter neared the hospital; I was unconscious. My blood pressure was dropping. The tourniquet had slowed the blood flow out of my leg, but I was bleeding from multiple other places that couldn't be tourniqueted or have a bandage stuffed in place. Blood was rushing out from nine different fracture sites and into my lungs and abdomen. A man my size has about nine liters of blood in his entire body. I had lost half of that.

As I continued to bleed into my lungs, I started to have more trouble breathing. I was coughing up blood from both lungs and a broken nose. My nose was moved to the side and my nasal passages were now blocked with clots, making it impossible to breathe. The blood draining down my throat was impeding my windpipe. Robert knew I would soon not be able to move enough air. As I fell again into unconsciousness, my breathing slowed and my lips darkened to a greyish blue.

Robert grabbed an endotracheal tube and a light. Without any fight from me, he opened my mouth and passed the tube into my windpipe. This tube would be my airway. It would keep my windpipe open, allowing air to be pushed into my lungs. Robert inflated a small cuff around the end of the tube to form a seal between it and my windpipe, preventing any more blood or saliva from going down into my lungs from above. This allowed Robert to force air into my lungs with a squeezable bag and ensured that at least I had some air moving whether I took a breath or not.

Again, Robert was buying me time, but there was simply no way to predict whether I would ever return to being the man I had been less than an hour earlier.

The helicopter landed on the roof of the University of Wisconsin-Madison Hospital, one of the best trauma hospitals in the United States. Four emergency doctors were waiting, along with sixteen nurses and support staff. I would need them all. As soon as the skids hit the roof, they charged in.

For Reflection

Now you are the body of Christ, and each one of you is a part of it. And God has placed in the church first of all apostles, second prophets, third teachers, then miracles, then gifts of healing, of helping, of guidance, and of different kinds of tongues. Are all apostles? Are all prophets? Are all teachers? Do all work miracles? Do all have gifts of healing? Do all speak in tongues? Do all interpret? Now eagerly desire the greater gifts. And yet I will show you the most excellent way. (1 Corinthians 12:27–31)

1. Have you ever wanted to quit doing something only to become better later? What did you do to get better? Why did you continue if you were not initially good at it?
2. Have you ever had a bad experience or mistake teach you something valuable?
3. Are mistakes bad?
4. How can we move forward after making a terrible error, especially one that hurts another person?

CHAPTER 5

MORE ANGELS

Robert was opening the helicopter door before the helicopter landed. Three nurses ran out to get me into a triage room just inside the hospital, where the rest of the staff was waiting. Robert didn't have to say a word; the expression on his face told the story. I was dying and dying fast. The gurney was soaked with blood and my abdomen was bloated with even more blood. My foot lay flat off the gurney, twisted ninety degrees to the side. There was a slight bend just above the knee wrapped in a bloody bandage indicating where the leg was broken. My left arm fell to the side as they began to move me out of the chopper. It bent and rotated both at the elbow and at the shoulder, obviously broken also. A nurse grabbed my hand and set my arm back over my chest, turning the palm back to as close to normal resting angle as possible. It is hard even for professionals to see hands and feet lying grossly, unnaturally contorted.

The nurses searched for a pulse on my wrist but found none. My heartbeat was audible but only barely. My heart was still pumping whatever blood was left, but there wasn't much there. Since very little of that was making it up to my brain, I was unconscious.

I had seen this myself countless times before as a veterinarian: people rushing their dogs or cats into our office after they'd been struck by a car. These injured animals would be unconscious, with blood coming out of their nose and mouth. Their gums would be pale like mine. Veterinarians often don't feel for a pulse since the animals are smaller and covered with hair, making it more difficult to find. We usually listen with a stethoscope for a heartbeat. Often the heart is slowing down as it starves of oxygen before it finally stops. My heartbeat was slowing to a dangerous pace.

The hospital staff jumped to action but knew it would be a hard fight. The organs die quickly when they lose blood flow, but a few—the brain, heart, and kidneys—are particularly sensitive.

A nurse immediately began the task of setting another IV line and hanging another bag of blood. The goal of my medical team was to stop the bleeding and replace the lost blood, but it was flowing out faster than it could be put back in.

Blood loss, however, was not the only concern. The team knew I had clots everywhere; any one of them could easily break off and end up in my brain. Trauma is one of the major causes of strokes, and I was a prime candidate. Usually, people prone to strokes are given "blood-thinners" to stop the blood from clotting, but I was still hemorrhaging all over, and the last thing I could afford was thinned blood. Increasing my pressure would ignite blood flow (stagnant blood immediately starts to clot), so for the moment, my medical team's first priority was raising my blood pressure.

Enter my third angel of the day.

Dr. Jerry Lang is one of the best trauma surgeons in the country. Though I had many doctors that day and over the following months, Dr. Lang and I would develop a special relationship. Doctors see thousands of cases. Although every case is special to the patient, most of them are fairly routine to the doctors and nurses. As a doctor myself, I knew that even the most spectacular cases become commonplace after a while. Today I was just another guy whose family was hit by just another drunk driver. Doctors and nurses see this all the time; I was simply an unfortunate victim of someone else's bad choices. Yet anyone who works in medicine knows there are certain cases that just stand out—the especially tough ones that demand all of our skills and knowledge. For Dr. Lang, I would be that case. He was the doctor I needed. In spite of my three other superb doctors, without Dr. Lang, I would die.

I would later learn how talented and skilled he really was. The nurses would all smile and sing his praises whenever I asked about him (especially the younger nurses, since he was handsome and ran marathons). We would have been good friends if we had gone to school together, given the fact that we were about the same age. We both loved what we did and would recount surgical cases like a high school football star recounting his experience of winning a state championship. Our kids were roughly the same age, giving us even more in common. Dr. Lang acknowledged that though he would use great skill to keep me alive, it was not all up to him; he had a great team around him and he would need every one of them that day. Even so, there is always more going on than even the best surgeon can control; ultimately, he could fix only so much. After that, it was in God's hands.

At that moment, I desperately needed all of Dr. Lang's skills. However, there was another doctor present who had seniority and was technically in charge. This doctor correctly suspected that my torn spleen was causing internal bleeding; therefore, he gave the order to get me into surgery ASAP because they had to get the spleen out.

Although this doctor's assessment was accurate, Dr. Lang soon realized I was bleeding more profusely from the torn femoral vein in my leg. Because a tourniquet had been wrapped around it, the femoral vein was not "spurting" blood, but it was hemorrhaging too quickly to postpone a surgical remedy. When Dr. Lang noticed the unusual amount of blood soaking into the sheets under my leg, he knew without a doubt that this had to be dealt with first.

They started wheeling me down to surgery to take out my spleen when Dr. Lang stopped them, contradicting the more senior surgeon—the spleen would have to wait until the leg was dealt with. Dr. Lang took a big risk by stepping on some toes, but he put me, the *patient*, first. If they did not get the bleeding from my leg under control, I would die before I got to surgery. This is where my respect for Dr. Lang originates: It takes some balls to contradict your boss for the good of the patient. And Dr. Lang's got 'em.

Dr. Lang removed the bandage Robert had put in place in the helicopter and searched for the vessel that was still gushing blood. Getting down to the bleeder was difficult. Although the tear in the skin and muscle was to the outside of the bone, the vessel ran along the inside. Cutting through the other side would take too long and create more damage; the best option would be to reach the inner side of the bone through the existing hole. Dr. Lang separated the muscles and moved bone fragments out of the way, shoving the various bone pieces deeper into the muscle so he would not lose them; he'd need them later to reconstruct the thighbone.

As my surgeon angel started his search, blood was suctioned away and muscle retracted. My entire lower left leg from just above the knee was now only attached by the muscle on the back and on the inside. Dr. Lang frantically sought out the vessel. He searched and grabbed with clamps, but the bleeding continued. Rarely is the vessel sitting out in the open like a garden hose, just asking to be tied off. The muscle retraction invariably pulls the vessel deeper into the remaining muscle, which has been transformed into hamburger. Finding this vessel and tying it off before the patient bleeds out requires great skill and a little luck. Dr. Lang repeated the search-and-clamp process to no avail; the blood continued to flow.

At this point, he made another fateful decision, one that would ultimately save my life. After failing to find the vessel and ascertaining the rapid pace of blood flow, he realized he would not be able to clamp it before I ran out of time. Since I was becoming progressively weaker, he did something extremely difficult for a highly competitive person like a surgeon: He gave up on tying it off.

Instead, he called for a large lap sponge and pressed it deep into the wound directly over the femoral vein. He then packed the wound with two more sponges and pulled the leg back to its normal position to close the wound and squeeze the bandages into the hole. Finally, he quickly surrounded the leg with more wraps to keep the sponges in place and apply more pressure. For the first time since the car dashboard had been lifted off of my crushed leg, the bleeding from the femoral vessel stopped. My biggest source of blood loss was now under control. Eventually it would have to be tied off, but not today. The doctors could now move onto the operating room.

Now it was time to examine my abdomen and stop the internal bleeding. Dr. Lang had given me the necessary time to shift focus to the second major bleed: the spleen.

For Reflection

But Peter and the apostles answered, "We must obey God rather than men." (Acts 5:29)

1. Have you ever been in a situation where God put you in the right place at the right time to use the unique gifts God gave you to help someone?

2. Have you ever had to go against someone you respected for a greater good?

CHAPTER 6

ARE YOU IN THERE?

Mona had a bruise on the right side of her head that traveled from her ear to over her eye. She continued to repeat herself: "What happened?" "Are the kids okay?" "My back is sore; can I have a pillow?" Stuck in an endless loop, her brain could formulate these questions repeatedly yet couldn't comprehend the answers because it had stopped processing any new information.

Although her back was the only injury she complained about, it was quite obvious she'd sustained a head injury also. Mona also shrieked in pain when her left arm was moved before quickly reverting to complaining about her back. Needless to say, she was of little help in evaluating her injuries.

A doctor began to examine her left arm, suspicious of a break. As he reached the elbow, she cried out again and pulled it back; a subsequent X-ray soon confirmed it was broken. They couldn't figure out exactly how her left elbow broke when she impacted mainly on her right side, but it didn't really matter. They just needed to determine the extent of the damage and decide how to repair it.

Since her back was the obvious problem, a CT scan was ordered. The test revealed what had been suspected: three spinal fractures, along with the broken elbow, a major concussion, internal bleeding, and a bruise on her pancreas (a likely source of the internal bleeding).

All in all, it could have been much worse. The internal bleeding was not severe and would be left to stop on its own. The doctors knew that this type of hemorrhage is usually self-limiting, with vessels clotting up within minutes. Surgery is rarely necessary to find the source unless the bleeding either continues or, as in my case, is severe. Giving her fluids and a blood transfusion to replace lost blood volume probably would work well. While confident they would not have to cut her open, surgeons monitored her carefully; in the end, Mona would emerge from this ordeal without a big scar.

That was important, because in Mona's world, bad times are to be forgotten; a scar would serve as a constant reminder of what had happened. Every day, it would force her to recall the worst day of her life. Thankfully, she got lucky; only a small scar from a cut above her lip would serve as her reminder.

They called in a neurosurgeon to evaluate Mona's spinal fractures. Two of the fractures were on the protrusions of bone that serve as muscle attachments. These are away from the spinal canal and the spinal cord and would not need surgery.

The third fracture was the fracture of the vertebral body, similar to where older people get compression fractures of their spine due to osteoporosis. The danger with these fractures is that the loose bone can move into the canal and compress the spinal cord. Any type of pressure on the cord or the nerves exiting the spinal canal results in anything from numbness or weakness in the legs to chronic, sometimes debilitating pain or even paralysis. It was determined that the fracture pieces had not moved toward the spinal cord to any significant degree. There was a narrowing in the canal, but the cord had enough room around it to move out of the way rather than compress. Had the fracture moved another eighth of an inch, she would have lost use of her legs, but so far she was okay.

Mona's neurosurgeon knew that spinal surgery is fraught with risks for even the most gifted surgeon, so her team ultimately decided surgery was a last resort.

The neurosurgeon walked into the trauma room and began the exam that would truly determine the extent of Mona's injuries. The CT revealed that the fracture was not compressing the spinal cord now, but it did not mean it hadn't done so before; there was a real possibility it could have impacted the cord when it was broken, then moved back to a better place when Mona came to a rest. Any impact to the cord, even if only temporary or fleeting, could have paralyzed her forever.

Mona complied when the doctor asked her to move her toes. Next, she felt his hand touch her toes and feet. Then, he pulled out his pleximeter—known as a "hammer"—raised her knee slightly, and hit it just below the kneecap. This is the classic reflex test with its resulting kick. Mona's foot reacted accordingly, indicating her reflexes were still intact.

The remainder of the neurologic exam showed no loss of nerve function. As long as this didn't change, she would not need surgery to stabilize the fracture. Instead, she would be fitted with a body brace that she would wear for the next three months. Custom-fit to her size, the brace would completely wrap her body like a corset, extending from under her armpits to below her hips. It was also hot and uncomfortable and would be worn twenty-four hours a day until the bones healed together. Mona would be permitted to remove it once daily for personal hygiene. During this time period, the muscles of her abdomen and back—her "core muscles"—would deteriorate to a point where simply standing up would be a struggle. Still, it was better than surgery.

Attention now shifted to Mona's concussion. A concussion is defined as the brain being shaken. The brain has a very limited ability to heal, which is why a major concussion can leave lasting effects. When Mona's head hit the side of the door, her skull stopped moving, but her brain kept going. The brain floats in a small amount of fluid. As the skull stopped moving, the brain continued forward and slammed into the skull, tearing up blood vessels and disrupting the nerves. Information becomes jumbled and the brain goes into shutdown mode, rendering the victim unconscious. This severe of an impact can even pull the brain apart as lighter areas (grey matter) have less momentum than heavier areas (white matter). Separation of these areas of brain tissue result in a person being "brain dead" due to all of the connections between the higher-thinking areas being sheared and severed. Breathing and heartbeat are controlled in the more basic and protected parts of the brain; therefore, a person can still be "alive" but no longer able to process any information. He or she is in a "persistent vegetative state," in other words, a vegetable.

Since Mona was still talking, her higher processes still worked; the doctors just couldn't ascertain how well. As a veterinarian, she could work only if her mind was clear. A concussion typically affects short-term memory, so she could not remember what happened or what the doctors had just said. It's also why she kept repeating the same questions.

This scenario would play out continuously in the twenty-four hours following the accident, restarting each time a family member entered her room: Mona would wake up, look around, ask the same set of questions again, and then fall back asleep.

The brain is a funny, complex machine, and when it is messed up, things can get a little strange. Mona would write the month of October, the month of the crash, every time she wrote out the date for the next four months. She'd consciously try to write the correct date to counteract this tendency, but as soon as she stopped thinking about it, the month would revert to October. Words would be substituted or reversed without her awareness, so a Christmas recital for the kids would become a band recital, even though none of the kids was in band. She would say her sister Carla just called when she knew it was her sister Theresa.

For Mona, this was a scary reality. Because the brain does not repair well, damage is often permanent. How could she do her job if she kept saying the wrong words? We spend a great deal of time explaining very difficult problems to pet owners; a few wrong words can spell disaster.

Unfortunately, nobody had any idea if the problem would correct itself. There is no treatment for a concussion; Mona would just have to wait it out and see if her mind would work properly again. We really wouldn't have a solid answer for months, which was harrowing because Mona had been a vet for fourteen years. Practicing veterinary medicine was a big part of who she was and the means by which we both supported our family. Now it looked like neither of us would return to our profession again because Mona might not ever be able to think clearly and I might not survive, much less work. Not even our stellar medical team could predict what would happen. Only God knew our future.

FOR REFLECTION

Do not let your adorning be external—the braiding of hair and the putting on of gold jewelry, or the clothing you wear—but let your adorning be the hidden person of the heart with the imperishable beauty of a gentle and quiet spirit, which in God's sight is very precious. (1 Peter 3:3–4)

1. How can scars be beautiful?
2. Where does God see beauty in humankind?
3. Have you known people with disabilities? How have they coped with their situations? Did they accept it as part of God's plan?

CHAPTER 7

God's Gift

By now I was in surgery—mainly an exploratory one since my medical team really had no idea what they would find.

The surgery would explore everything, from the liver sitting up under the ribs to the bladder down by the pelvis and all body parts in between. I'd emerge from the experience with a big scar from my sternum to just below my navel—ruining my dream of posing with my shirt open on the cover of *GQ* (strike that one off my to-do list!).

In cases like this, there is no care given to making the incision look pretty; a small incision does not allow for adequate visualization of the various organs.

Dr. Lang would perform the surgery. As he entered the abdomen, taking great care not to inadvertently cut anything just under the surface, blood began shooting out and flooding onto the floor. My engorged abdomen was under so much pressure, it poured out like water rushing out of a fountain. My surgeon couldn't see anything; all the organs were submerged. He called for suction, but the blood flooded out much faster than suction could catch it, spilling onto the floor and splattering all over his shoe covers. He immediately extended the incision and reached for the spleen.

The spleen lies on the left side of the abdomen just below the stomach. This highly vascular organ has two main functions. First, it is an important part of the immune system; it is basically a factory that produces white blood cells to guard against and fight infection.

The second function of the spleen is to act as a blood reservoir. When a large amount of blood is lost, as in my case, the spleen contracts and forces red blood cells directly into the bloodstream. Essentially, it provides an automatic blood transfusion.

Unfortunately, this is not a good thing if the spleen is ruptured. In that circumstance, the injured spleen contracts, pushing blood into the abdomen, *not* into the general circulation. Blood is then lost even more rapidly, negating the benefit of that built-in blood reservoir. My blood was now pumping out of the spleen through a large tear and had to be stopped or I would bleed out on the operating table.

Dr. Lang grabbed my tattered spleen and pulled it out of my abdomen to work on it. He could see it was torn in half. He grabbed the largest clamps available and placed one across the vessels feeding each portion of the spleen. Of course he would have to come back, tie each vessel individually, and remove the spleen, but first he would arrest the bleeding so he could examine the rest of the abdomen.

Systematically, he began to check everything. The liver was severely bruised with a deep purple swelling about the size of a baseball in the lobe near the spleen. It was weeping blood but not bleeding profusely. An absorbable sponge was placed over it to slow the bleed and assist the blood in clotting. It would be left there after they sewed me up again because the body would dissolve it in a few weeks.

Dr. Lang then examined the bile duct and gall bladder coming out of the liver, both of which held green bile, making a leak easy to spot. Both were okay.

He moved on to the stomach and intestines. Any type of break in these organs releases bacteria into the abdomen, resulting in a deadly and incredibly painful infection inside the abdominal cavity (peritonitis). Bacteria released into the abdomen make it feel as if it's on fire; a temperature will spike and toxins will be absorbed. It is nearly always fatal.

The whole tract is a long tube, so Dr. Lang simply began at the stomach and worked his way down, pulling intestines out, then shoving them back in until he had inspected it all. A few areas were severely bruised and beaten but not ruptured, so they were left alone to heal.

Then Dr. Lang checked the rest of the organs. Right away, something seemed wrong with the fluid he saw in the abdomen. Yes, it was bloody but also more watery than it should have been. By this time, I had received a lot of fluids, so Dr. Lang easily could have explained it away, but he followed his gut feeling: Something was leaking, and he had to keep looking for the source.

He immediately reached for my bladder. This is usually a fluid-filled sack, but mine was empty and flaccid, containing no urine at all. Of course, most people who notice a Jeep about to hit them head-on at accelerated speed would have emptied their bladder (as well as their bowels) out of fear. My bladder, however, was completely empty, never a normal state for this organ. Dr. Lang knew immediately that there had to be a tear, so he pulled the bladder out of the abdomen and inspected every inch. A large bruise made it hard to see, but sure enough, there was a half-inch hole where the urine had blown out the side. Once again, Dr. Lang's gut feeling had been right on; this had to be repaired.

My potassium levels were rising due to the urine leaking into my abdomen. If Dr. Lang had not checked the bladder, I probably would have died from potassium slowing and ultimately stopping my heart. Instead, with six sutures, the tear was fixed.

With everything inspected, the surgeon turned back to the spleen, which is fed by three major pairs of arteries and veins, each about the size of a pencil. Each one was separated and double-tied before being cut. The spleen was thrown onto a tray and the abdomen was washed out with saline to remove any contamination, along with the remaining urine. As the saline was suctioned out, Dr. Lang moved the organs out of the way and watched the deepest part of the abdomen, where any continual leakage of urine or blood would pool. After a few minutes, he saw none. He could now close me up and deal with the rest of my injuries. I had made it through the first part but was far from out of the woods.

No major vessels or nerves seemed to have been torn in my arms, so they would be splinted temporarily and wrapped to my chest to prevent further damage.

Because I had been under for a while, the doctors wanted to get me off the surgery table quickly, knowing my weak heart could give out at any time. As they kept pushing blood in, they started gaining ground now that the biggest sources of blood loss were all under control. Still, I'd lost a ton and my pressure was dangerously low. The average human body holds about nine units of blood; I would require twelve units that day. They simply did not have time to fix all my fractures until I was more stable.

However, the thighbone fracture presented a problem. Putting off its repair would leave the lower leg attached to my body by only some muscle because the outside muscle of the thigh had been sliced in half by the bone. The fractured bone had broken so violently, there were at least five separate pieces to put back together. It would need a plate, but plating can take a long time and I couldn't stay on the operating table much longer.

Casting was not an option since any cast or splint must extend one joint above and below the fracture to be effective. This meant the cast would have to extend above the hip – nearly impossible to do because the cast then extends up around the waist. I would still need to urinate and defecate. How would I do that when casted up to my waist?

Dr. Schumacher now became involved as a secondary surgeon to relieve Dr. Lang, who had been working on me for hours and needed a break. Dr. Schumacher was assigned to stabilize my leg. She would later repair my elbows also. Until a plate could be put on permanently, she decided to place an external fixator temporarily on my leg. I was familiar with these because I place them routinely on animals with similar breaks.

External fixators work by placing threaded pins into the bone above and below the fracture site. These pins travel perpendicular to the bone and are driven through the skin and overlying muscle right through the bone underneath. They are long and are left sticking out of the skin, often on both sides. Then all the pins coming out of the skin are clamped to a rod on the outside of the leg—thus the name external fixator. It sounds primitive and barbaric but is very strong and, in skilled hands, can be placed very quickly. There is no need to carefully realign the various fracture pieces since the surgeon works only with the larger pieces of bone. The smaller fragments were ignored for the time being.

With the fixator in place, the wound in the thigh could be addressed. There was a hole in the outside of the thigh as big as my fist filled with glass, upholstery, dirt, and plastic deeply embedded in the tissues. (Dr. Lang would later tell me it looked like a shark bite.) This would have to be meticulously cleaned out before it could be plated. Foreign material like this introduced bacteria and even fungal spores into my system. The doctors would have to wait to plate my leg until the infection brought into my system by some piece of glass or plastic was under control—otherwise it could cost me my leg or even my life.

Dr. Schumacher removed the sponges placed in the leg wound by Dr. Lang and quickly cut away any muscle that was obviously dead or beyond repair. She washed the hole with a jet of saline. This removed a lot of the dirt and debris from the wound, but she knew she could not get it all; glass and debris were imbedded too deeply in the wound. The end of the bone had exited the skin and was therefore contaminated; sewing the skin closed would just trap the infection. Dr. Schumacher decided to leave the wound entirely open. This would allow for it to be washed daily until it was clean enough to plate, giving the body time to "push out" any infection through the open hole. The external fixator would hold my leg in place long enough for the wound to become clean, so they would plate it a few days later (if I was still around).

There was one last thing to do: place an intracaval filter. This is basically a big strainer, shaped like a daddy long-legs spider. It is placed in the main blood vessel returning blood to the heart. The reason is simple: A blood clot breaking off from my thigh fracture could travel upstream, pass through the heart, and lodge in the lung. Known as a pulmonary embolism, this phenomenon is almost instantly fatal and doctors can't predict if or when it will happen.

What they do know is that it often occurs after trauma, especially with fractures to the large bones. Once a blood clot lodges in the lungs, not much can be done. Dr. Morris was called in to address this specific issue. He was a quiet man—not the loud, cocky type you envision for a surgeon. He is an interventional radiologist; that is, he uses imaging systems like X-rays and fluoroscopy (taking multiple X-rays to create a "movie," made from a series of still pictures) to place things like stents in hearts or, in my case, a filter to catch blood clots. The filter is placed through a vein in the thigh and fed up the venous system to just below the heart. Here the "spider legs" of the filter are allowed to open and it lodges itself in place. Any clot heading from below the heart hopefully will be caught by the filter before it can get to the lungs. This filter can stay in place for months as the body heals and is eventually removed when the risk of blood clot is gone. For me, it would be a long time.

Dr. Morris worked quickly, knowing I could not handle much more. It was time to get me off the table. It had been eleven hours since our world had changed, and my heart was still weak. They needed to end this operation ASAP.

Dr. Lang had stayed in the hospital while the other doctors worked on me, waiting to speak to my family. He had started with me when

I came in and was now personally involved. Good or bad, he wanted to be the one to break the news to my loved ones. It was now eleven o'clock on a Sunday night, and he was exhausted. He was supposed to have been done at noon. In fact, he hadn't originally been scheduled to be at the hospital that day. Dr. Lang had switched his weekend schedule to help coach his son's Pee Wee football team, so for several weeks he had covered Sundays instead of his usual Saturdays. This week was his last Sunday because the season had ended the day before. That simple decision to coach his kid had placed the doctor I needed at the hospital on the day of the accident to save me.

Still, he should have been gone by the time I got there because his shift had ended at noon, an hour before we arrived. He'd been finishing some paperwork and dictating notes when the call came in that we were on our way. Dr. Lang stuck around to see if he could help, putting his weekend on hold and losing his half day off for some guy he had never met.

He certainly could have left and let someone else handle it; we were just another family hit by another drunk driver, and he had seen hundreds of cases like ours. But for whatever reason, he stayed. He stayed so he could be there to stop my bleeding femoral vein; he stayed to remove my spleen and suture my bladder; he stayed to get me through the ups and downs that were yet to come. He stayed because he was supposed to—not because of hospital rules but *higher rules*. God had given him a gift—the ability to save lives—and He expected that gift to be used for His will, not in obedience to some hospital schedule.

This is why Dr. Lang hung around. He really had no choice, though I am not sure he knew it. Yes, he could have left, but his conscience prevented him from walking away. The choice was made for him when he accepted his gift as a surgeon. He stayed because, like most people who have found God's gift, he knew he could do it better than anyone else. He would never tell anyone this, especially not another surgeon, but Dr. Lang understood the meaning behind his rare and precious talent. He wasn't about to walk away.

In that sense, he and I are a lot alike. If a dog had been rushed into my hospital after being hit by a car, I would have done the same thing. Although I employ many great vets in my practice, I had been given a gift to be a veterinarian-surgeon. Dr. Lang stayed because he knew he'd been blessed with the skills required to pull me through. There were plenty of good doctors around, but my injuries demanded the very best. Dr. Lang was yet another angel in the right place at the right time, without him even knowing why. His belief that he was the only man for the job was vindicated in the end, because his decision to stop the gurney, contradict the doctor in charge, and get my bleeding leg under control had saved my life. God put Dr. Lang there that day to keep me alive because His purpose for me was still not finished.

I found out later that there was another reason for Dr. Lang's remarkable competence, skill, and dedication. He was a father to three sons, one of whom had severe autism. Raising kids is hard enough, but discovering your son has autism and will have to struggle in life is simply heartbreaking. Dr. Lang and his physician-wife certainly had the means to pay someone else to raise their child; they easily could have hired a team of nannies or sent him to an institution to enable them to go on with their lives just as they had planned.

Instead, Mrs. Lang gave up her career and Dr. Lang reduced his schedule so they could be with their boy. They accepted God's plan for them instead of trying to make their own plan work. In doing so, Dr. Lang became the surgeon who would save me. His autistic son taught him true dedication to others, to put his wants and needs on hold for the benefit of someone else who needed him more. That day, I needed him, and he would stay—something he might not have done had it not been for the gift of his son. God had provided Dr. Lang with a difficult personal challenge in order to make him stronger, to fashion him into the surgeon God intended. Not to improve his technical skills, because Dr. Lang constantly worked on that, but to improve the other necessary traits that would mold him into the medical professional and human being God desired him to be: things such as dedication, patience, attention to detail, and the ability to clearly explain very complicated situations to people whose minds are clouded with fear and shock. Dr. Lang's autistic son had imparted these lessons to him; in many ways, *he* was the one who truly saved me that day—something nobody could have foreseen when he was diagnosed with autism.

For Dr. Lang, being a surgeon was a gift from God, but it had come with a price. His conscience—God's voice in his ear—simply would not allow him to walk away. He would have been haunted forever if I'd died that night because someone else had made the wrong decision, or if the surgeon taking his place did not have his skills. He would have been reminded of his failure, his lack of dedication, every time he looked into his son's eyes. Would his son doubt that his dad would stay with him when he needed him the most? Dr. Lang could not let that happen.

If I was going to die that night, I would die with Dr. Lang, one of the country's most gifted trauma surgeons, doing everything he could to save me. God had placed me in his hands, another angel in the right setting at the right time.

For Reflection

For the Lord *gives wisdom; from his mouth come knowledge and understanding; he stores up sound wisdom for the upright; he is a shield to those who walk in integrity, guarding the paths of justice and watching over the way of his saints. Then you will understand righteousness and justice and equity, every good path; for wisdom will come into your heart, and knowledge will be pleasant to your soul. (Proverbs 2:6–10)*

1. Have you ever had a "gut feeling"? Did it turn out to be correct? Do you believe your "gut" is actually God telling you what to do?
2. Is our conscience the voice of God?
3. Why is it that we often do not recognize God speaking to us?

CHAPTER 8

WORSE INSTEAD OF BETTER

By midnight, I was in recovery. It had been eleven hours since the Jeep had crossed the median and put me there; eleven hours since our great plan for our life had been completely thrown out the window. My wife was broken and mumbling, Alexa was recovering with a broken arm, and Victoria and Chase were bruised and terrified. All because of a loser who just had to down a twelve-pack before one o'clock on a Sunday afternoon as he drove around with nothing better to do.

Our families had started to arrive at the hospital after many frantic hours on the road, and Dr. Lang was ready to meet with them. My parents and three sisters were there, along with two of Mona's sisters and her brother. Mona's parents had just walked in after an exhausting nine-hour drive. They all gathered in a small room after visiting Mona and receiving updates on the extent of her injuries. They had spent hours holding and comforting our kids, who were now fast asleep on the floor and on couches, completely spent from the day's activities, their youth protecting them from truly under-standing the changes yet to come. Everyone was incredibly tired from the drive yet unable to sleep due to relentless fear and adrenaline. A nurse came in and told everyone to gather around; Dr. Lang would be in in a few minutes.

As they waited for the news that would upend their lives, they spoke very little. Nobody knew what to say, so they mostly prayed in silence.

Dr. Lang knocked before entering. He had been working for seventeen hours straight between his regular shift and then jumping in to work on me. After introducing himself, he sat down while our families anxiously gave him their full attention, waiting to hear the extent of the damage and an answer to the question of me ever regaining consciousness again.

If I did, would I walk? Would I be on permanent disability? They all knew I would hate not being able to work and would drive them all nuts if I was stuck in the house for the rest of my life. *Would they have to move closer to help with the kids?* They braced for the news about how their lives would drastically change.

Understanding they did not want small talk, Dr. Lang got right to the point. I had survived the surgery, but my chances were still fifty-fifty at best, and things could go downhill at any time. He explained that they would need to perform multiple surgeries to repair my various fractures over the next few days but would not put me on the operating table again until I was more stable. As for my mental status and prospects for working again, he could tell them nothing definitively. I had been unconscious when I arrived and would remain in a medically induced coma for a few days. Dr. Lang predicted a two- to four-month hospital stay and another six months in a nursing home at a minimum; I would be lucky to work again in a year. Furthermore, he warned them that the next twenty-four hours were critical and a lot could change. My body had taken a terrific beating and I probably would get worse before I got better. He was partially right; it wouldn't take twenty-four hours—it would take only one.

It started with a couple drops of blood. Not much, just a few drops. But in a strange place. Because my face had hit the airbag with such force, my nose had been relocated off to the side, with nose bleeds fully expected. However, blood was trickling from my eye like a teardrop.

On the surface, this would seem to be a very minor problem. Surely with nine fractured bones, massive internal injuries, and cuts and scrapes everywhere, a drop of blood from the eye wasn't a big deal. But the trickle of blood was not due to an injury. I had not bled from my eyes in the aftermath of the crash. The trickle had started because my blood had stopped clotting—my body was now bleeding out. My nurses knew I was probably a dead man.

In reaction to my multiple injuries—bruises, breaks, torn blood vessels—my body had started to assemble a variety of proteins called clotting factors. Now these clotting proteins were almost depleted. Without them, the whole process of clotting stopped. As a result, I was beginning to bleed spontaneously and soon would be bleeding in all kinds of different areas, including out of my eyes.

This is how rat poison works. The poison, Warfarin, stops the blood from clotting. Anything that ingests it bleeds to death from even the slightest little bump.

Now, I was like a poisoned rat beginning to bleed with no way to stop it. Soon I would start hemorrhaging in my lungs, brain, or anywhere else. I would bleed to death, experience a hemorrhagic stroke, or bleed into my lungs and die from asphyxiation. Immediately, the nurse ran for Dr. Lang and caught him exiting the doctor's locker room after just putting his coat on to leave.

My exhausted surgeon threw off his coat and rushed to my bedside. He recognized the problem immediately, having feared it from the start. All of his skillful work, hundreds of thousands of dollars spent, a Sunday with the family lost, and he would soon have to break the tragic news to my father and mother, my three sisters, my wife, and my three battered children that I was gone. He was familiar with the exact words: "We tried everything we could but were unable to save him. He passed away."

They would all explode into sobs, and my parents, now nearing seventy, would collapse. Their lives would be ruined because they would never recover from the loss of their child and would spend the rest of their days in a sorrowful funk. Family gatherings would forever be clouded with the emptiness of a missing family member. Christmas would now be about trying to act happy for the kids while the adults would be dying on the inside. One dead, and two whole families destroyed.

Blood naturally forms a clot by what is called a "cascade." A cascade is a series of steps, each step multiplying the effect of the previous one. It is like a snowball rolling down a hill; it starts as a small ball that picks up more snow as it rolls. The faster and bigger it gets, the more snow it can pick up. A blood clot is formed by proteins in the blood that begin to stick together, causing different proteins to glom on and eventually form a clot. They are triggered to stick together by the tear in the blood vessel that exposes the underlying tissue and provides an irregular surface for blood proteins to adhere to. Each clotting protein (called a "factor" and numbered in sequence) multiplies the next protein until there is a huge amount of them all congealing together. It forms and looks much like Jell-O. Ultimately, it is a big wad of protein that sticks to the torn vessel and seals it off.

The problem for me was that I had used up one of these factors in the sequence, making it impossible for clots to form. I still had numerous torn vessels and broken bones oozing blood, but there were only so many of these factors in the body at any time, and I had run out. If even one factor in the chain that makes a clot is missing, the entire process stops. Hemophiliacs can't clot blood well because they are short on a single clotting factor and thus are at constant risk of bleeding to death. Thanks to my ordeal on the interstate, I was now one of them.

The blood trickling out of my eye was the first sign. It was soon followed by a trickle of blood out of my ear. This kind of spontaneous hemorrhage is called disseminated intravascular coagulation, or D.I.C. I had seen this in animals, either from trauma such as this or with other systemic disease such as infections or cancers. In veterinary school, we used a different name for D.I.C.; to us it stood for *dead in cage*. I had seen it dozens of times in my practice, treated each animal aggressively, and never saved one. They all were "dead in cage" within hours.

I had been given twelve units of blood by now, but all of it contained an anticoagulant. More blood transfusions would make it worse instead of better.

There was one chance to stop the bleeding, but it was a long shot: a product called factor VIII, one of the blood clotting proteins and the one that the body typically depletes first. It also cost $15,000 for the single dose. Knowing it was probably too late, probably a waste of money and probably doomed to fail, Dr. Lang ordered the factor VIII anyway. He was not optimistic; he had used it many times before with no success. Every patient had bled to death while he stood by helplessly.

After calling for the injection, Dr. Lang watched and prayed as it was administered through the IV port. Then he called Dr. Gibbs, Mona's primary physician. After informing him of my status, they both agreed; Mona should be told about my situation and allowed to come to my room. She would be able to see her husband and the father of her children before he passed away. This had to be done immediately.

Dr. Gibbs had treated Mona when she first came in and also had stayed well past his shift to monitor her. Now he had to tell her about me. This was what every physician hates, telling someone that their loved one is about to die. But before he told Mona, he and Dr. Lang had to meet with the family. They asked a nurse to find Mona's mother, Anne, and her father, Joe. It was past midnight and they were both sleeping. The nurse found them on chairs in one of the hallways and woke them gently.

"Dr. Gibbs and Dr. Lang need to speak to you both," she announced. Sensing their fear, she added, "Mona's condition is unchanged. It is about Scot."

Joe and Anne sat with their hearts racing. They both knew that the nurse waking them up and the doctor coming in to talk to them could only mean something bad. Although they had considered the possibility that I would die, they had not discussed it at all during the long drive to the hospital. They did not want to even bring it up.

What would they have to do with the kids, and how would they help? Should Anne quit her job to help raise the grandkids if they did not have a father? How would Mona support the family by herself in my absence? How would she work with a broken back?

Dr. Gibbs and Dr. Lang entered the room and asked Joe and Anne to sit down. They were both ready to collapse as the adrenaline surged through them, with Anne starting to tear up even before Dr. Gibbs could speak.

"We have run into a complication with Scot. His blood is no longer able to clot. We call the syndrome D.I.C. I don't need to explain the acronym, but he can't clot his blood, which is usually fatal. He is very likely to die tonight. We believe Mona should be brought in to see him while he is still alive."

Mona's father was fiercely protective of his family, and his instincts won out over the doctor's recommendations. "Absolutely not! She has been through enough. Seeing her husband dying will kill her."

Dr. Lang then took over, employing the patience he had developed in dealing with his autistic son. "Mr. Anderson, I understand your concern, but the chances of Scot surviving this complication are only one in a hundred."

"What do you mean one in a hundred?!" Anne asked as Joe stormed out of the room.

"We have given Scot a medicine to get his blood clotting again, but it is rarely successful. If one hundred people need the shot, only one will survive."

"Isn't there anything else you can do?"

"We are doing everything possible, and Scot is currently stable. That is why we need to decide quickly. I do not know how long he will remain so."

"We need to bring her up. She needs to see him," Anne decided.

"We agree," Dr. Lang replied gently. "It is the best thing."

Anne left to find Joe, having come to the realization that this was necessary, and the two entered Mona's room, where she was hooked up to monitors and IVs. The huge deep-blue bruise on her head encompassed a third of her face. She was in a back brace from her armpits to her hips and lay flat on her back, unable to move. Anne gently spoke her name, asking her to wake up.

"Mona, Mona, wake up." It was the same voice she had used when waking her for school thirty years earlier.

"Mona, wake up. You need to go see Scot."

Mona's eyes slowly opened and she began to comprehend. She was still on a morphine drip and her brain was still rebooting after the concussion, but this time she understood right away.

The nurses gathered around the bed to help her into a wheelchair. In the brace, she could no longer bend to get up. With her broken elbow, her left arm was wrapped to her side.

"Why are you bringing me now? It's still dark out."

"Mona," Anne said gently, "the doctor asked that you come see Scot."

"Why? Is he dying?"

"Mona, he is very injured. They thought you should go speak to him."

Mona was still in a fog but soon realized that the doctors must have been thinking *I was not going to make it.*

She arrived in my room and began to sob, having not seen me since the crash. I lay there on a respirator, my eyes shut and unresponsive. She could see all the splints and wraps and my obviously broken nose. She knew on sight that I probably would not make it through, but she could not even get out of the chair. All she could do was reach over and touch my hand.

I was in a medically induced coma and had no awareness of her presence. She cried softly, trying to keep it muffled so as not to wake me, knowing the pain would be unbearable if I were to regain consciousness. She did not want that for me even if it meant that I could not hear her final words. She simply said, "I love you. You saved me and the kids. You are a great father and husband. Just please keep fighting. I don't want you to leave me; we need you here."

She cried there for a few minutes. When it became clear she'd said what she needed to say, the nursing staff came in to wheel her back to her room. She was now supposed to try to get some rest—an impossible feat when you are waiting to hear if your husband is going to live or die. She sobbed in her wheelchair as they transported her back to her hospital bed.

What would she do? How would she tell the kids that their dad was not going to be there anymore? She mostly worried about Chase. *Who would show him how to be a man? Who would play football with him in the yard and teach him how to throw a baseball?*

She knew the girls needed me too. They would soon be coming into their teen years when girls need a strong father figure to act as their safety net and the thing that keeps them grounded when all the boys start coming around. Now Mona knew I probably would not be around anymore to provide that sense of protection; it was gone for all of them.

On the way back to her room, she prayed. She had not had the time or mental capacity up to that point to ask God for help, but then in an amazing moment of clarity, she did. Her mind cleared, making it possible for her to pray—not in an endless loop, but lucidly and concisely. With all of her might, she prayed to save me, begging God to let me live; there was nothing else she could do.

"God, please let him live. I don't care about anything else. He doesn't have to get back to normal. Just let him live and we will adapt to anything else. I don't know how to raise these kids by myself; I need him with me. I am begging you, just let him live."

There was no reply, no booming voice from heaven. She was hoping for a comforting feeling that everything would be all right. She got nothing, just silence. It scared her even more and she felt completely alone. Although her mom was in the room with her, she still felt like her life would be a very lonely struggle. As a thirty-eight-year-old widow, she would be raising the kids by herself. Both our parents and all our siblings were scattered all over the Midwest. If Mona wanted their help raising the kids, she would have to sell everything we had built together and move. The thought of uprooting the kids and starting all over scared her more than her injuries. She very well might have been facing the loss of her husband, her source of income, all her friends and contacts, and her home. She confronted these horrifying possibilities in a wheelchair with three breaks in her back, a scrambled brain, and no message from God that He had heard her prayer. She felt so incredibly alone.

Then her anger flared: at Jacobs who had just destroyed our lives, at God who wasn't listening, at the inability of the doctors to save me. All this advanced technology, all these highly trained doctors and nurses, and they were all standing by watching helplessly. It wasn't fair; we didn't deserve this. We had tried to be good people. We went to church on Sundays and attempted to do the right thing always. Sure, we weren't perfect, but we didn't deserve *this*. Mona could do nothing to help as she lay there on a morphine drip, her mind still wanting to repeat and jumble her words. Everything was completely out of her control. Our plan for our lives had been destroyed.

She pushed the button for another dose of morphine—not for the physical pain but the emotional—and drifted off, assuming that upon awakening she'd be a widow before her fortieth birthday.

Dr. Lang had apprised my family of my condition just as he had done with Joe and Anne. Now he waited to see if he would have to go through the "death speech" with them. Everyone just passed the time in quiet fear and desperation, knowing that the bleeding probably would continue in spite of the factor VIII shot. It probably would fail and either my oxygen level would start to drop precipitously as my lungs filled with blood or I would start to hemorrhage profusely in my brain. I would "stroke out" and never wake up. The room was quiet except for the constant rhythmic beat of the monitors signaling my heart was still beating. As long as that was going, I had a chance, though not much of one.

Margaret was the E.R. nurse watching over me. She had been with me from the time I left the helicopter almost half a day ago. Now she carefully wiped the blood from my eye and ear waiting to see if more came. She had to be gentle so as not to incite any more bleeding. At this point, any small bump, any disruption to a blood vessel could bleed for the rest of my endangered life.

Blood continued to slowly drip like tears while Margaret waited, wanting to give it a chance to clot, only to see another drip trickle out. She repeated this process every few seconds with the same result, and each time her heart sank a little lower. She had seen it before dozens of times, an innocent victim cut down in his prime due to some stupid act of another. Drunk-driving crashes; gunfights in which only the bystanders get hit; domestic disputes in which an abusive husband beats his wife repeatedly for some perceived wrong and finally puts her into a coma, resulting in death. As she wiped away tears of blood, Margaret recounted them all. She had seen the factor VIII shot administered dozens of times but had yet to see it work. She had no faith in this last-ditch effort to save my life.

She continued for a half-hour, never leaving my side, while my parents sat silently in the room. My sisters were waiting outside in the hall so as not to be in the way of the staff.

Then it happened: The tear trickled down more slowly the next time. Unsure if what she was seeing was real or a product of her imagination, Margaret did not want to say anything. She wiped the tear away again, but it seemed to take a little longer for a new tear to form. The third time it was clear: The blood was slowing down. It took several minutes to refill my eyelid and overflow down my face. She wiped it again, not sure if the blood was going to truly stop or just slow for a while and then restart. She did not say a word. It had to stop completely in order for me to live; a temporary slowdown would not be enough.

The next time she wiped it away, it did not refill. That's when she ran to find Dr. Lang. My parents came to my side, and my sisters entered my room. Everyone began to cry. The shot had worked! The trickles of blood from my eye and ear had stopped. Margaret could not believe it. I was the one in a hundred who would live after getting the factor VIII shot.

Dr. Lang took stock of where I was. The major sources of bleeding had been controlled, the ruptured spleen had been removed, and the torn femoral vein was packed off. The fracture in my leg had been stabilized with the external fixator, and the open fractures of my elbow and heel were cleaned, bandaged, and splinted. My arms were wrapped to my chest waiting to be fixed later on; no more blood dripped from my eye. For the moment, I was stable. It was time to let me rest and go talk with the rest of my family filling up the chairs in the hallway. They had been kept updated since they had arrived and had been expecting to hear the worst. Dr. Lang gave them the good news that I had dodged another bullet and said the same words I have often told my clients after getting through a nearly fatal injury or surgery on their beloved pet: "I have done all I can do. It is in God's hands now."

My family had been praying nonstop, so they did not have to be told to ask for God's help, but Dr. Lang told them to keep it up anyway. "We will re-evaluate his status in the morning. Now we all need some rest."

Mona was in the same boat, with the work done for the day. Anne had come to her room to tell her that my bleeding had stopped, for now. Mona's elbow was splinted, her abdominal bleeding halted or at least slowed to the point where it was no longer life-threatening, and her concussion was not getting worse. However, it would be days before they would know how badly her brain had been injured. Her back was fractured, but she was in a body brace and sedated— bruised and battered but stable.

The kids had all been checked out also. The two youngest were bruised and cut up but physically in one piece. Alexa had a broken arm that was in a sling. They were not sure if surgery would be necessary since many broken arms do very well with this method; the bones are pulled into place by gravity and allowed to heal. Being only ten years old, she would heal quickly. She had been given pain medication and was doing okay. Mona's parents and sisters were sitting in the same waiting room along with my parents and sisters. They all took shifts taking care of our three children.

We had made it through Day One. The only family members missing yet were the dogs.

For Reflection

So whoever knows the right thing to do and fails to do it, for him it is sin. (James 4:17)

1. When have you been in a place where you normally would not have been and it resulted in a good thing (i.e., the right place at the right time)? A bad thing (the wrong place at the wrong time)? Are such things merely coincidence?

2. If you don't listen to your conscience, is that a sin?

Do not be anxious about anything, but in everything by prayer and supplication with thanksgiving let your requests be made known to God. And the peace of God, which surpasses all understanding, will guard your hearts and your minds in Christ Jesus. (Philippians 4:6–7)

3. Have you ever had an experience when things got worse before they got better? Did you ask God for help, and if so, what was the response?

4. Do you believe God listens to all prayers? Do you believe God responds to all prayers? Why?

CHAPTER 9

WHERE ARE THE DOGS?

Now that the reality of what had happened was beginning to sink in, the kids realized they were missing their dogs. Mona and I were in no position to inquire about them, but the kids knew they were no longer with us—Olivia, our little Yorkie-Poo, and Annabelle, our rescue Golden Retriever. In all the chaos, they had not been accounted for.

Olivia was found lying on the side of the road when paramedics arrived, having been ripped from the warmth and safety of Chase's lap and thrown out the window on impact. She lay in the ditch with a fractured skull and a massive brain injury, going immediately into seizures. A bystander had covered her with a blanket to prevent the kids from having to watch their tiny, beloved pet experience convulsions and die on the side of the road. It was not until all of us had left for the hospital that a paramedic checked under the blanket, fully expecting to find a dead dog. To his surprise, Olivia was still alive. She had suffered major head trauma and was in and out of seizures but alive nonetheless.

A dog lover himself, the paramedic gently picked up her eight-pound body and brought her to his vehicle, where he wrapped her in a spare towel and decided to drive her to the veterinary emergency hospital. He had seen the kids and the parents and figured their little dog would either die on her own or have to be put down, but he could not bear to leave her on the side of the road to perish. Having helped to free me from the van, the paramedic was sure I would be dead soon; he also knew Mona had sustained serious head trauma and might never be the same again. As he contemplated the tragedy of these kids losing their dad and their dog on the same day, he began to tear up. At the very least, he could ease the little dog's suffering. He drove with Olivia on his lap to the animal E.R.

On the way, the dog had two more seizures. Her body would tense as the seizure came over her, extending her neck backward until it was over her shoulders, looking back behind herself. Her front legs would extend out fully and her lips would pull back in a terrible grin. Then, when her muscles were as tight as possible, the seizure would start: Her body would shake violently and she would cry out. Her tongue would turn blue, as she was not able to move her diaphragm and pull in any air. This would continue for about a minute and then pass, the muscles exhausted and the brain's chemical messengers depleted. She would then relax and start to breathe again.

The paramedic arrived at the veterinary emergency hospital and presented Olivia. A situation like this always puts vets in a tough spot because we need to treat the dog but have no permission from the owner to do so. Without permission, we have no sense of how much treatment to administer. Would the owners want to do anything to save their pet, or would they want her put down? She was seizing and obviously had major head trauma, so she probably would need days or weeks of treatment and medications before anyone would be able to determine if she'd ever function anywhere close to normally again.

From a business point of view, there was also no guarantee that the hospital would ever be paid for its services. Nobody wants to make this decision based on money, but there are real costs involved here: A veterinarian would have to examine her, determine how to best treat her injuries, and decide the proper drugs and dosages to administer. He or she would need to monitor Olivia's response and decide if and when she needed more. Our little dog also would need an IV catheter that costs about twenty dollars and medicine that is relatively cheap but requires someone to stand and administer it effectively and then monitor afterward. Realistically, the hospital's cost for the first day of her care would be in the hundreds of dollars. Not nearly as much as Mona, Alexa, and I were going to cost, but eventually the expenses could rise into the thousands of dollars.

Unlike human hospitals, there is no government assistance for the veterinary E.R. treating Olivia; the cost would come directly out of the pocket of the hospital owners if they didn't get paid. Of course, they had no way of knowing if we, the owners now broken and struggling to survive, would have a dime left to spend on a dog that might never come back from a major injury.

Without permission to do any treatment, they decided to administer the drugs needed to stabilize Olivia but not do any diagnostics such as X-rays or bloodwork. They would have to keep their costs down but would do what was humane: stop her seizures and keep her pain under control.

The paramedic had tears in his eyes as he handed off our helpless pet. "Please do everything you can to save her. These kids may lose their dad tonight and don't need to lose their dog also. I don't make a ton of money, but here is $165, all the cash I have on me, if they can't pay."

He was another angel sent to us that day. Not only had he been part of the team that got us to the hospital, but he had taken it upon himself to help this scruffy little dog that probably had little chance of survival. Now he volunteered to give up some of his own paycheck for a family he didn't know because he just couldn't bear to let the kids lose their dog. Yes, another angel.

The emergency hospital took Olivia in. The vet on call determined that there were no broken bones except for a possible skull fracture and an obvious bruise to her left eye. The bones on the side of her face felt intact, but Olivia had major head trauma. If the bones of the skull had broken, the pieces did not appear to have moved significantly and would not need surgery; they would be left to heal on their own. Dogs have much more muscle around their heads than we do, so the bones heal much faster. There was obvious brain injury with the seizures and the fact that she was unconscious, along with the history of being ejected from a vehicle onto the interstate. They would have done an MRI to ascertain the extent of the damage if they'd known someone would pay for it, but for now, they would just stabilize her.

The doctor ordered a catheter to be set in Olivia's front leg and a bolus of valium to be given. If the seizures continued, she could get another 0.2 milliliters until they stopped, up to a total of 1.2 milliliters (the high end of the dose). If this did not stop the seizures, she would administer another drug and put Olivia into a coma. Dogs with this kind of injury often die fairly quickly as the brain swells and the seizing becomes uncontrollable. Still, the hospital would do the best it could.

After the first bolus of valium was given, Olivia was transported to a cage for observation. But before they could even place her inside, she threw a seizure again, prompting them to give her more of the drug. Afterward, she fell unconscious, her breathing slowing to a point that made everyone nervous—yet she kept going. This tiny little dog was surviving, at least for the moment.

She also was given a bolus of steroids with the goal of stopping the swelling in the brain and stopping the seizures. They gave her the steroid injection along with a second drug called Mannitol and waited to see if it would work. Olivia was one of God's creatures just like us; she was in His hands now.

The paramedic had told the vets about the crash, so the office receptionist began calling hospitals. Figuring I'd been taken to the university, she started there. She was told that, yes, there was a family brought in after a terrible car crash but there was not yet anyone available who could talk with them. They were working on stabilizing the parents and the family had been notified. The family was hours away yet, but they would pass on the message as soon as possible. Then the hospital receptionist said to the vet's office, her voice cracking with emotion: "There were three little kids in the car. It is likely they will lose their dad today; anything they could do to save the little dog would be greatly appreciated."

Hours later, the hospital receptionist went to tell my family about Olivia. She approached my mother, Diane, who was still pale and crying from realizing the extent of our injuries but had had some time to process everything.

"I know your son and daughter-in-law are your biggest concern, but I wanted to let you know that the animal E.R. in town called and they have their little dog. She is alive but has a head injury. They wanted me to tell you she is stable for now but she may not survive."

My mother just nodded. She knew how much the kids loved that little dog, but she just couldn't think about the family pets right then.

The receptionist turned to leave.

"Wait," Mom spoke up, "what about the other dog?"

The woman turned back to face her with a puzzled expression.

"They only mentioned a small tan dog. Was there another?"

"Yes," she continued, "there would have been a Golden Retriever with them also."

"Sorry, they did not mention another dog. Just the one."

Grandma went to tell the kids who still hadn't grasped the seriousness of Mona's and my condition and were very worried about their dogs. Knowing that Olivia was in the hospital and alive sent them off running and yelling for joy. That is, until Victoria asked, "What about Annabelle?"

"They did not say where she was," Grandma replied. "Maybe she is at a different hospital."

With that, the celebration was over. The kids' hearts sank as they realized nobody knew what had become of our Golden Retriever; she was still missing. Victoria had seen her take off at a full run as soon as the doors to the van had opened. Preoccupied with the human occupants, no one on the scene had stopped her. Now she was gone. Annabelle was a great dog, but there was no stopping her when she panicked. She had been last seen diving into a cornfield next to the highway. Our dog was sixty miles away from home, wandering around outside in October in Wisconsin. The temperature would drop into the thirties at night when she normally would be safe and warm inside the house. Now Annabelle was wet and scared, completely on her own.

All the family could do was wait. There was a good chance by morning they'd have to break the news to the kids that their parents were no longer able to care for them and that they would have to leave behind everything they knew to go live somewhere else. At the very least, it seemed more likely the children would have to deal with the loss of their dad. Their world was being shaken to its core.

Every face the kids saw had the look of dread, as if everyone around them was hiding something that they didn't want to say.

I, of course, was unaware of anything that was going on; the kids had seen it all. They would remember everything.

FOR REFLECTION

But ask the beasts, and they will teach you; the birds of the heavens, and they will tell you; or the bushes of the earth, and they will teach you; and the fish of the sea will declare to you. Who among all these does not know that the hand of the LORD has done this? In his hand is the life of every living thing and the breath of all mankind. (Job 12:7–10)

Your righteousness is like the mountains of God; your judgments are like the great deep; man and beast you save, O LORD. (Psalms 36:6)

1. How do you think God sees the animals in our lives?
2. Do animals have souls?
3. How does God want us to relate to animals?
4. What can our animal friends teach us about dealing with tragedy?

CHAPTER 10

DAY TWO

The second day brought some good news: Mona was becoming more lucid. She was recognizing the people around her and had stopped repeating herself. Another specialist was brought in to evaluate her brain function. Mona was told at the start of the exam to remember four things seen in the room—a pen, a table, a chair, and a pillow. Then she was asked to repeat those four things. She started with the pen but then stopped, unable to remember the other three. For someone whose entire life revolved around retaining knowledge—diagnoses, treatments, complicated medical jargon, the kids' schedules and homework—this was troubling to say the least. If she lost her ability to remember small details like a few objects in a room, how could she ever go back to being a vet and a mother?

The neurologist tested a few basic reflexes before excusing herself. As she turned to leave, she advised Mona she'd be back in a week to retest; only then would she be able to determine if this memory loss would be long- or short-term. If Mona could pass the test in a week, great; if not, she would be looking at a very long road to recovery (if she ever did recover).

My wife was in full panic mode; a brain injury would be catastrophic. If I died or could not regain the ability to work and she could not remember simple things, we would have to sell the clinic and Mona would have to go on disability. Since our income would plummet, she probably would have to sell the house and eventually move closer to family for help with raising the kids. She loved where we lived now, and the disruption would be very hard on everyone, especially if I was dead or not the man I had been. The "what-ifs" were terrifying.

Luckily, she had not yet fully comprehended all that had happened. She knew the kids were okay and under the care of family. Although she'd been apprised of my injuries, her brain hadn't stored the information. She asked if I could be brought down to see her, not realizing that I was on a respirator with multiple broken bones yet to be fixed. For the umpteenth time, her sister Carla patiently recounted the previous day's events for her. Mona had no recollection that the doctors had brought her to me to say goodbye the night before. She was still experiencing acute pain, eased by a morphine drip that further clouded her mind. This would take a while.

The most important thing was that Mona's spinal cord was intact and her brain function had not worsened. Yes, the recovery process would be long and grueling, but she was not going to die. Our kids would have at least one parent.

As for me, I was becoming more stable but had been put in a coma and would stay there for the first three days while the doctors put me back together, one bone at a time.

First, the thighbone had to be plated. Since my condition had stabilized some more and the antibiotics had had some time to work where the bone had exited the skin, Dr. Lang decided to remove the external fixator and apply a bone plate.

The thighbone had a number of problems. First, it had shattered at about the lower third of the bone and the fracture had extended down through the knee. There were multiple bone pieces present, while still others were missing, having been blown out the side of my leg. The knee part of the bone was cracked in half. Also, that torn femoral vein had to be tied off once and for all.

Dr. Lang began by first removing the external fixator that had been placed previously. A plate would be placed directly over the bone and would not damage any muscle. This would enable the muscle to continue to slide and the knee to bend during recovery. I would be able to do some rehab and use a wheelchair until the bone was healed.

Dr. Lang removed the external fixator, but before he plated the bone, he'd have to fix the torn femoral vein that nearly killed me a day prior. The temporary bandage he'd wrapped into the wound had gotten me through the first day, but it could not stay there forever.

The torn vein had retracted into the muscle, making it hard to find. However, Dr. Lang had an advantage: The vein was torn, but the artery was still intact. These two normally lie right next to each other, so if you follow the artery, it will lead to the vein. Better yet, the artery was easy to find. It was as big as my index finger and it had a pulse. Feel for the pulse and you find the artery; follow the artery and you find the vein.

A large clot covered the entire area, filling the void where the muscle had been. It was the clot that initially had saved my life, stopping the bleeding that had been killing me.

But now this life-saving clot had to be removed because the torn vein could bleed again at any time. Once the clot was removed, Dr. Lang could identify the vein itself, isolate it, and tie it off.

With the bleeding under control, it was time to get the bone back together, at least as much as possible. With a minimum of five separate pieces to reassemble, it was like a 3D jigsaw puzzle.

The problem was that the lower part of the bone (the part that forms the knee) had split in half; there was no solid piece to hold the end of the plate. Before the plate could be placed, the end of the bone comprising the knee would have to be put back together so the plate could be secured to it.

If Dr. Lang could screw together the pieces and reform the knee, then a plate could be placed to reconnect the knee to the thighbone. It would be critical that the pieces of the knee lined up exactly so the surfaces are not irregular and the kneecap has a smooth place to slide. If the joint is not realigned perfectly, the cartilage won't heal, creating bone-on-bone contact. The knee will be painful and never function well. Dr. Lang had to get it right.

Lining up the two pieces of bone, he pressed them together. The jagged bones of the fracture locked back together like those afore-mentioned 3D puzzle pieces. Three screws were placed across the bone to hold it together, with care taken to leave a spot for the plate to be attached. The end of the bone was now solid; the first step was over.

Putting the rest of the bone together would not be an easy feat, since the entire middle third had shattered. Dr. Lang started to sort the pieces out. From about halfway down the thigh to about three inches above the knee, the bone was completely smashed; some of the pieces were crushed beyond recognition. Even worse, it soon became apparent that a crucial piece was missing. The bone shard had shot through the muscle and out the side of the leg. Most likely, this bone fragment was rolling around the floor of the car somewhere. I'd have to heal without it.

Since not all of the pieces could be reassembled, the goal would be to hold the two ends—one from the hip to the middle of the thigh and the other at the knee—in place and let the middle part "just heal." A special bone plate was used that would span the shattered part of bone. The plate holds the ends in place until the pieces can "knit" themselves together underneath. I would have to rely on the plate to bear all my weight until the bone was healed, so the team employed a bigger, thicker plate made out of titanium. Despite the strength of this plate, it still would not support a one-hundred-seventy-pound man; I would be in a wheelchair or crutches for two to three months.

Three screws through the top of the plate and two more through the bottom fixed the plate to the bone. These would bear all the weight for the bone during the healing process.

Dr. Lang had one more trick up his sleeve: He wanted to help fill in the missing bone. Instead of a graft, Dr. Lang decided to use bone morphogenetic protein; this is a hormone that tells bone to grow and stimulates it to fill in what is missing. It is soaked into a collagen sponge that eventually will be absorbed. The doctor's assistant opened a package and shoved the sponge into the hole where the bone was missing. It took just seconds. Now, we'd have to wait and see if bone could fill in and heal.

With the vein tied off and the bone fixed, Dr. Lang could address the torn muscle, and that would be enough for one day. My pulses were steady, but my blood was still in danger of not clotting again. I still had two broken elbows, a broken arm, a dislocated and broken shoulder, and a broken pelvis and nose, but they would have to wait.

Meanwhile, Mona spent the day in a drug-induced haze. She was increasingly cognizant and could really feel the pain, although morphine kept it at bay. It also prevented the realization of what had happened from fully sinking in. Therefore, she didn't yet have to deal with my situation and the effect it would have on our lives.

Alexa had received some good news concerning her dog at the veterinary emergency hospital. Olivia had survived the night, having been medicated in an attempt to stop the seizures, and was still alive. Dr. Chris Welch, our partner at our veterinary hospital, was coming to Madison that day to see us and would stop at the E.R. to check on Olivia.

Our Golden Retriever, Annabelle, was still missing, but some of the police officers who had helped us at the crash were coming back during their time off to look for her. These officers were complete strangers to us. We did not live in their community, and the fields were muddy and cold. These angels went anyway to search for our lost dog.

The kids knew their mom was pretty banged up but saw she was talking, so they were not too worried. They hadn't seen me yet and really did not comprehend the extent of our injuries; their worry was focused on the dogs. There was nothing to tell them yet; nobody really knew the fate of our pets. The doctors couldn't predict Mona's and my final outcomes either, but at least we were all alive.

The sling holding Alexa's broken arm caused concern among the surgeons. The bones were not in the right position but instead were overlapping. They had hoped that the weight of the arm would pull the bones back into place, but that hadn't happened. The doctors had no choice but to ask Mona for permission to perform surgery.

Mona was in no shape to make any decisions, so her sister Carla had to make the call. Our daughter was only ten years old, and surgery is always a concern. Additionally, Alexa *hates* needles. Carla carefully explained to Mona that her child needed surgery and Mona nodded her head. Everyone knew that Mona was not really understanding the question, but this was all the doctors needed. They allowed Carla to sign a release.

Within thirty minutes, Alexa was being wheeled into the O.R. for surgery. Unlike my fractured leg, Alexa's arm had only two pieces to get together, which easily aligned. She would spend the next month in a sling but would heal quickly; youth was on her side.

We had all made it through another day. The risk of anyone dying was decreasing by the hour. The doctors still could not say how "normal" we would be, but at least it looked like we would survive.

For Reflection

And he took a child and put him in the midst of them, and taking him in his arms, he said to them, "Whoever receives one such child in my name receives me, and whoever receives me, receives not me but him who sent me." (Mark 9:36–37)

1. How important do you think it is for children to have faith in God?
2. How can a church community support children through crisis?
3. Do you think kids understand that God is with them?

CHAPTER 11

God's Will Be Done

Over the next few days, they would fix my elbows and shoulder. I was still in a medically induced coma and hadn't awakened since I'd arrived at the hospital. Once again, they wheeled me into surgery while my family stood vigil. They all sat waiting, knowing that my small steps forward could, at any moment, turn into a huge step back. My heart could fail, I could throw a clot and have a stroke, I could have a problem with anesthesia—so many things could go wrong that everyone held their breath every time I went in to the O.R. All they could do was wait and pray. Pray that I would make it through one more day. Pray that Mona's brain would continue to improve, that her broken back would not shift, making her legs go numb. The ever-present tension of the last few days continued unabated. Nobody really slept and everyone was quiet.

As they sat in silence, the same question reverberated through all of their minds: *Why?* Why did this happen to *their* loved ones? We were a nice family, we never made enemies, we went to church on Sundays (some of the time), and we worked to help injured and sick animals. Surely we didn't deserve to be crushed in an auto accident by a drunken scumbag, especially one who walked away with nothing but a scratched nose. Everyone struggled to make sense of it all.

About two hours later, a nurse walked into the waiting area to announce I'd made it through another surgery. Another piece of Humpty Dumpty had been put back together. Tomorrow my upper arm would be plated and my shoulder put back into place. The day after that, my nose would be set.

I still had a couple of pelvic fractures, but my medical team decided these would be left to heal on their own. Encased in muscle, the pelvis heals well. The biggest muscles in the body are in the buttocks. Because of their thick size and great blood supply, these muscles help to hold everything in place. Good blood supply and stable breaks allow for bone to heal well; therefore, they expected the pelvis to fully recover on its own in a few weeks without any medical assistance. I would be flat on my back for two months anyway; these breaks were the least of my worries.

With me in a medical coma, nobody had a clue as to my mental status. Was my brain going to work again? Would I be the same person as before or would I be unable to think or speak? This was the elephant in the room that nobody wanted to talk about.

What if, after all this work and all these surgeries, I never woke up? What if I didn't remember who I was or what I did for a living?

My profession demanded the use of an incredible amount of information every day; what if I was not able to retrieve it anymore? Bones could be put back together and would heal in a few months, but the brain is an entirely different thing. My brain was severely concussed. I would be in too much pain if they woke me up now, but they decided to give it a try in twenty-four hours. Tomorrow, they would bring me around just enough to see if I was still there. For now, they'd keep me in a coma to facilitate my recovery from this latest surgery. As I slept, the rest of my family could do nothing but wait and continue to pray. Tomorrow would be the day they'd discover if they had lost the husband, father, brother, or son they had always known. Tonight, it was just more waiting.

As I slept, our church pastors, Mark and Mary Ann, arrived. This husband-and-wife team had taken over a dying church a few years before we got to town. At the time, membership was less than one hundred and the average age of the congregants was over seventy. Torn apart by internal bickering and a complete loss of mission, the church was in total disarray; Mark and Mary Ann had been sent to save it.

Upon their arrival, these enthusiastic pastors had great visions of cultivating a youth program. They would offer a Sunday school that was fun and engaging, along with Bible camps, and retreats for the teenagers. Their natural energy was infectious. This would be a youth-centered church.

Of course, God had sent them here specifically, which meant it would not be easy. They spent the first few weeks heartbroken, wondering if they had made the right choice. Although they had worked their whole lives with the goal of leading a church that fulfilled their vision of ministering to the youth, they had discovered that there could be no children's Christmas choir the first year. How could there be? There were no kids in the congregation—not one.

Mark and Mary Ann had faced what we were facing now; their plan for their lives looked like it was not meant to be. How could they have a young, vibrant church when they had no kids or young couples attending?

God had a plan; it just was not *their* plan. Their job was to accept it.

They had immediately won people over with their energy and faith. By focusing solely on the church's mission of bringing people to Christ, they completely changed the culture and ended the squabbling. With that, the church took off. Mark and Mary Ann retained the traditional service with its slow, somber hymns for the older members but added a contemporary service complete with a rockin' band and loud, upbeat music.

At first, the band consisted of a piano player and a single vocalist. Many times, they had fewer than a dozen congregants in the seats. But soon, new people began to show up; word was spreading quickly about this new church that *celebrated* on Sundays. They made church fun and pertinent, focusing the sermons on real-life problems. Pastor

Mark even made sure to leave a few windows open and the door slightly ajar during the more modern service. He wanted the music to emanate outside to allow people down the street to hear it—a little free advertising that things had changed.

In the six years since we had known them, the church had grown exponentially and there were dozens of kids now singing in the Christmas services. Mark and Mary Ann exuded love and compassion and had come to offer their prayers and support as soon as they had heard the news of our crash.

They walked in and introduced themselves to my family just as the doctors were leaving. The surgery to fix my elbows had gone well, but since elbows are notoriously unforgiving, I probably would not get back full range of motion on either side. I would have to be in splints for a month, which would cause my joints to scar down. Before I could ever gain the use of my arms again, I would need more months of rehab and possibly even more surgeries.

When asked if I would be able to work or if the damage was too severe, the doctors just shrugged; they simply had no idea.

Pastors Mark and Mary Ann knew not to stay long. The family was under a great deal of stress and did not need a protracted visit from strangers. After my sister Julie updated them on our condition, they requested that everyone bow their heads and join hands for a prayer, prompting a slight hesitation I could have easily predicted had I been awake. My family is very conservative in some ways; we do not touch each other much. It is more customary for us to *fold* our hands for prayer, not *hold* hands. However, Mark and Mary Ann persisted until my parents, sisters, and brothers-in-law awkwardly grasped each other's hands. They then all bowed their heads. As the monitors beeped and the ventilator gave me breath, they prayed for healing and strength. Mark prayed for all of us to make it through this difficult time and accept God's will. He prayed that we'd remain faithful in our understanding that there is a higher plan—*His* plan—that we cannot see or anticipate. We just needed to accept these trials and use them to strengthen our faith and bring us closer to God. He ended with, "God's will be done."

With that, they headed to Mona's room where she was being weaned off the morphine. A side effect of those drugs is lack of GI (gastrointestinal) motility; your guts slow to a crawl. Over the last few days, she had become terribly bloated and constipated as indicated by her distended abdomen. Her brain was still not functioning well and she was in the haze of lingering morphine, which had altered her personality, making her combative and paranoid. Mona was convinced that the nurses were sending drugs through the inflatable compression stockings placed on her legs to keep her blood moving and to prevent clots from forming. She was absolutely certain they were all conspiring in the nurse's station to overmedicate her and keep her sedated.

Of course, the nurses were doing no such thing. The drugs had made Mona delusional, but her thoughts made perfect sense to her. All the consoling and reasoning of her family didn't help. In fact, it just proved that they were all in on it together. Everyone was lying to her, preventing her from getting up and going home, and keeping her drugged. She was sure of it.

As the pastors came in, she was being wheeled for a CT scan to evaluate her abdominal distension. She truly believed it was due to uncontrolled and undiagnosed internal bleeding and she was dying. This was further confirmed in her mind because she had gotten her period (this commonly happens after major trauma) and was obviously bleeding internally.

In her altered mental state, Mona had convinced herself that the doctors were all sitting around doing nothing while she slowly bled to death. She was dying and they were just not telling her. She called for Carla and had a long discussion about her taking the kids after she was gone.

All this was going on as Pastors Mark and Mary Ann entered the room and tried to say a prayer. Sensing that this was a bad time, they prayed with the family as a nurse came in and sedated Mona for the CT scan.

"Don't worry," the nurse assured them, "it is just the drugs talking and making her bloated. We will get her off them as soon as possible."

Mark and Mary Ann repeated the prayer they had said for me asking for strength and acceptance that there was something bigger going on, something we simply do not have the means to understand, all part of "God's greater plan."

Knowing this was not a great time for them to be there, they advised Mona's mother, Anne, that they would visit again in a few days and keep the congregation informed. Eventually, the congregation would form the backbone of the support we needed. For now, all they could do was pray, and that they did with gusto. Mark and Mary Ann spread the word that we needed prayer, and the congregation responded. They not only said prayers at the services but also formed prayer chains in which members asked family and friends— most of whom did not even know us—to pray also. There were people praying constantly for us, not because they all knew us or had taken their animals to our veterinary practice, but because they cared and had faith that it would help. We had worked hard to become part of the community; now the community would be there for us.

For Reflection

And we know that for those who love God all things work together for good, for those who are called according to his purpose. (Romans 8:28)

As he passed by, he saw a man blind from birth. And his disciples asked him, "Rabbi, who sinned, this man or his parents, that he was born blind?" Jesus answered, "It was not that this man sinned, or his parents, but that the works of God might be displayed in him.

We must work the works of him who sent me while it is day; night is coming, when no one can work. As long as I am in the world, I am the light of the world." Having said these things, he spit on the ground and made mud with the saliva. Then he anointed the man's eyes with the mud and said to him, "Go, wash in the pool of Siloam" (which means Sent). So he went and washed and came back seeing. (John 9:1–7)

1. Why do you think God lets bad things happen to good people? Why doesn't God allow bad things to happen only to bad people?
2. What can we gain from bad things happening to us?
3. What might God be teaching us when we have to adapt to a new plan?

CHAPTER 12

CAN I GO BACK TO MY COMA, PLEASE?

After fixing the elbows, the doctors were ready to wake me up. They still needed to repair my shoulder, but first it was time to see if I was still there.

Waking someone from a medically induced coma is an agonizing waiting game. The doctors stop the drugs and wait for them to wear off while the entire family sits in the room hoping for some sign that the patient is still the son or brother they knew. With each passing minute and no reaction from me, they couldn't help but believe that the Scot they knew was never coming back. The thought that this was as good as I would ever get crept into everyone's minds, though no one would dare admit it out loud. They kept telling themselves that it was just the drugs and I needed more time, but the thought of permanent brain damage kept hounding them, becoming increasingly frequent as time dragged on. No response, no sign that I could feel any pain or that I could hear their persistent voices trying to wake me.

"Scot, time to wake up," my sister Julie kept repeating.

No response.

My oldest sister, Kim, a registered nurse, tried also. "Scot, if you can hear me, squeeze my hand."

Nothing.

My parents stood at the foot of the bed, fear etched plainly on their exhausted faces. It had been four days and they had barely slept.

The consuming dread that their only son might be forever changed crushed their spirits. After all of their constant prayers for some kind of sign I'd come back, they got nothing in return.

It takes massive amounts of drugs to keep someone in a coma. This is not just sedation or sleep but the actual shutting off of the brain. The brain fights hard against the drugs, because it is always trying to sense and feel. That's why it takes a massive dose to induce a coma. When the drugs are stopped, it takes a long time for them to disappear.

My family gathered around my bed and waited. Mona's family stood in the hallway outside knowing that the next few hours would determine their fate as well. There was silence except for the beep of the monitors and Julie and Kim's voices every few minutes trying to wake me up. Occasionally, someone would break the silence with some nervous chatter about their schedule and how long they could take off from work, but they all had other things on their minds. Today would determine how we would all spend the rest of our lives. If I wasn't there mentally, who would take care of me? Mona and I lived about two hours from my nearest family and eight hours from her parents; there was just nobody close by to help out for a long period of time. Rearranging schedules for a few weeks was one thing, but months or years of around-the-clock care would be impossible. They all sat and waited.

Mona, the one who would be the most affected by my recovery or lack thereof, was not in the room. Under the influence of heavy pain medication, she was sleeping soundly in her room, unaware that they were trying to wake me up. Her concussion was resolving and her brain resetting, but she was confined to the bed. Her back injury made it very difficult to move her, because every time she was taken out of bed, there was a chance her spinal fracture could displace and cause paralysis. Getting out of bed was not an option, so it was decided that Mona would not be present when I came out of the coma. Her sisters stayed with her while her brother and brother-in-law kept the kids busy. My family watched and waited.

It took about two and a half hours after they stopped the drugs. They kept the morphine going so I would not come out screaming but stopped the drugs that kept me unconscious. Because morphine specifically blocks pain, I would definitely still need it, but they had to let my brain start working again.

The doctors stood ready to see if I could breathe on my own. If not, they would put me back on the ventilator. They would also know that I probably would lose all cognitive function. Breathing was one of the most basic brain activities. If I couldn't do that, I wouldn't be able to do much else; I probably would never wake up.

As I came around, my body first realized that there was something in my throat. I began to gag and cough as I tried to expel the tube they had inserted to keep me breathing. The nurse gently pulled it out and the coughing abated. I took my first independent breath since Robert had inserted a tube in my throat on the helicopter flight in. Everyone in the room was excited. At least I could breathe on my own and would not need a respirator. So far, so good.

It took about twenty minutes for me to start moving and emerge fully from the coma. I started with a groan. Kim assured everyone that the groaning was normal.

Julie, a year older than I and my closest sibling in age, continued asking me to wake up. This would be my first memory since leaving the cabin three days earlier. Julie was a social worker who specialized in elder care, so she knew how to communicate with people with decreased cognitive function. She kept it very simple, telling me only what I needed to know. As my eyes opened, she said very plainly, "Scot, you are in the hospital. You were in an accident, but Mona and the kids are all right."

At first, I didn't really comprehend what she had said. She repeated: "Scot, you are in the hospital. You were in an accident, but Mona and the kids are all right."

Slowly, it started to sink in. I was on my back looking at the ceiling. The walls looked like a hospital room, very clean and plain. To my right was the monitoring equipment, an ECG for heart rate, and a pulse oximeter for oxygen level. We used these daily in our hospital, so I recognized their rhythmic beep immediately. There was also an IV stand with a fluid bag attached. I was sure that it fed into a catheter somewhere in my right arm.

As my brain processed where I was, I began to take inventory. From the time I was a child, I could see well out of only my right eye. My left eye was so bad that I could not make out the E on the top of the eye chart. I was always terrified that I would lose my good eye and end up legally blind. I looked around, taking it all in. I could see pretty clearly, so I knew immediately that my one good eye was working. At least I would be able to see.

Kim asked me to squeeze her hand. In a bit of a panic, I thought, "They are asking if I can move; this must be bad."

For me, paralysis had always been another huge fear. I concentrated hard and squeezed. Kim smiled and said, "Good job." I knew that hand worked. Julie, standing on the opposite side, held my other hand.

"Now, squeeze your right." Julie smiled and said, "Good job." They both knew I could not only work my hands but that I was understanding their simple instructions also.

Both my arms felt extremely heavy. I was flat on my back and unable to raise my head; I couldn't see that both arms were splinted. I could feel my fingers so I knew the nerves must be working down to my chest.

Next, Kim asked me to move my toes. I quickly realized they were checking for paralysis. I concentrated and sent the message for my toes to move, praying that they would respond. First, the left toes moved. Then, the right toes. A wave of relief swept over me—I could move all my limbs! I could not comprehend why my arms and legs were so heavy, but I didn't care. I knew that as long as I could feel them, the nerves were working. I had no idea how bad everything was, but as long as I could feel them, I had a good chance of using them again.

My family watched the process and with every movement felt a wave of relief. By the end, they were all smiling. All the prayers for me were paying off. Not only could I move my limbs, but I could follow instructions. This meant I was hearing and processing information. These were primitive tests, but at least my brain was functioning at some level. I might not be completely back to normal, but I sure could be worse.

I soon found out there was a downside to being out of the coma. The nurses arrived in my room for the sole purpose of changing my sheets. I had a urinary catheter in place that drained urine into a bag, so that was not a problem, but I had numerous open wounds that had to be kept clean. Using a bedpan was out of the question, since that would require them to lift me over it; consequently, I had to defecate in the sheets. This wasn't a problem yet since I hadn't eaten for three days, but the sheets had to be changed. The two nurses who had arrived to do it got on one side and rolled me over, pushing the bedding underneath me. My left arm was still not fixed, so as they rolled me, I felt (and heard) the bones moving. Being on a high dose of morphine, the pain did not really register, but having felt hundreds of broken bones in animals, I remember thinking, "Boy, that's a bad fracture," as the jagged ends of the broken bone in my upper arm popped and ground against each other. It suddenly hit me that what I felt moving were *my* bones and that it was *my* arm that had this bad fracture. I hadn't realized that my arm was broken until now. I wished for the coma again.

Having established that I could see, hear, and think, the nurses gave me more sedation. I needed to rest because there was more surgery scheduled for tomorrow.

My family was thrilled, and my mother rushed to tell Mona the good news. I had a long way to go but had cleared another hurdle.

For Reflection

For I know the plans I have for you, declares the Lord, *plans for welfare and not for evil, to give you a future and a hope. (Jeremiah 29:11)*

1. Have you ever faced a time when you were not sure of an outcome that would change your life's direction?
2. In what instances have you asked God for help?
3. When the direction of your life has changed, how have you come to accept that?

CHAPTER 13

Monkeys in the Room

In four days, I had had four major orthopedic surgeries, had three dislocated bones repaired, had my spleen removed and bladder repaired, nearly bled to death a few times, and been in a coma. Needless to say, I had had better weeks.

Every day I got a little stronger, but there were still more surgeries to go. My medical team had to clean and debride some wounds and straighten my nose; however, these were relatively minor compared to everything else I'd endured. Mona was allowed to come and see me, but neither one of us could move enough to do more than touch hands. Still, I could see she was also going to take a long time to heal. I also knew that, for the time being, she and the kids were on their own. As parents, we would not be able to do much to help our kids get through this hardship. We'd have to rely on family to support us; fortunately, we both had strong ones. Until we could get back to them, the kids would be cared for by grandparents, aunts, and uncles. At least they could have people they trusted around them to make Mom and Dad's absence a little easier.

We decided not to let the kids see me in this state, with two casted arms, two casted legs, major black and blue eyes, and a feeding tube coming out my broken and bandaged nose. They'd already been through enough and didn't need to witness this spectacle; talking on the phone would have to do. My kids were still young enough to believe their dad was indestructible, and I didn't have the heart to steal that from them. I certainly didn't feel indestructible anymore.

My night nurse was Andrew, a very dedicated and caring individual whose personality fit perfectly with a night shift. Not only was he professional and kind, but he worked independently. Like Dr. Lang, Andrew believed that *he* needed to be there for his patients since only *he* could do the job as well as it truly needed to be done. For me, he was yet another angel sent to guide me through my hell.

I was now out of my coma but still on heavy doses of morphine, which began to do some funny things. That night I decided that I had had enough. I distinctly remember telling Andrew that I was "leaving this dump and nobody could stop me" as I pulled out my IV and got up to pack my clothes.

Of course, this memory was a hallucination. It is one of my most vivid memories of that first week, but it never happened. I had both arms and both legs in casts and was weeks from sitting up, much less walking out the door. Still, I was convinced I needed to leave; I didn't need any of these quacks, even though these quacks had saved my life.

A few hours later, I apologized to Andrew for my outburst and for calling his hospital a dump. He just smiled because he had seen it before. He advised, "Come find me when the drugs wear off. Then you can tell me if you think this place is still a dump."

Due to the heavy morphine doses, I was lucid only at times. In spite of the steady stream of visitors and well-wishers who came in to see how I was doing and give me words of encouragement, I remember nothing. While I appreciate their intentions to this day, I have no recollection of anything.

Even when I appeared to be there, I wasn't. One of my best friends whom I grew up with traveled all the way from Atlanta to see me. We talked for hours and he fed me ice chips to keep my mouth moist. He told me later that I was making perfect sense and we talked about everything from the crash to politics. Yet I don't remember *any* of it, not a second. Later on, his visit completely forgotten, I would wonder why this good buddy had never even called to see how I was doing, when in fact he'd traveled eight hundred miles and spent several hours in my hospital room with me.

My family was working in shifts to ensure that someone was in my room at all times. This was very nice and demonstrated their incredible loyalty, but it was preventing me from getting much-needed rest. Finally, with Julie monitoring me, I very nonchalantly told her to watch where she sat, because "there were monkeys running around the room." I was seeing monkeys climbing over my bed and swinging from the curtains.

Julie looked confused and asked, "Did you say there were monkeys in the room?"

I said, "Yes, but don't worry. They are nice monkeys."

She paused momentarily, then replied, "I'll be right back," before she quickly ran to the nurse's station to alert them about this latest development. About fifteen minutes later, another doctor entered my room and introduced himself as Dr. Jacobs from psychiatry. Yes, within fifteen minutes after seeing the monkeys, they sent a psychiatrist to evaluate me—pretty good service!

Dr. Jacobs said, "I hear you see monkeys running around the room."

"Yeah, they are kind of fun to have in here." (I was oblivious to how insane that sounded.)

In response, he asked a simple question, "Do you see the monkeys when your eyes are open or closed?"

I looked around. Not seeing any, I closed my eyes and the monkeys reappeared.

"I guess only when my eyes are closed," I answered, again oblivious to any connection to reality.

He smiled and advised, "Get some sleep and call me if the monkeys are around when your eyes are open."

Then turning to Julie, he plainly stated: "No more visitors except family. And only for two hours a day. Scot needs his sleep."

Julie replied, "I have known him his entire life and have never seen him sleep more than eight hours in a day. In fact, he usually only sleeps about six."

"Not anymore," the doctor ordered. "You heal better when you sleep. Any visitors, family included, are only allowed in his room for a maximum of two hours a day. He will probably be sleeping for eighteen to twenty hours a day for a while now."

Realizing the good sense in the doctor's words, Julie agreed and quickly informed the family and the staff at our veterinary practice, who called our church pastors so they could announce it at the services. All of these people were advised to send cards and emails but not to come to the hospital. As hard as it was for them to hear it, they conceded that it was best for me and my recovery.

The next day, the doctor who would straighten my nose entered my room. My sisters, not having to be in the room anymore, had gone home. My mother and father came in with the doctor not knowing if I was conscious enough to comprehend what she was going to tell me. She pleasantly introduced herself, but I could tell she was all business. After quickly informing me about what she was going to do, she asked if I had any questions.

"Just one," I said. "I always thought this nose was a little big. While you are fixing it, could you take a little off and make it more like Brad Pitt's?"

My dad broke out into laughter while my mother just stood there shocked. The doctor stared at me in bewilderment.

"I think I will just put it back where it is supposed to be instead of smashed over to the side like it is now." With that, she turned and walked out of the room.

Dad looked at Mom and remarked, "His brain is working well enough to be a smart-ass. The crash didn't knock *that* out of him."

I smiled for the first time since the crash, and it hurt. I didn't care; I was starting to come back.

FOR REFLECTION

And we urge you, brothers, admonish the idle, encourage the faint-hearted, help the weak, be patient with them all. (Thessalonians 5:14)

1. Visiting the sick is considered a work of mercy. But how can we perform that work and help others when visits might not be appropriate?

2. What are some additional ways you can show support for someone you cannot physically be with?

3. Andrew was a night nurse with a gift for working alone. Generally, we are taught the importance of working with others. How is it a gift that Andrew could work on his own?

Jesus replied, "A man was going down from Jerusalem to Jericho, and he fell among robbers, who stripped him and beat him and departed, leaving him half dead. Now by chance a priest was going down that road, and when he saw him he passed by on the other side. So likewise a Levite, when he came to the place and saw him, passed by on the other side. But a Samaritan, as he journeyed, came to where he was, and when he saw him, he had compassion. He went to him and bound up his wounds, pouring on oil and wine. Then he set him on his own animal and brought him to an inn and took care of him." (Luke 10:30–34)

4. How is Andrew's work similar to the actions of the Good Samaritan?

CHAPTER 14

WHERE IS ANNIE?

The day also had brought some good news regarding the dogs: Olivia had stopped seizing. Dr. Welch, our partner at our vet clinic, had come to Madison and taken her back to the office for monitoring. When Olivia first arrived, the doctors at the E.R. had recommended that she be put down due to her brain injury and nonstop seizures. Dr. Welch had made the decision to keep going and give her a chance to recover; he had kids of his own and knew that ours would be devastated to hear about the death of their dog on top of everything else. Instead, he would take her back to our hospital, where our staff would nurse her along until she either improved or died, but he would not put her down. They had lots of drugs to use and could put her in a coma if needed; Olivia would be given every chance to live. They set up a schedule with either a doctor or a trusted technician in charge of monitoring Olivia every night. Our dedicated staff alternated taking her home at night in a little carrier to watch her for seizures. If she had one, they had meds at the ready that they could administer. Dr. Welch told them all to call him any time if there was a problem.

Despite all of this excellent care, it would be very tough for our little dog. Even after she stopped seizing, she could not get up because her center of balance was thrown off. She would try to sit up but get dizzy and fall over. Because she couldn't eat or drink, she was on an IV. Three times a day, they would hold her up to a bowl of wet food or chicken in an attempt to get something into her. She would try but then get dizzy and fall to the side, unable to swallow or chew more than a few bites. They were not sure if they could get enough food into her and considered placing a feeding tube, but as she was gradually able to eat more, they decided to wait. They kept this up for a month, rolling her from side to side to prevent pressure sores and hand-feeding her until she could eat on her own and start to sit up.

A whole bunch of angels.

Annabelle, our Golden Retriever, was still missing after three days, having fled the crash terrified and confused. She'd been hiding in a cornfield, afraid to approach anyone. The police and the farmer who owned the field had walked the area for days calling for her, but she would not come out. Soon the farmer would need to harvest but was delaying it, fearing Annabelle might get into the machinery and be killed. He had never met us or our dog but had seen the damage to the van and heard on the news that there were kids involved. He waited to harvest the field because he did not want to cause more pain for these people he didn't even know.

On the fourth day, the medivac helicopter crew called in and said they thought they had seen Annabelle in a field and gave the location. They were the same crew that had flown me in to the hospital, and they had been watching the area as they flew over on another run. The fact that they would even think to look for our dog, as busy as they are and without knowing our family at all, was amazing enough. That they had found her was a miracle. More angels.

Now knowing her location, my father and father-in-law decided to go look for Annabelle. They had been out every day up until this point with no luck; Annabelle was just too afraid to come out of hiding. The evening temperatures had been plummeting to below freezing, and rain was expected. Annabelle would be hungry and freezing and would not survive much longer outside alone.

As my dad and father-in-law were leaving, they had an idea; they would bring along eight-year-old Victoria. They stopped at a store on the way to buy her a pair of boots, because it was muddy and cold in the field. When they got there, they handed Victoria the leash but stayed in the car. Our little girl walked along the edge of the corn calling for her dog. She walked and walked but got no response.

Her grandfathers drove up to get her as she started to cry. Poor Victoria had been so hopeful that Annabelle would be found. She knew how cold it was getting and how wet everything was. She could sense that this was their best chance of finding her dog, and it had failed. Furthermore, she knew about coyotes, since there are a lot of them around our home, and that they would gang up and kill a dog like Annie.

Her grandfathers tried to coax Victoria into the car, but she refused. She wanted to walk a little farther into some woods nearby just to check. The men once again sat waiting.

Victoria continued calling for her dog, becoming more and more desperate.

Then she heard it, a rustling in the woods. Something was moving in there, probably just a deer or a squirrel. She called again, and the rustling got faster. Whatever it was, it was moving toward her. The thought of the coyotes returned and she started to panic; she was just a child and all alone. What if this was a pack of hungry coyotes? When Victoria looked back, she could not see the car anymore; she had gone too far.

Then she spotted it: a flash of wet, muddy hair in the trees. Her heart raced as she called again. Out of the brush it came at her at full gallop. It was Annie! She ran up to Victoria and almost knocked her over. Her tail beat wildly and she rubbed up against Victoria's legs doing circles around her and smearing her with dirt. Victoria had found her, and she was okay!

They ran back to the car and Annabelle leaped in, muddy feet and all. My dad looked at Joe and smiled, "Glad we took your car, not mine."

Although Joe was a fanatic about keeping his car clean, to him this outcome had been worth any inconvenience. He was a true dog lover, having bred, raised, and trained hunting Labradors for most of his life. The pure joy on his granddaughter's face was something he would never forget. Time to take Annie home.

For Reflection

For everyone who asks receives, and the one who seeks finds, and to the one who knocks it will be opened. (Matthew 7:8)

1. When have you had angels step in to help you?
2. Victoria's grandfathers left her to search for Annie by herself. Have you ever had to step back when you wanted to help because the situation demanded it? Are you still doing God's will by stepping back?
3. Has somebody or something you loved ever been lost? How did you feel when that loved one was (or was not) found?
4. How does this chapter recall the return of the Prodigal Son?

CHAPTER 15

LET THE MIND GAMES BEGIN

Now that my surgeries were winding down, the psychological battle was ramping up. My family kept telling me how lucky I was to be alive, and I could see that was true. Still, it was hard to feel lucky in my condition. Both arms and legs were in casts and I was coping with constant pain on a morphine drip while contemplating the possibility of not being able to support my family again. It's hard to feel lucky when your doctors tell you that you will be in the hospital for two to three months and then in a nursing home for six more. I had been an active, thirty-eight-year-old man in good shape; now it would be a miracle if I ever walked again.

Upsetting me even more was that I was forbidden to see my kids. I looked so scary, I would give them nightmares. On top of that, my wife had three breaks in her back that could paralyze her or at least keep her in chronic pain. She also might be facing the inability to do the things she loved to do: work as a veterinarian, tend to her horses and goats, even be a good mom. Mona and I both were suffering from enormous pain, physically and emotionally. The doctors refused to predict the extent of my recovery, not because they didn't want to, but because they had no way of knowing. Yes, the bones would heal, but the messed-up joints were a whole separate issue; there was a real chance I might never be able to use them again.

Beyond the physical healing, the best-case scenario also assumed that Mona's and my relationship could survive this kind of ordeal. Many couples—over half—that live through this type of major crisis end up divorcing because the stress and pain take a toll, not to mention the loss of income and mounting hospital bills. The disruption of one's life is more than many can bear. Mona had been working part time but kept both the business and the home running on a day-to-day basis. At the office, she handled a lot of the tedious but necessary things—from ordering supplies to dealing with staff issues—in addition to seeing clients. At home, she kept the kids where they needed to be, the house organized, and the bills paid. It was truly amazing the number of tasks my wife could complete in the course of a day. Now we weren't sure if she could even be weaned off the pain meds or if she would spend the rest of her life lying in bed in a haze.

My job at the animal hospital was to perform the major surgeries that so many of our clients had come to expect. Those long, complicated procedures distinguished our hospital from most others and brought in a significant portion of our income. It was our bread and butter. Now I didn't know if I would be able to walk again, much less stand over an operating table and concentrate for two or three hours at a stretch. The crash would force both of us to change our roles—at least temporarily—and dramatically reduce our income, which would impose an incredible amount of pressure, leading to much resentment and frustration. Soon we would be fighting with each other and miserably questioning if we'd made the right decision by getting married in the first place. Divorce would follow.

Was I lucky to be alive? Yes. Did I feel lucky? No.

For the first few days after waking up, I had very few emotions. I drifted in and out of consciousness, still in shock that this could have happened to us. I had had our lives all planned out, and this crash just wasn't a part of it. I didn't know if I believed that this was real.

Maybe it was just a dream?

But reality was starting to settle in. I had been in the bed for nearly a week with various family members rotating through. Although my parents still drove down every day to visit with me, conversation had just about stopped; there was just nothing else to talk about, and I was on so many drugs I couldn't think clearly. My visitors had been restricted to a few hours a day to allow me to get enough rest, and I was sleeping twenty hours daily. Mona was permitted to come in once a day for a few minutes, but it was risky and difficult to move her, not to mention incredibly painful.

I went through the gamut of emotions. First, joy that we all had survived and the kids were not severely hurt. That joy quickly turned to anger at Jacobs for being such a jerk and driving around drunk on a Sunday afternoon. What did he think was going to happen? Then, as I started to comprehend the extent of my injuries, fear took over as I envisioned what my new, post-accident life was going to be like. There was real dread that this was going to be my new normal: crippled and lying in bed. I had worked hard for the preceding ten years to build a business so I would not have to work as hard when I hit this age; now I wasn't sure if I or the business would survive. If I did pull through, I figured the business would be much less valuable than it had been in the past and I would no longer be able to pull my own weight.

The partners would tolerate it for a while, but eventually reality would hit home: If I would not or could not produce, I'd have to step aside. Our veterinary practice simply couldn't sustain the dead weight of a veterinarian who couldn't stand on his own two feet, move around, and treat patients. With the amount of damage to my feet and legs, I couldn't visualize myself standing long enough to perform the long, complicated surgeries that had built our practice. The reason why many of these surgeries were done at our hospital was because the pet owners did not have the money to take their pets to a referral practice where these same surgeries cost thousands of dollars more to do. If I was physically unable to save them, these pets would be euthanized. Consequently, our practice would be just like any other, and our patients and their owners would start to go elsewhere. I would be half the man I was before, crippled and in pain for the rest of my life, living on disability. I would be a failure.

For me, the thought of not working, of not doing the job I knew I was perfectly suited for—the one I had been born to do—scared the hell out of me. I had never intended to be unemployed; boredom would kill me. Spending the rest of my life watching TV on the couch while my kids played outside was as frightening as anything. I would get lazier and lazier, and my mind and body would wither away. All the years I'd worked to hone my skills as a vet, as the "fix-it guy" around the house and office, and as the "fun dad" out running around with the kids had been for naught. I had worked hard to stay in reasonable shape and maintain good health and had been able to handle long days on my feet without a break. But now, it would be months before I could stand, and nobody could predict if I would ever be close to normal again. So much of what I had worked for was gone. My spirit and drive started to waver as I felt the first onset of depression.

I kept telling myself I was lucky: I survived, and my wife and kids had all survived. But I just didn't *feel* lucky. My life was in turmoil and not because of anything I had done. I simply didn't deserve this. Why was this happening to me? I hadn't done anything wrong. Why did I have to endure so much pain? Despite the high doses of morphine, pain dogged me relentlessly. Every move—even the simple act of breathing—hurt terribly, and it wasn't looking as if that would end any time soon. My injuries might never heal to the point that they were no longer a source of intense discomfort. The drugs certainly helped, but I did not want to spend my life on narcotics, which at best only lessened the pain. It had never really ceased since I had awakened from the coma; it was just less intense when I was still and worse when I moved. I could not even lie on my side, with both feet and both arms wrapped in heavy bandages. And the simple *thought* of pain kept me immobile, too scared to move at all.

The worst part was realizing the pain would be around for a very long time. When you experience excruciating pain from hitting your thumb with a hammer, at least you know it's temporary. If you can handle it for a few minutes, it will quickly subside. My kind of pain in the aftermath of the accident was dramatically different, not only because it was much more intense but because it had no foreseeable end. This debilitating pain was completely sapping my will to fight. Every move I made involved a long thought process weighing the cost of pain versus the benefit of motion. I even tried not to urinate or defecate, which I had to do in my sheets since I could not lift myself to use a bedpan. Afterward, the nurses would have to come in and roll me side to side so they could change my sheets and wipe my ass. Needing a twenty-two-year-old nurse to first insert a suppository to enable a bowel movement (the morphine was making me terribly constipated), then come back to change my soiled sheets and wipe my butt like a baby was absolutely humiliating. I wasn't sure I could just "tough it out" and handle the pain or the embarrassment. What if Mona or, God forbid, *the kids* would have to do this for the rest of my life? No way could I live like that.

As for Mona, I figured she would walk again but might have back pain forever. I knew in all probability she would not function as she had before. She loved riding horses, but that part of her life was almost certainly over. Neither of us probably would be able to work as we had before either. It had been ten years since we'd built a large, modern hospital with lots of staff and all the newest "toys" for helping our patients, but now I figured we'd be lucky to keep it all afloat. We had just upgraded the X-ray from plain films to digital to the tune of $50,000, which did not include the X-ray machine itself (another $35,000). Without Mona and I there to see clients, our income would dry up. The debt payments, however, would hang around and eat up a large portion of our take-home pay. Owning a business is great when it is going well, but there is no guaranteed income. We did not have a pension that would continue to finance us and our expenses; we were reliant on generating income by doing our job as veterinarians. As owners, we were the last ones to be paid. If a business fails to make a profit, the owners don't get paid at all. If I couldn't get function back in my arms and legs, I would be forced to sit home collecting disability for the next forty years, bored out of my mind. With the business failing, I would be unable to sell it for even half of what it had originally been worth. Anyone interested in buying it could just patiently wait while it continued to wither away, then buy it for next to nothing. Or, worse yet, they could just set up next door and outcompete us. All our work would circle the drain, taking all of our plans with it.

I would hate this new life. I can't even stay on vacation for more than a week without going stir-crazy. Now I'd be confined mostly to bed. Would we lose our house in the country? Would we have to move into town and give up the horses, goats, and chickens the kids loved? I dreaded the thought of losing the life we had worked so hard to attain.

I sank deeper and deeper into depression. I could feel it happening but didn't really know how to stop it; I'd just wait for the next dose of morphine so I could fall back asleep and get through another boring day of watching TV while trying not to move.

My depression evolved and grew as time went on. It changed from sadness at what had happened and what I had lost to hatred for the man who had caused it. As I became more able to understand what people were telling me, I absorbed more details about what had happened. I had no recollection of the crash or anything that transpired for three or four days afterward.

Mark Jacobs, the loser who had slammed into us head-on, was about my age, but that was probably the only thing we had in common. We were as opposite as could be: I was married with children; he was unmarried with a child out of wedlock. I worked hard to support and provide for my kids; he was years behind in child support. I taught my kids the importance of always telling the truth regardless of the consequences; he ran away and left us to die rather than face what he had done. I had been employed continuously since I was sixteen years old, and my employers always wanted to hire me back; he could not hold a job because of his endless drinking. He was an alcoholic who couldn't stop; I had never faced addiction and regarded it as a failure of will by a pathetic human being. To me, it was simply an indication of a lack of strength to be addicted to anything. Real men would suck it up, get their life back in order, and quit screwing up. Jacobs's addiction meant he wasn't a real man but a weak, sniveling wuss.

The man who did this to my family was everything I despised. In fact, I have a hard time calling him a man, because I believe a man takes responsibility for his actions and supports his family. Jacobs did none of this; therefore, he was not a man by my definition. He was easy to hate, and I hated him through and through.

In many ways, hating Jacobs was natural and expected. My family despised him also; I could tell when they talked about him. I felt I *should* feel hatred for him after something like this. Isn't it right to hate the man who could do this to an innocent, perfect family, one with a perfect plan for how their lives were supposed to go? Jacobs had screwed up everything.

Thus, I alternated between depression and hatred. Being brought up in a family that did not show much emotion, I kept my feelings to myself. When I talked to visitors or family, I did what I had been taught to do: I smiled and said I was doing fine. I didn't complain about much and did not want anyone to create a fuss over me. Not eating was okay because I was being fed and nourished through a tube; I said my pain was a three out of ten, when it was more like an eight. I told everyone I was positive I would get back to work in four or five months when the doctors were telling them I would spend at least two months in the hospital and six months in a nursing home, with no guarantee I'd ever go back to work again. I'm not sure if this is a Midwestern thing, a Polish thing, a male thing, or a combination, but I didn't think complaining about my condition was acceptable. I would not show anyone I was in trouble; I just had to suck it up. I had handled everything else myself; this would be no different.

I was caught in a cycle where the more I thought about what had happened, the angrier and more depressed I became. Having never been through anything this bad, I figured I did not need help from anyone, even though I was in a hospital with psychiatrists on staff. All I had to do was stop telling the doctors I was fine and they would have sent me a doctor specifically trained to help me navigate the emotions of what had happened. I was too mule-headed to ask for help. Instead, I became more isolated as I struggled to hide my hatred, depression, and fear. The isolation just caused me to focus on it more and more, while my anger increased exponentially. Round and round it went, getting worse every day.

For Reflection

For if the readiness is there, it is acceptable according to what a person has, not according to what he does not have. (2 Corinthians 8:12)

Love is patient and kind; love does not envy or boast; it is not arrogant or rude. It does not insist on its own way; it is not irritable or resentful; it does not rejoice at wrongdoing, but rejoices with the truth. Love bears all things, believes all things, hopes all things, endures all things. (1 Corinthians 13:4–7)

The LORD will fulfill his purpose for me; your steadfast love, O LORD, endures forever. Do not forsake the work of your hands. (Psalms 138:8)

1. Have you ever had people tell you that you were lucky when you did not feel lucky?

2. Many married couples end up divorced after a major trauma. Why do you think that is the case? What steps can be taken to avoid this?

3. How would your life change if you were unable to work? How would you feel about that?

4. Does your work give you a sense of purpose? If not, what does?

5. Does work or purpose make one happy?

CHAPTER 16

My Plan

After all the surgeries, I was moved out of intensive care. At that point, I mostly needed time to heal, but the doctors were talking months. I was going to survive but still had no idea what my new life would be like. My bucket list had included things like fishing in Canada, touring Australia, and hiking the Grand Canyon—all activities that required a sound body to accomplish. Now those dreams looked impossible.

I had been in the hospital for a couple of weeks, spending most of my days alone. Mona had been discharged and gone home to be with the kids. They were over an hour away, and with the coming winter and Mona's injuries, travel was difficult. We talked nightly, but they were seldom able to visit. My other family members were an hour and a half away and could not be at the hospital every day anymore either. My sisters had families of their own to care for, and my parents knew they couldn't do much to help me. Consequently, I had all kinds of time to stew on just how much this sucked—all due to some inconsiderate asshole driving around completely drunk at one o'clock on a Sunday afternoon. What a complete LOSER! I hated him more and more each day.

The sheer hate, depression, and boredom were taking a toll. These emotions were making me want to sleep more just so I could wake up and have another day behind me, but I was finding it harder and harder to sleep because I could not do anything when I was awake. I was just never really tired. The more trouble I had sleeping, the more irritable I became and the more the hate and anger grew. I relied on the pain medicine increasingly when I should have been needing it less often. But when I got the next dose, I felt no pain and zoned out, plus I could escape the hate and sadness for a while. So I kept asking for more. The doctors were very aware of the drug-seeking that often occurs after severe trauma and remained cautious. However, I had a great excuse for wanting pain medication and was still in the recommended dose range—just nearing the top with every request. I found myself overstating the pain level to get "enough" OxyContin. They would ask to rate my pain on a scale of one to ten, with ten being the worst. I found myself rounding up, whereas before I was always rounding down. I would tell them six when it was really a four. I told myself I was blocking the physical pain, but in reality, I was medicating the emotional pain. I was on the slippery slope of drugs. It had begun.

My family saw it too. I was interacting less. I wasn't speaking about when I could get back to work or when the fractures would be healed. I was speaking in ifs—"if" I would get back to work and "if" I would walk again. Although they noticed the change, they did not breathe a word about it, as per our family's way of dealing with things. They needed to stay positive and avoid the negative vibe I was emitting. It was natural for trauma victims to be hateful and angry; maybe it would just pass.

The change in me was quite evident to the nurses also. I wasn't the self-confident, "I can beat this" person I had been before. I was broken, both physically and mentally. How could I be confident in the future when my plan for it had been completely torn apart? I had figured out every step in my life and up until now had been executing each step perfectly. I had never thought about not being healthy and having to stop working. I had no plan for *this*.

I had lost all control of my life when control had worked so well for me before. I had been the boss—and a bit of a tyrant at that. My staff was intimidated by me, but the business had prospered so I wasn't going to change. I had excelled at everything in life so I must be *really* smart and *really* blessed. God must like me, right?

Now I wasn't so sure. I had failed at things in life before but not anything that I had genuinely put my heart into. I had failed at being an athlete, but that hadn't bothered me because I was born with only one good eye and had no depth perception. Sports were not my focus. I had failed at playing a musical instrument, but that was not how my mind worked. Music required feel, not logic, and my brain was purely analytical.

In the end, I was good at remembering facts and using logic to figure things out. Plus, I worked incredibly hard. I felt that what I lacked in physical and musical talent was compensated for by my smarts and work ethic. From high school on, I had just memorized everything I could and outworked everybody. I had brains and drive so I was *supposed* to be successful at the things that required those qualities—things like medicine.

Now everything I was good at was in jeopardy. Since my body was a mess, outworking everyone was no longer a guarantee; my job could not be done at a desk. My mind was fogged, maybe with drugs or maybe due to bouncing my brain into an airbag at seventy miles per hour. Therefore, I just couldn't be sure if I would be able to think the way I had before the crash. My family's *modus operandi* was to simply state that everything would be fine, but I was a long way from that. Though I would never admit it, I was just plain scared.

It was all Jacobs's fault. He should rot in hell for what he did to me. I was sinking deeper and deeper into the hole of hate and self-pity, and I honestly didn't know how to get out of my downward spiral.

I needed revenge, the sweet revenge I thought would make me whole again. I needed to get even, but I knew I couldn't do that physically. I couldn't break Jacobs's bones the way he broke mine, but I could work to send his pathetic butt to jail for as long as possible. Jacobs had been caught after literally running away after the crash.

He'd taken one look at Mona and me bleeding and dying in the car, and our terrified, crying kids in the back seat, and fled like a coward. He disgusted me.

About a week in, two of the policemen from the scene showed up in my room to update me on Jacobs, who had been arrested. Another motorist who had driven around the wreck when they opened a lane of traffic had been heading down the next off-ramp when he'd spotted a man walking on the side of the highway. Jacobs turned to look at him as he drove past, and the driver noticed blood on Jacobs's face, quickly surmising that this guy was probably the other driver involved in the crash. When he pulled over to ask the hitchhiker where he was going, Jacobs told him his house was a few miles away. The savvy driver replied that he needed to drop off his girlfriend but then would give him a ride; he left her at the nearest convenience store and came back for Jacobs. Meanwhile, his girlfriend called the police, who were waiting at Jacobs's home when they arrived. He was arrested and given a Breathalyzer. Over an hour after the crash, Jacobs blew a 0.22, almost *three times* the legal limit.

It was critical that this driver picked up Jacobs. Not only did this ensure Jacobs's arrest, but it prevented Jacobs from using the trick so many repeat drunk drivers know about: When you get in an accident, run to the nearest bar or get home and start drinking. It then becomes impossible to determine if the drinking occurred before or after the incident, creating enough reasonable doubt that the driver avoids a DUI charge. Jacobs couldn't use this tactic because he had no opportunity to drink after the crash. The police had taken pictures of the open beer cans and the half-empty case in the back of his car. They had even taken DNA swabs off his airbag where he had left blood in order to prove that he, and not someone else, had been the driver. Good police work.

The police arrested Jacobs for his eighth DUI; he was on probation from his sixth and seventh already. More importantly—the policeman smiled as he informed me—Jacobs would be charged with three counts of hit-and-run with great bodily harm because he fled the scene with three of us injured in the car. The eighth DUI in Wisconsin would come with a maximum of six years in jail, of which you serve four. However, each count of hit-and-run carries a maximum penalty of fifteen years, of which you serve ten. With three counts, the loss of probation from his sixth and seventh DUI, and the eighth DUI, Jacobs faced more than forty years in prison. Nearing forty himself, he probably never would be let out. Surely this was the revenge I needed to stop my descent into darkness.

After the policemen finished speaking, I smiled and thanked them for their great work. My mother was in the room and nearly jumped with joy. This was the news I needed to hear, right?

Somehow the news didn't change a thing. Deep down, I knew it wouldn't. I told my mother this was great and served Jacobs right, but my smile was fake; I felt no joy. I kept telling myself I got even and I should be happy. But like everything else since the crash—including the facts that I'd survived and would eventually heal—the news that Jacobs was caught and would be sent away for life did not make me happy. Nothing did. That is, nothing except OxyContin.

I began to wonder if I would be joyful again without pills. How could I be? My life would consist of living on disability and waiting on the couch for the mail to bring a check that I really didn't earn. *Would I be sitting there consumed with anger at no longer being able to do my job? Would I hurt every day and no longer be able to play with my kids?* My son was four, and I didn't know if I would ever throw a football with him again. *Would I be the strong rock of a father figure, something that is so important for my girls to have growing up, or a hobbled, weak shell of my former self stuck in the house watching TV, popping pills, and getting weaker, dumber, and fatter?*

I looked at my casted arms and splinted legs and doubted my recovery. I felt the anger bubbling up inside me again and figured that being in a constant state of anger, being a victim, was now my life. Yes, it was better than being dead but not by much. After my mother left for the night with a big smile on her face, I cried for the very first time. I was losing hope that I would ever be close to the man I was before Jacobs literally crashed into my life; I was also angry at God for putting me through this, because I deserved better. I had done everything right, and I was still in this mess. It wasn't fair.

The next day, I had a meeting with the hospital staff about my long-term care. I was no longer critical and had to leave the intensive care unit even though I could not even sit up and required months of rehab. I was just starting to eat on my own but could not take in enough calories and had lost twenty-five pounds. The staff was talking about the best nursing homes for me.

I was too drugged to participate in the conversation and too depressed to care. Sure, a nursing home; great, *whatever*. It was just another reason to hate my new life.

Thankfully my sister Julie stepped up and acted as my advocate. In her career as a social worker, Julie placed the elderly in situations where they'd receive the level of care they needed: in-home, assisted living, or a nursing home. She knew all about these facilities and the types of care they could provide. There was no better angel to help me with the next fateful fork in the road.

The hospital staff was convinced that a nursing home would be the best option. They had round-the-clock staff and the equipment and staff to care for me.

Julie was adamant that she could do better. Nursing homes are basically set up to help people in the last stages of life, to guide them through their inevitable decline toward death. Patients there are not really seeking to get back to the activity level of a man less than forty years of age.

I needed a different goal in care: intense rehabilitation to regain the strength I'd had just a few weeks ago. My sister knew I needed to be in a hospital in order to heal and receive the physical therapy designed to push me and push me hard. She felt I could take the more intense regimen she had in mind, completely unaware that I was beginning to believe that rehab wouldn't help. I was starting to believe I was done and my body wasn't going to get much better. I had lost my drive.

The staff looked at her like she was crazy. A nursing home was the only option based on my level of care needed. My broken body demanded intense care for months, not weeks, and was in no shape for rehab yet because my bones were nowhere near healed. They wouldn't come out and admit it, but they really didn't think I would get much back either, and they did not want me to take up space in a rehab unit. Other patients who had a better chance of recovery might need it more than I did.

Julie and the staff argued as I drifted in and out of sleep. They left the room to allow me to rest and sat down in a conference room, where the fight became intense. Julie is a consensus maker; her job is to work with distraught families about their ailing loved ones. Now she was on the other side as she fought like hell to keep me out of a nursing home.

The hospital brought in a third staff member to argue their side, but Julie held fast. She had it all set up; I could go to the hospital where she worked in my hometown. My parents and two sisters all lived there, and Julie had arranged a place for me on the rehabilitation unit. She already had spoken with the physical therapist she wanted to handle my case. It was all arranged; she just needed this hospital to sign off on it.

The hospital argued that I was not ready for rehab; I still could not bear weight on my leg or lift either of my arms.

After an hour of arguing, the staff gave up. I was moving out of their facility and would be someone else's problem; I'd be transferred by ambulance at the end of the week. My sister's boss had signed off that my rehab would start immediately even though at this point I could not even sit up in bed. Julie was doing more than stretching the truth about my condition, and in the process, she was putting her job and career on the line. By getting me into the rehab unit when I was not physically ready, she could have been fired if the insurance company refused to pay. Yet she trusted in the Scot she'd known all her life, the guy who would do whatever was necessary to get better.

At least that was who I was *before* the crash. I was not at all sure this was still true. I knew the rehab would be hard and painful, and I had started to doubt that it would be worth the effort.

Finally, the hospital gave up and signed off on the transfer; I would be someone else's responsibility if it didn't work out.

Every day got worse as I sank deeper into depression. I watched endless TV and had realized that 90 percent of the shows were just stupid. It hurt every time I tried to move, which wasn't much. I had splints on both feet and both arms, so I was stuck lying on my back like a turtle. It seemed every day the casts and splints got a little looser; I knew I was losing muscle quickly. Great! If I ever got home, I would not only be a useless, pill-popping couch potato, I'd be weak and scrawny too.

I needed to find a way out of the depression but didn't know how or where to begin. I was discovering it wasn't about being tough; I was depressed because I was confronting major problems in my life that I might not be able to fix. That made me sad—incredibly sad.

I needed a new plan, but how could I plan out my life now? I couldn't really do anything until I knew how much progress I could make along my path of healing and rehabilitation. Months of rehab awaited me without any clues or guarantees as to how well I'd emerge from the experience when I was done.

I had never been without a plan before; my life was on hold, which just added to my depression. It wasn't fair that my life was in such shambles, because I'd figured it all out years ago and my plan had been perfect.

Then I heard it.

It was a whisper—not a booming voice that you hear in the movies or from behind a burning bush—but I heard it clear as day.

"It is not your plan."

The still, small voice stopped me dead in my tracks. My mind had been racing; I hadn't been able to sleep more than a few hours because I kept trying to figure out my life. But as I lay there, the thought kept reverberating through my head.

"It is not your plan."

I tried to ignore it, but it wouldn't go away. Instead it grew louder, if a thought could be loud.

"It is not your plan."

It blocked out everything else. I concentrated on it fully, trying to determine if it was real or imagined.

"It is not your plan."

I didn't get it at first. I was always in control of my life. How could it not be my plan? It was *my* life, so I was in control, wasn't I? I was the one who made the decisions in my life, and if not me, then who?

"It is not your plan."

FOR REFLECTION

Whoever says he is in the light and hates his brother is still in darkness. (1 John 2:9)

1. Should we be happy when those who hurt us are punished? Does revenge help us heal? Why or why not?

2. Have you ever had somebody stand up for you when you needed help? Have you ever stood up for somebody else who was unable to speak for himself? What does Jesus say about this?

Whoever is of God hears the words of God. The reason why you do not hear them is that you are not of God. (John 8:47)

3. Have you ever heard God's voice? What made you think it was God speaking to you?

4. Why might someone not hear God's voice or recognize a message as coming from God?

CHAPTER 17

But I Want It to Be My Plan

"It is not your plan."

This repetitive thought in my head wouldn't go away; I couldn't make it stop or conform to what I wanted. I wanted to be in control, but the voice was stopping me. Why?

At the same time, I sensed I'd heard this voice before, although I couldn't place where or when. I was just certain I had heard it previously. It was familiar.

Well, of course it's familiar, I told myself. *It's in your own head. It must be you. It's your own thought.*

But I didn't believe what I was hearing. After all, *I* was in control of my life. Up until that asshole slammed into me, I had made all the right decisions. I sure as hell wasn't about to let anyone else control my actions.

The thought persisted, over and over again. It was loud and clear and wouldn't be denied.

As I sat alone in my hospital bed, hooked up to IVs, immobilized in splints and casts with the TV tuned into a Judge Judy episode I'd already seen three times, my mind raced. *What did this mean? Why couldn't I get the thought out of my head?*

I fought to deny the simple truth the thought conveyed. *I* was in control! It was *my* life!

I was railing against the obvious and the inevitable.

Could this *really* be the voice of God talking to me? God doesn't *actually* speak to us with a voice like that, does He? I had never been *that* religious before. I went to church and called myself a Christian but never figured God would address me directly. Of course I'd heard of other people who claimed to have "spoken to God," but I always rolled my eyes and figured they were "Bible-thumpers." In their zeal to have a true experience of God, they'd convinced themselves He'd spoken to them, creating a self-fulfilling prophecy. I figured they had so little going on in their lives that "speaking directly to God" was their way of making themselves feel more important than they truly were.

But I was far from a Bible thumper. Truth is, I had never even read the Bible. Yes, I attended church, but I rarely listened to the messages imparted through the services. Why should I? I had it all figured out and used that hour in the pew to plan out the day or refine my next great idea. While I could recite the Lord's Prayer by heart, I had no clue what it meant. I wasn't desiring to talk to God, nor had I considered listening to the prayers that Pastor Mark and Mary Ann were reciting. I was too drugged up and arrogant even as I lay in my own feces and urine. I hadn't even thanked God for keeping me alive. I hadn't thanked him for Mona avoiding paralysis and for the kids being all right.

Why?

I was too busy worrying about what was going to happen to *me* and how I, the smart guy with the plan, would handle it. I was completely self-focused. After all, I was the strong one who had beaten the odds and survived in a situation where everyone else would have died. That meant I was simply better than most. Right?

What an ass!

In spite of my selfishness and ingratitude, I was getting the help I needed to start my recovery. It was like when I was a kid and had a problem I couldn't figure out; my dad would walk in as I floundered and solve it with a few words. Then I became a teenager and *I* knew better; I didn't need my father's advice anymore. Of course, like most teenage boys, I had made mistake after mistake because I thought I knew it all. Could this be God, my other Father, solving a problem for me with just a few words also? Could this be me, the arrogant teenager once again, not accepting His wisdom and trying to do it all myself?

It soon became apparent that the thought wasn't going away no matter how much I resisted. My belligerence wasn't going to prevail over it, so I stopped fighting the voice and said, "Okay, God, it is not my plan. It must be Yours. But what is Your plan? I need to know why this happened and how I am going to make it through, so tell me what Your plan is for me."

Silence.

I asked again, expecting God's voice to answer my questions. I was such an important and special person; I had just heard His voice, so I must have a direct line to God.

"What is your plan, God?"

Silence.

Okay, I guess I didn't have a direct line to the Almighty after all. He wasn't on my speed dial. But I thought about His words: *It is not your plan.* I got it; it was *His* plan.

Maybe I wasn't in control as much as I thought. I kind of felt like the Grinch who stole Christmas when he realized, "Maybe Christmas doesn't come from a store; maybe Christmas means a little bit more." I almost felt my heart grow three sizes that day, just like the Grinch. I smiled for the first time since the crash; I was getting it.

Although I wasn't in control the way I'd thought I was, I was beginning to realize this was okay with me. I had always said that I would only worry about the things over which I had control, but it was becoming obvious that I wasn't in control of much. Moreover, as I lay there unable to even roll over, I realized that I had *never* been in control. With respect to the accident, I'd been in control of my car yet could do nothing to stop this drunk driver from hitting us. I had controlled my veterinary hospital, but now it was functioning without me. For crying out loud, I didn't even have control of my body! I smiled as I figured out that God was making His point by reducing me to this. *"You are not, nor have you ever been, in control. I am and I always was."*

Even I, the arrogant, follow-my-great-plan guy, could see that I had been wrong—nearly dead wrong.

Now it made sense; this was the reason I had survived. It wasn't that I was special or Superman; it wasn't because I was such a great person that God didn't think the world could survive without me. It was because He had decided I would survive. It was *His* call, not mine. He had a reason, even if I did not understand what it was. I had no control over my survival because it was His choice whether I had lived or died that day—whether I lived or died every day.

That night, I finally slept well. I had fallen to the bottom of the pit of depression and vengeance, and I was lost. My life would turn on how I dealt with this—something I had never had to deal with before—a total lack of a plan. But I knew if I stayed like this, struggling to regain control, I would never pull myself out of the pit and my life would continue to be crap. I had changed. This voice, this simple thought, had led me out, and all I had to do was what I was struggling to do. All I had to do was listen.

Once I understood and acknowledged it was God—not me—who was in charge of my life, I realized the same was also true for Jacobs. God had allowed all the steps to align perfectly in order to put our two cars, the van and the Jeep, in that exact spot at that exact time. It was He who had permitted all those things to go right that day to keep all of us alive.

I had been mad at God for letting this happen. Really? Did I honestly think *I* knew better? After admitting He was in control of my life—including the accident and my recovery—did I still want to question *Him*? Was I arrogant enough to think *I* knew better than *He* did? I just couldn't be *that* self-centered anymore; I just couldn't declare that *I* had a better plan than *God* did. What a selfish prick I had been! Not anymore.

Now I felt I would find peace. I wasn't entirely there yet; I still became angry every time I thought about the drunken man who hit us, but I knew I would be all right. It still bothered me that I couldn't recall when or where I'd heard the voice, but for tonight, I had had enough. I sensed I'd turned a corner. Tomorrow would be a better day, all because I had accepted the fact that I couldn't control anything. My life was in *His* hands, not mine. I accepted the fact that this had been true from the very beginning, in spite of my long-held, misguided belief otherwise. God was in control.

For Reflection

Many are the plans in the mind of a man, but it is the purpose of the Lord *that will stand. (Proverbs 19:21)*

1. Can we control our futures?
2. Do you think God used the crash to show that He was in control?
3. Does putting your future in God's hands make life easier or harder? Does it bring you peace to know you're not in charge?
4. Have you ever thought you knew best and then been shown the opposite? Why do we think we know better than God?

CHAPTER 18

The First Step Out

I woke up determined to get stronger each day. I began sleeping less and becoming increasingly cognizant of my surroundings. The staff wanted to wean me off the feeding tube and try to get me to eat again. Although it had been providing some nourishment, it is nearly impossible to feed enough calories into the body through a tiny naso-gastric tube, which has to be small enough to fit through the nasal passages, down the throat, and into the stomach without causing a gag reflex. At the same time, the high-calorie fats and proteins traveling through the tube are thick and tend to cause blockages. The result? I wasn't getting more than eight hundred calories a day and was losing weight quickly.

It was time for me to eat on my own.

I had lost about thirty pounds, including most of the muscle around my arms and legs; my face looked skeletal. A large part of the problem was the OxyContin pain medicine that had shut down my gut, creating a stalemate of sorts in which nothing was moving. Also, in the two weeks since the crash, my stomach had shrunk to a third of its normal size; I could not eat a large meal even if I wanted to. Now was the time to slow the pain meds and try to get calories in.

The thought of intense pain made me very nervous. In reality, I was becoming addicted to the meds and did not know if I could make it without them.

So, I swallowed my pride and asked God for help. I understood the whole "not my plan" thing and had given up on trying to do this on my own. I knew I needed His help in order to wean myself off the drugs.

God, please help me handle my pain better. I want to eat and get stronger. Then I can heal and follow your plan. I will follow wherever You lead. I know that it is all up to You.

This was a 180-degree swing for me. Relinquishing control? Giving up on having everything figured out because I was soooo smart? I had not been without *my* plan since I was in high school. To accept that I was not in control was tough. Still, I reached out to my Creator for help, seeing clearly that the next few months or years would be more than I could do alone. The long, painful healing, the fear of being permanently disabled, of not playing with my kids anymore—these were all too much for me to bear by myself. I needed a Father.

I knew I had to take fewer pain meds, but I was also aware that I could not just stop all the drugs cold turkey. The body doesn't work like that. I still needed pain meds; it had only been a few weeks since the horrific crash, and my bones were still broken. At the same time, the drugs were keeping me in a daze and sapping my will to do anything. I was just waiting for my next pill and the blissful sleep that would soon follow. This was not me.

So, I started by taking less, cutting the dose by 25 percent. Then I waited for the pain to come.

An hour later, I noticed the pain wasn't so bad. It was mostly a dull soreness as long as I didn't move. Since both of my arms and legs were still splinted, it wasn't hard to stay in one spot. I just lay there on my back watching TV. Boring, yes, but at least I knew I was healing.

I dozed off for a few hours; Judge Judy wasn't real exciting that day. When I awoke, I felt hunger pangs for the first time in two weeks. The pain was manageable and I was ready to eat. I looked up to the ceiling and offered, "Thanks."

I buzzed the nurse and asked her to have the cafeteria send up a cheeseburger and fries with a chocolate milkshake. I wanted calories. In a half-hour, it was delivered to my room. By this point, I was starving. The tantalizing aroma of the fried food was overpowering; all I wanted to do was wolf it down and then ask for more. I knew the more calories I could take in, the faster I would heal and the stronger I would get. With gusto, I dove into the burger with large bites.

For the first time, I discovered God has a sense of humor. While this was the one time in my adult life when I could eat as much of anything I wanted—ice cream, pizza, cheeseburgers dripping with grease—my stomach had shrunk so much that I could not eat more than a few bites of anything. One half of a burger and I was stuffed full. I couldn't even finish half the fries and a quarter of the milkshake. I smiled. It was God's little joke.

Now I had to figure out something else. I needed the calories, but I could not eat the volume of food required. Therefore, I decided to add more calories to the food I was consuming. Foods with the most calories in the smallest volume are fats, and the best source of fats is cream.

While God may have a sense of humor, He was also willing to give me a great way out of my predicament. I loved ice cream and started adding it to just about everything. For breakfast, I would order sugary cereal and add in two big scoops. It was cold, chunky, and overly sweet, but I got the calories I needed. For lunch, I would add more ice cream and even more at dinner, plus a bedtime snack. In fact, I ate so much ice cream that I soon became sick of it. I could hear God laughing at his little joke again; the one time I could eat as much ice cream as I wanted, and I no longer wanted it—real funny!

I had decided that it was time to start working on getting back to normal. My kids deserved a father who was as physically close to what they'd become accustomed as I could possibly get. I played a lot with my kids—baseball, football, and soccer depending on the season.

My goal was to get back to the physical condition I was in before the crash. I knew I had to give it my all. I would not want my kids to think I could have done more but chose to do less.

The Chinese have a great expression: "A journey of a thousand miles starts with a single step." It was time to start the journey. It was time to take that first step.

The first step wasn't a step at all. I had been flat on my back for weeks, and the staff wanted me to sit up. *No big deal. This will be easy.*

A group of nurses surrounded me. *Wow, what service,* I thought, reverting to my arrogant ways. *They must really like me.*

Then I found out why they were all there. Each grabbed an arm, and they started to raise the bed. I reached vertical and was sitting up, not on my own but just with the bed being raised (my first step). I was sitting upright and figured I would soon be ready to try to walk down the hall. I would be home in no time.

This lasted all of about ten seconds.

Then the room started to spin and everything went black. I had passed out and the nurses were waiting to catch me before I fell out of bed.

I came to in a few seconds with a dazed look on my face, lying flat on my back again. One of the nurses smiled and said, "You did great! You made it ten seconds." I had never fainted in my life, so I wasn't sure what had happened.

She explained, "You have been down for all this time. Your heart doesn't remember that it needs to pump harder when you sit up to get the blood to your brain, and you passed out. Keep trying; your heart will have to learn again."

I couldn't believe it. My heart has to learn to pump correctly? It has been doing this for almost forty years, and it forgot in a few weeks?

But the body will adapt to what it needs in the moment. It hadn't needed to pump harder, so it lost the ability—a classic "use it or lose it" response. I would have to work on it a few times each day, and each day it would relearn some more. Yes, the nurse told me, I would get nauseous and nearly vomit each time I passed out, but I had to keep trying if I would ever sit up again. The more I lay flat, the harder it would be to get up.

Wow, did I have a long way to go! It seemed like I really did have a journey of a thousand miles ahead of me.

The nurse let me recover and then tried a second time with the same result; I passed out in about ten seconds.

"You did great," she complimented. "We will try again tomorrow." With that, all the nurses left the room.

This was doing great?

I could not even sit upright. That's when it hit me just how weak I had become. The frustration I'd been holding in for a long time came flooding out. As a man, I was taught never to cry, but my world was upside down, and I didn't really care. If crying was what I needed, then I would wail away. I was alone in my room and did not want anyone to be there to console me. It was time to let it out, and I did. I had been told that crying was normal and I should let myself indulge. Of course, I, the arrogant bastard I was, thought the rules did not apply to me. I was stronger than everyone else. I was a man and I would handle this without sobbing like a baby.

Now I knew crying was part of the healing process and part of releasing the arrogance. It was God breaking me down enough to accept Him fully. I was ready, and I decided to let it fly, no holding back.

I cried and cried and cried.

After what seemed like forever, the crying stopped. The room was dead quiet. *God, help me. I have such a long way to go. I can't even sit up. How will I walk again? How will I run with my kids again?*

I was finding out just how hard this journey was going to be, and my will was already starting to falter. Maybe I could learn to accept lying in bed? Everyone would understand that my injuries were just too much to overcome.

After hearing His voice before, I waited for it again. I heard nothing.

This time I didn't get angry or ask again. Instead, I thought about why I hadn't heard a response. Finally, I said, "God, I am in Your hands. I will work as hard as I can and be satisfied with what You give me. It is Your plan, not mine, so what I get back is up to You, but I will put in the work. I know You could heal me in a second, but You want me to go through this for a reason. I need to learn to fight, to push harder. Getting strong again will be the toughest thing I have done, but I will do it. I will do it through You."

Nothing. I smiled anyway; I knew He had heard.

Over the next week, the nurses kept coming in to help me sit up. Each time, I got stronger—first thirty seconds, then fifty, then a minute. Soon it was five minutes and they were moving me to a chair instead of the bed. My heart was remembering how to get the blood to my brain. There were times when I dreaded it, because each time I passed out I would want to vomit and was nauseous for hours, but I kept going. I had taken the first few steps in my thousand-mile journey.

For Reflection

Bless the Lord, *O my soul, and forget not all his benefits, who forgives all your iniquity, who heals all your diseases, who redeems your life from the pit, who crowns you with steadfast love and mercy. (Psalms 103:2–4)*

1. How can you relinquish control to God? *Should* you do that?
2. How have you felt when you've had to accept a new reality? Scared? Angry? How did you cope?

3. Do you think God has a sense of humor? If so, give some examples.

Therefore, since we are surrounded by so great a cloud of witnesses, let us also lay aside every weight, and sin which clings so closely, and let us run with endurance the race that is set before us, looking to Jesus, the founder and perfecter of our faith, who for the joy that was set before him endured the cross, despising the shame, and is seated at the right hand of the throne of God. (Hebrews 12:1–2)

4. Have you ever been in a situation where the road in front of you looks very, very long? How did you handle that?

CHAPTER 19

THUD

As I mentioned, the only family that still visited daily by this time were my parents. Having returned to their busy lives, my sisters were stopping by less frequently, and of course Mona and the kids were home. I spoke to them at least once a day but noticed we talked very little about the crash; whenever I brought it up, they would quickly change the subject. Even Mona avoided any discussion of it. After a while, I asked my father why. He noted that every time we talked about the crash, everyone ended up crying and angry; it was just easier to avoid the topic altogether. Exhausted physically and mentally, we hated what we were going through, thanks to Mike Jacobs, the loser who had hit us and run away. We couldn't even watch the news reports about the crash because everyone would break down in tears.

Dad continued: "I hadn't cried in years, and now I am crying every day. It's just hard to face the reality of how close you came to dying and how much work is still ahead of you."

This anguish had continued unabated for weeks, and I realized something had to change. Understandably, every time anyone thought about the crash, it resulted in anger and sadness. There was no escaping it. Every time I gazed at my bandaged arms and legs, or felt excruciating pain as I tried to move, it was a constant reminder. I had never really hated someone before, having been raised not to hate anyone, but Mike Jacobs deserved it. He was an easy guy to despise.

But in my heart, I knew it was wrong. I had seen other people in difficult situations who were mad all the time. Nothing was ever good enough; nothing ever went right; they were always being persecuted and unfairly deprived. Not surprisingly, they ended up divorced and alone—which just confirmed to them that the world was against them.

Now I was becoming "that guy," the downer nobody really wanted to be around. My family would tolerate me for a while but slowly find excuses to keep their distance. And really, who could blame them?

That's when I decided I didn't want to be that resentful person anymore. One of Mona's favorite sayings is, "Happiness is a choice." No matter what, you can choose to be happy or you can choose to be sad. Anything else and you are a victim; you have given up your power.

It was time to put those words into action. We had talked the talk, but could we walk the walk? A tragic, devastating event had wreaked havoc on our lives, but I still had the power to choose whether I would let it control me or whether I would put it in my past. Bad things would happen in the lives of my kids; they already had. How could I tell them to fight through it and not be a victim if I was acting like one myself? Victims stay angry; they thrive on hate. Yes, on the day of the crash we had been victims, but that day was over.

I was told once that when you change in the way God intends, He changes your name. When Simon became the disciple of Jesus and chose to follow him, Jesus changed his name to Peter, meaning "Rock," and told him He would build His church upon him.

Now, if we would let go of the anger and accept God's plan, we would no longer be victims but survivors; our names would be changed. It was time to start acting like survivors; it was time to stop the hate. Because it was my choice, I chose happiness, right in that moment.

Excellent plan, right? There was just one catch: I wasn't sure how to do it. I had taken the first step already when I had accepted that God had a different plan for us, but Jacobs's stupidity and inconsideration still made my blood boil. *How could anyone be such a loser?*

What did he think was going to happen that day?

Though my family did not want to talk about it, I knew that ignoring the elephant in the room wasn't going to work anymore. If they were ever going to return to normal, the kids would need to talk about it, as would Mona and I. The hate we were holding for Jacobs eventually would destroy both of us, our marriage, and ultimately, our family. I decided I wasn't going to let Jacobs destroy any more of our lives. He already had inflicted more than enough damage.

I tried to tell myself that there must be something positive about the guy and that it wasn't his fault. That sounded nice, but I am a big believer in personal responsibility. Jacobs made the choice to drink that morning and drive around. He'd also decided long ago to evade responsibility for his alcoholism after four stints in rehab and five years in jail. No matter what had happened in his past, he chose to make the same mistakes over and over again, which ultimately resulted in a head-on collision with a car full of kids. It *was* his fault; trying to make excuses for him only pissed me off more. This cycle continued for days. I just did not know how to get past the hate.

Then as I lay there watching the news alone in my room trying to figure this out, a story was broadcast from Pennsylvania. A local man had gone into an Amish school with a gun. He ordered all the adults and boys out before lining up the girls against the blackboard. His daughter had died shortly after birth some nine years earlier, and he hated God for putting him through that tragedy and grief. He just had to kill these innocent school girls because, in his twisted mind, this would punish God for taking his daughter.

The adults had called 911 (some of the people in the school were not Amish and had cellphones), and the boys and teachers huddled together outside and prayed for their classmates. The girls inside the room, ages six to sixteen, asked the gunman to pray with them. Instead, he lined them up and shot them one by one in the back of the head, killing five of the ten girls before killing himself. His anger over the death of his daughter had destroyed him and a room full of innocent children; his hate had rotted his mind to a point where he thought killing innocents would make things right.

As I watched this horrific report, I realized I was on that same path; I had to find a way off or I might just as well have died on impact. If I couldn't let go of the hate, I would be like the gunman, devoting all of my time to plotting my revenge and driving myself to insanity.

Next, a reporter interviewed an Amish father and mother who had lost a daughter in the shooting. The reporter asked what they thought about the man who killed the girl and her schoolmates. Their response shook me:

"We have forgiven him, and our child is now safe in the arms of Jesus."

The stunned reporter followed up with, "You have forgiven him? Forgiven the man who just shot your daughter?"

Equally stunned, the parents of the murdered child looked at her and replied, "This is what Jesus teaches us to do: 'Forgive us our trespasses as we forgive those who trespass against us.' We must forgive him."

Then I understood. It was like someone had turned the light on in my darkness. For the second time, I had heard the voice of God, this time in a news story out of Pennsylvania. It now made perfect sense. This family could deal with the tragedy—a much greater tragedy than mine—only by forgiving the man responsible. It was only through forgiveness that the hate would go away. I had tried to bury it, to not speak of it, to live with it, but it was clear that none of that was going to work. The only pathway available to me was the hardest and most unnatural; I had to forgive the idiot who had nearly killed my entire family, nearly paralyzed my wife, and put me in the hospital for the foreseeable future. I had to forgive him even though he did not deserve it and had not asked for it. It wasn't fair, but I knew it was the only way.

That day I decided to forgive; I would no longer hate. Jacobs was a despicable human being who didn't deserve forgiveness, but I would forgive him anyway. I told myself that this was not my plan and that God must have used Jacobs for some other reason; I just was not able to see why. In the end, I didn't need to see why since it wasn't *my* plan but *His*. I didn't need to understand it; I needed only to accept it.

Could it really be this easy? Could the Amish, stuck in the simple ways of two hundred years ago, have figured it out so much faster than someone like me, schooled in the modern world with all this information at my fingertips? It seemed pretty obvious that they had. The Scripture they had quoted was from the Lord's Prayer, something I had repeated since I was four but somehow had never given much thought. I just recited the words without ever contemplating their meaning. Those people were smarter than I because they really meant what they were saying. They followed God's Word exactly, literally and without question, and it was leading them through the darkness of their tragedy. Now, it would lead me through mine. They were more angels, grieving a terrible loss three hundred miles away and saving me from my own hatred and anger.

With that, I felt the hate start to go away. It was like coming through a tunnel and emerging into the light. The tunnel was cold and dark; the light was warm and bright. It was the joy that comes with letting God back into one's life. I felt happiness returning. I could envision the devil himself, a demon that was living inside of me, being driven out by the simple words of the Lord's Prayer: "Forgive us our trespasses as we forgive those who trespass against us."

As I thought about it, I figured Jacobs would feel so much better when he realized I had forgiven him. I would be seen as a great guy who could forgive the man who did not deserve it. I would be seen as a role model for forgiveness, a really special human being.

I stopped. The anger started to come back. Why would I care if Jacobs felt "better"? His feeling better about what he did would only compel him to repeat it. I wanted him to feel terrible about what he had done for the rest of his life. If we had to be in pain, so should he.

Whoa, back up! I thought about it again. Once more, I was not really following what Jesus would do. I was wrong; I wasn't getting it. I realized I couldn't truly forgive Jacobs simply because others would see me as a hero. (Since he hadn't been tried in court yet, I was banned from speaking to him. I couldn't tell him I had forgiven him even if I wanted to.)

I needed to forgive Jacobs for *me*, not for him. It was kind of selfish, but in a good way. Forgiveness is the path through tragedy. It was my way out.

I realized that hate is the barrier that stops everything, a wall we put around ourselves that ultimately becomes our prison. How many times have we heard of two people who hate each other but neither one can remember exactly why? Maybe something was said or done by one person and completely misinterpreted by the other. As a result, they didn't speak again for thirty years. Hate does this. It clouds the memory and distorts the truth. Now, it was preventing me from being thankful that we all had survived, that my kids had come through with relatively minor injuries, that my wife would walk again. The hate was depleting my drive to do the rehab; it was pushing my family away; it was even making the nurses hesitant to come check on me in my room as often. Because I alone had built this wall of hate, I alone could tear it down.

I discovered an interesting thing about forgiveness; it has just as much or even more impact on the *forgiver* as on the *forgiven*. It is like giving a gift; the giver feels just as good as—or even better than—the one who receives it. I had to forgive Jacobs if I wanted to survive, to get back to where I was before the crash psychologically more than physically. I had to do it whether anyone else knew about it. God had arranged it so that it would be done without others knowing. No witnesses would be there to admire me; that was too arrogant and self-serving. It had to be done because "that was what Jesus teaches us to do."

Hate is the lazy way out. It is just so easy, much like a drug; it makes you feel superior and strong but soon takes over your life until all you can do is hate. It is a temporary fix that makes you feel good for a moment but ends up isolating you from everyone, with only your anger for company.

Forgiveness, on the other hand, is not our natural response but a learned behavior (the Amish did it quickly because they are taught from day one to forgive others). For most of us, it takes time and effort. It brings people together, it makes people happy, but it is hard to do. How tough is it to call that no-good brother-in-law you haven't spoken to for a year and apologize? Forgiveness takes work.

I had to choose: Did I want to keep hating, or did I want to forgive?

I decided that day that the man who nearly wiped out everything I cherished would be forgiven. I asked God to help, knowing I could not do this myself. There had been many times in my life when I'd asked for and received forgiveness (I was taught that Jesus forgives all our sins); now I would forgive Jacobs. No, he hadn't asked to be forgiven, but that didn't matter. I needed to complete the process of forgiving Jacobs so I could move on with my life. I wasn't about to wait for an apology from him. I asked God to help me forgive him regardless. I wanted to let go of the anger and bitterness.

Again I wondered, *Could it really be that easy? Could it be that if I forgave him, with all his faults, I would finally be happy again?* Once more, I remembered those words I had repeated since the first time I went to church: "Forgive us our trespasses, as we forgive those who trespass against us."

This was the Lord's Prayer, the prayer Jesus instructed us to use when we spoke to God. There were no qualifiers as to whom or what should be forgiven. It just said to forgive, period.

If I wanted Jesus's help getting through this, I had to do what

He wanted me to do without question. Nothing is free, including happiness.

With that, I forgave Jacobs. I would no longer see him as evil. I would no longer hate him. I would put it in the past.

Immense relief washed over me. It felt as if I had finally dropped a heavy weight I had been carrying, and I could almost hear the thud as the baggage dropped. I felt physically lighter. I had been carrying this bag of hatred and anger for almost a month. Now it was gone, and I knew I could go on. In that moment, I knew I would not fail at this.

For a month, I had walked through hell. While I knew the journey was far from over, I could see my way out. It was like I had been lost and now saw something I recognized; I knew I had found my way. For the first time since the crash, I felt like I was going to get my life back. We would be okay.

For Reflection

Therefore, if anyone is in Christ, he is a new creation. The old has passed away; behold, the new has come. (2 Corinthians 5:17)

1. Give some examples of how God changes your name when God changes you.

And whenever you stand praying, forgive, if you have anything against anyone, so that your Father also who is in heaven may forgive you your trespasses. (Mark 11:25)

Judge not, and you will not be judged; condemn not, and you will not be condemned; forgive, and you will be forgiven. (Luke 6:37)

2. Think of the story of the Amish school shooting. Could you be so forgiving? How would your life be different if you chose to forgive instead of choosing to be angry or hateful? Would you be following Jesus if you did not forgive? Is there another way to get rid of hate and anger?

3. Is happiness a choice?

CHAPTER 20

TRUST IN ME

Forgiving Jacobs was like turning a page in a book: The dark, terrible chapter in my life was over and a new story was beginning. This chapter would be one of recovery now that the weight of my anger and hatred was gone, along with the depression and the asking "Why me?" Sure, there would be times when they'd come back for a visit, but each time I could take heart in the words that had initiated my recovery: "It is not your plan."

I found comfort in my belief that there was a reason for all this—a reason I did not fully understand, but a reason nonetheless. I could now focus on my recovery and rehabilitation, not my sadness over being stuck in a hospital, or the pain with every movement, or the injustice of being the victim. I reminded myself that I was no longer a victim; I was a survivor. God had changed my name.

I was coming to realize that there was an explanation for why bad things happen; I just wasn't smart enough to see it. God was not going to give me the details of His plan because He knew if I had advance notice of what was in store for me, I would try to change it to fit my perception of what the plan *should* be. But my vision was far too narrow; I would not know how it should really play out.

Absolute faith in Him was required, pure and simple. When He put me on this course, I was lacking in the faith I needed, but it was now growing inside me. I was beginning to understand if I just placed my trust in Him, I could follow His plan for my recovery and the rest of my life without fear. I could relax about the details of why it was happening, stop complicating everything, and just keep moving forward.

The fact is, bad things happen to us all—good people and bad people. It is not about who deserves it. Bad things happen to you because they are part of life. I had to accept that I was on this earth, susceptible to both good and bad developments.

What had happened to me and my family wasn't fair, but a lot about life isn't. If I was waiting for life to be "fair" or to "get even" with those who had wronged me, I would always be disappointed. "Fair" and "getting even" just don't happen in this life. I had to accept this reality and move on. Looking back and asking, "Why me?" would not help me walk again, especially not when I had to endure the pain of rehab. "Why me?" and "This sucks" were dragging me down and eroding my will, just more unnecessary weight I was hauling around. I had realized that the idea I didn't *deserve* the car crash or someone else didn't *deserve* the disease or the downsizing or the abuse had no relevance. I figured that there were things in the past that had happened to Jacobs that were not right either. *Yeah, Scot, life isn't going to be fair. Tough shit; you need to get over it.*

Although I might not have deserved it, maybe I needed it. Maybe it was a vehicle for me to get stronger, to have more faith, to change course. I don't know. What mattered was that I would live my life in a different way—a better way. Would I learn the lesson God meant to teach me, or would I wallow in self-pity? In the end, that was the choice I had to make.

I decided I was not going to fold. It was my time to man up. It sounded harsh as I lay there with both arms splinted and both legs immobilized, unable to even roll on my side. I still could not eat much or even use a bedpan. Nobody would ever tell me, as I lay there, that I wasn't tough enough, that I needed to suck it up and deal with it, but I knew I had to. Others might be afraid to say this to me, but I could say it to myself. Mental toughness was what I needed now. That was the next step on my road to recovery.

I began to see my recovery as God's challenge for me and decided He had given me an opportunity—yes, *opportunity*—to see what I was made of. I had been the "smart kid" and never was particularly tough. Growing up, I was always afraid of getting into a fight on the playground and would usually back down. I was of average height and skinny; I had stopped playing football in eighth grade and wrestled for only a year. At my large high school, the other kids were just bigger and faster. In college, I worked out regularly and was no longer as scrawny, but I had never really been physically stronger than average. Now I would have to work harder than ever to regain my strength. It was time to get tough.

I started to see this event as a great challenge. I had never gone through a really tough time and had always wondered how I would respond. Soldiers going into battle always wonder about how they will act when the real bullets start flying. This crash became my war, my test of character.

Malcolm Gladwell refers to this in his book *David and Goliath*, in what he calls the "near-miss" phenomenon. It was seen in the English during World War II when London was bombed for fifty-nine days straight in the "Blitz." There was great fear among the leaders of England, Winston Churchill included, that the civilians would panic if bombs started falling from the sky on London. The government did not even build bomb shelters because they were afraid civilians would not come back out, fearing the English people would not have the courage needed to make it through the toughest, most horrific parts of the war.

Instead, the opposite happened. Bombs fell, but there were no civilians running through the streets in a panic; after a while, people barely even looked up. It is a strange part of the human psyche: We are all afraid of how we will react to a terrible event, but once we make it through, the fear starts to go away. In London, the people who survived the bombings (those in the "near-miss" group) began to feel invincible, as if not even bombs could touch them; they'd drop on someone else, but not *them*. They had been "chosen" to survive, therefore the bombs would miss them time and time again. Fear of the bombs diminished and was replaced with resolve. The Londoners defiantly went on with life to show those German bastards they were tough. Screw the Nazis. Let them drop their bombs—the Londoners were invincible. Funny thing was that those who survived were right. The bombs did not hurt them. They *were* invincible.

I began to feel the same. I had *nearly* died, but this had been my "near-miss." Screw Jacobs. I was better than him and I would prove it by walking again. He would not keep me down; I would win. I had survived against all odds; I was invincible. Let the bombs come.

I would push myself harder than I had ever pushed. I would get back as close to normal as I could so my kids would never question my effort. I would try every avenue from traditional to non-traditional. I would research things I had never put much faith in before, such as meditation, acupuncture, and nutritional supplements. Of course, I also would get serious about my relationship with God.

Only one thing still bothered me: I had heard that voice before, that voice that kept telling me, "It is not your plan," but I couldn't remember where. I had figured it must have been some other life-changing event, but there hadn't been any until now. I just couldn't place the voice.

Then it hit me.

The voice hadn't been some "burning bush" like Moses encountered in the desert—my life wasn't nearly so dramatic, and I certainly wasn't Moses. In fact, it hadn't been a voice at all, just a thought. Like the *It's not your plan* thought, it was accompanied by an urgent feeling that I should listen; I intuitively knew this one was important, that I needed to pay attention. Although I wanted to dismiss it as random, I sensed clearly that this thought was crucial and that I should remember it. The realization sent chills down my spine.

It had occurred the night before the crash and was one of my few memories still left from the weekend. I was getting ready for bed when the thought popped into my head out of the blue for no particular reason, seeming completely out of place. The words were simple but clear: *If a car comes across the median, your job is to keep it from hitting the kids in back.*

At first, I had kind of laughed it off thinking in my usual know-it-all manner, *That was a strange thought. Why would I be thinking about car crashes? Besides, cars come across the center line, not the median. Medians are there to keep cars from crashing into each other in the first place. There's no way a car would cross the median and hit us!*

But it wouldn't go away; this persistent thought kept reverberating. Eventually I had to stop and think about it.

If a car comes across the median, your job is to keep it from hitting the kids in back.

Yes, I was the dad—it's my job to protect the family at all costs. That meant that if a car was coming at us, I would prevent it from hitting the kids. I guess it makes sense, but it just would never happen. Of course, at the time I had no idea that less than twenty-four hours later, a Jeep driven by a drunk driver would careen across the median and collide head-on with our van.

Now I understood. With that thought, God was just instructing me to do as He said: Keep the car from hitting the kids, and He would take care of the rest.

I don't remember the crash and don't know if I did anything in particular to protect the kids. I doubt that I consciously thought about anything; there was no time. All I know is that we were hit in just the right spot to be injured but not killed.

Our family had a near-miss. Jacobs's car had hit mine at the driver's-side headlight at about a 30-degree angle. It had sent us spinning, thereby dissipating a great deal of the energy. A few more feet to the left and he would have hit on the side by my door—and three inches of a van door would not have stopped a Jeep coming at seventy miles per hour. My head would have snapped to the side into the door instead of forward into the airbag; this certainly would have broken my neck and fractured my skull. Jacobs's thousand-pound Jeep would have collapsed the side of the van and landed on me.

In that case, not only I but also Chase, who was sitting behind me, probably would have been killed or paralyzed instantly. Instead, we all shot forward first and were stopped by our seat belts, while Mona and I hit the airbags. The forward, not sideways, impact kept our necks from breaking. Colliding at high speed, we needed to hit *head-on*, but not *straight* head-on, in order to survive.

I had done exactly what I was told to do, exactly what I had to do for all of us to live: *If a car comes across the median, your job is to keep it from hitting the kids in back.*

I had been guided by God's voice, the voice that had seemed like just a random, illogical, unrelenting thought. In the end, God rewarded us for my obedience. We would emerge from the experience stronger, perhaps not physically, but mentally and spiritually—which was ultimately more important. It proved that God had a plan for us. Some would call it luck, and no doubt we had been lucky, but why, if it was just plain luck, was I given a warning the night before the crash? God had informed me in very simple terms, "Don't swerve. Do what I say and I will take care of you. Have faith and trust in Me."

For Reflection

Again I saw that under the sun the race is not to the swift, nor the battle to the strong, nor bread to the wise, nor riches to the intelligent, nor favor to those with knowledge, but time and chance happen to them all. (Ecclesiastes 9:11)

1. How can you accept things that are not fair in your life? What does Jesus say about life being fair?

Rejoice in hope, be patient in tribulation, be constant in prayer. (Romans 12:12)

Not only that, but we rejoice in our sufferings, knowing that suffering produces endurance, and endurance produces character, and character produces hope, and hope does not put us to shame, because God's love has been poured into our hearts through the Holy Spirit who has been given to us. (Romans 5:3–5)

2.   Give an example of a time in your life when adversity made you a stronger and better person.

And your ears shall hear a word behind you, saying, "This is the way, walk in it," when you turn to the right or when you turn to the left. (Isaiah 30:21)

3.   Have you ever had God give you a warning? If so, did you understand the message? What was the result?

CHAPTER 21

ANGELS, ANGELS EVERYWHERE

After about three weeks, Mona was discharged. She joined the kids back home, having been fitted with a solid plastic body brace that went from her armpits to halfway down her thighs. It was sweaty, hot, and confining (it completely encircled her), and she had to wear it twenty-four hours a day. As you can imagine, it made sleeping very uncomfortable. Mona's broken elbow was splinted, making that arm totally useless since she couldn't bend or lift it. Her body ached all over due to the violence of the crash, which had inflicted terrible muscle and tendon damage.

Of course, they'd prescribed OxyContin to ease her suffering, but it made her sick to her stomach and constipated so she was rarely able to take it. Most days it was simply Tylenol as her sole pain medicine. *Tylenol* for three spinal fractures, a broken elbow, head trauma, and severe soft tissue damage all over her body.

Most people have no idea what it is like to cope with unrelenting, long-term, chronic pain. It's debilitating, and it saps the will of even the toughest people, knowing it will hound them every minute of every day for months, with no escape. Mona had already proven her toughness, so it wasn't a matter of being tough; it was about getting to the point of wondering if life would be worth living like this. Life with this kind of pain would be no life at all.

But she was a mom to three little kids and a wife to a husband who might not be of much help anymore; she had to persevere and keep her family together. The maternal drive to protect her kids kept her strong and determined. Mona had no choice but to get better. Since I probably wouldn't be coming home for a long time, the kids needed her. She simply prayed for the pain to subside.

However, daily maintenance of family and home activities was a real struggle for a variety of reasons. First of all, Mona could not be left alone. She couldn't drive in a brace, so transporting kids to school and running the typical household errands were out of the question. Her injuries made even simple chores like laundry, vacuuming, and meal prep impossible. How do you make dinner when you can't stand for more than a few minutes or even drive to the grocery store? The kids could get themselves on and off the bus, but they couldn't participate in after-school activities. Still, we did not want them sitting around watching TV for months while their dad was convalescing in a rehab facility and their mom was confined to bed.

Enter more angels. Mona's mom and sisters stayed with her in two-week shifts, putting their own lives on hold and using up vacation time to help us out. Her sister Carla came first for two weeks, followed by her mother, Anne, and then sisters Theresa and Denise. Their assistance was invaluable in feeding the kids and getting them to school, keeping animals (dogs, cats, goats, chickens, and horses) fed and watered, doing the laundry, and shopping for groceries. Some normality returned for the kids as they got back into the routine of school and friends, taking their minds off all the trauma and putting them into the swing of fall.

At just ten years old and with her arm in a sling, Alexa stepped up to the plate. She was a lot like her mom in that she just focused on what had to be done and did it. When it was time for her mom to bathe, Alexa would help her to the bathroom and in and out of her back brace. When Mona needed anything, Alexa ran to retrieve it. She even helped feed and dress Victoria and Chase, ensuring they were ready for school every day. This experience forced her to grow up and take responsibility, which she did without complaint. She proved to be one tough kid and, as I said, very much her mother's daughter.

Victoria did what she could, mainly babysitting Chase to enable whoever was there to focus on other things, such as meals and laundry. Even though Chase was only four, he realized that things had changed and took over a lot of the animal care. He also helped with the laundry. It was amazing to watch these kids rise to the occasion. They saw that they were needed and thrived on it. At that time, without any at-home nursing care, we had to rely on the kids and other family to help out.

The assistance we received from our community was simply incredible. We hear so much about the bad things people do in the world, but those we knew—and even some we didn't—consistently demonstrated kindness and generosity in the aftermath of the accident. They were truly angels among us. We'd moved to Lake Geneva ten years earlier when we bought a very small one-person veterinary practice with Mona as the only veterinarian and a single employee named Karen. We'd worked six days a week, including seeing emergencies, which required being on call every night and every weekend for the first five years. Our diligent work ultimately paid off in the form of a new building and a four-doctor veterinary practice that served thousands of clients and pets.

Initially I'd believed that all that sweat equity was for the sole purpose of building the practice and paying the bills; now I realized it had yielded so much more than that. These clients had become friends, and we had become an important part of the community, helping all these people when they needed us. Now, it was the community's turn, because we needed them. That our kids attended the public schools and had lots of activities and that we attended an active church had given us the opportunity to meet a large percentage of the population—even those who didn't have pets or, *God forbid*, took them somewhere else for medical care.

Due to the nature of our work, we tended to get to know our clients very well. Often, we'd see them through some of their toughest moments as pet owners. When someone who has just watched their beloved dog get hit by a car comes rushing into your facility—usually in the middle of the night—and hands their pet over to you with trust and confidence, it creates a bond. No matter what, we had always made an effort to ensure our clients knew that we cared and were doing all we could.

Being the person who can help someone else when he is at his lowest and most frightened forges a relationship in ways that few other professions do. I would develop the same type of friendship with my surgeon, Dr. Lang.

Now we were the ones at our nadir, and people rallied around us.

Lake Geneva is a small town, so word of the crash had spread quickly. Some of our clients had relatives in the Madison area who had called them when the news reported a "terrible crash involving two veterinarians from Lake Geneva." The crash had taken place on a Sunday, and as soon as our office opened Monday, calls began flooding in.

"Is it true? Were Dr. Scot and Mona really in a crash? Are they going to be all right? How are the kids?"

People were not asking when we would be back to see their pets or when we could help *them* again; they were asking how they could help *us*. Angels.

Friends and clients arrived to assist. One of our neighbors plows snow in the wintertime; every time a snowflake hit the driveway, he was at our house. He'd plow the drive while his teenage son would shovel the walk. His son even brought out a broom and swept any remaining snow to prevent anyone from slipping.

A client who owns a dry cleaner and laundromat called the office and told them to have our family assemble everything that needed washing; they would do our laundry for free. Once Mona and the kids were home, the dry-cleaning office would call the night before to inform us that someone would be there in the morning to pick up the laundry and bedding. That same night, they'd return it washed, folded, and pressed. They did this twice a week to help us keep up.

A local pizza place delivered lunch to our veterinary office every Friday, knowing the staff was overworked and could use a good lunch. The owners were a young couple with a big Lab whose shoulder I had fixed. During the process, we'd become friends. We shared some things in common in that they also had a business that required lots of time, dedication, and late hours. Their restaurant was the local favorite, known for its great food. It was packed every weekend and most weekdays. Despite being so busy, they never failed to deliver lunch to our staff every week.

Another friend came and installed a wheelchair ramp and a hand-held showerhead to enable Mona (and eventually me) to shower sitting down. He also installed handicapped bars around the house to give us something to hold on to.

One of our clients had a daughter Alexa's age, and we'd gotten to know the family over the years through school and 4H activities. They owned a gas station in town and offered free gas to anyone coming to visit us—for months.

We also had an angel named Earl, who lived down the street. He may have been in his upper sixties, but he had the strength and determination that characterized so many of his generation. He rarely sat still and would normally take care of the horses, chickens, and goats when we were on vacation. Now, he showed up twice a day to feed and water them, as well as maintain the barns. It was winter, which meant he had to carry five-gallon buckets of water over snow and ice. Here was a man close to seventy years of age hauling water up and down ice-covered hills to make sure Mona and the kids didn't have to. Having been taking care of the animals for us while we were at the cabin that weekend, he just kept coming once he heard about the crash. This incredibly generous man even made sure the maintenance was done, fixing latches and doors so they would close. We had always paid him for his services, but now he would accept nothing.

There were also the people who own a small farm where Mona had purchased our goats. These goats were just pets and not much work, but they still had to be fed and watered. We kept them in a little shed at night to protect them from coyotes so we had to go out twice a day to let them out or lock them up. Goats are somewhat ill-mannered and tend to jump on people, especially if there is food around. Obviously, Mona was in no condition for that.

Hearing about our injuries, that family came, got the three goats, and took them back to their farm. They cared for them for six months until we could handle them again. We did not even have a good way to transport the animals, so they picked them up and dropped them off for us. Again, they would accept no payment.

One of my favorites was my barber, Bill Huntress. Bill was born and raised in Lake Geneva, smoked fat cigars, had been divorced twice, and sported a bumper sticker on his truck that said, "If they call it Tourist Season, why can't you shoot them?"

For nine dollars, you can get a great haircut and all the local gossip you can take in. Bill owned the classic old-time shop on Main Street with the red-and-white-striped pole out front and an old TV that seemed to always be playing *Gunsmoke* reruns. He came across as a tough guy that loved to hunt and had even named his best dog "The Loser" because she had once failed to find a bird. She was only about four months old at the time and just learning how to retrieve, but she became The Loser from then on—even after she'd retrieved hundreds of birds. Of course, Bill would also spend twenty minutes after each hunt with that dog in his lap, picking out burrs and looking for ticks. That was just Bill.

He called me in the hospital and asked to come up because he wanted to give me a haircut. This man drove two hours to the hospital to give me a nine-dollar haircut and then refused payment. I don't know if anyone ever called Bill an angel before, but he *was* one—a gruff angel with a bit of tarnish on his bent halo, but an angel nonetheless. More proof that they come in all shapes and sizes.

The church also jumped in quickly. Our pastors, Mark and Mary Ann, visited us two to three times a week to pray with us and our families—over an hour's drive each way for two very busy people. After they announced what had happened at all three services the following week, they kept the congregation informed of our progress. They led prayers for us in church and organized prayer chains in which people prayed for us and then asked their friends to pray for us also. Many of the folks participating in these prayer chains had no idea who we were, but they didn't care. They prayed for us anyway. We literally had hundreds, maybe thousands, of people storming heaven, and we'd probably never even met half of them.

Mark and Mary Ann provided more than just spiritual help. Though they believed in the power of prayer, they recognized the real-life challenges Mona and I were facing and were determined to do more than pray. The church organized volunteers to deliver dinners to the house as soon as Mona and the kids were home. Though the prayers were important and helped us heal, the food saved the day. People cooked fantastic meals so Mona and the kids did not have to make many suppers. They enjoyed lasagna, meatloaf, even fresh-caught Alaskan salmon a friend had just brought home from a fishing trip.

The food was delivered by five o'clock every night and was one of the greatest gifts we received. Having meals delivered allowed Mona to rest and heal at a time when it was a struggle even to sit up in bed. Alexa would meet the people at the door, take the food, and thank them. Those delivering the food had been instructed by the church *not* to come in; they did not want Mona to feel pressured to get out of bed and try to keep herself "presentable" for guests. Their instructions were to hand off the food and keep any conversation short. It was all about making life easy for us, not about the volunteers getting recognized for what they did. Since Alexa rarely knew the person delivering the food, it was a lesson in anonymous giving and the pure joy that accompanies it.

One of the angels delivering food was a twenty-year-old college student named Sara. She had signed up to deliver a meal but had run late at a class. When she called the house in a panic, Mona's sister Carla answered.

"I am running late," she apologized, "and I don't have time to cook anything."

"Don't worry," Carla replied. "We have plenty of food for the night."

"No, I *want* to deliver something," Sara insisted. "If you don't mind, I will pick something up. My sister has little kids and they love Happy Meals. I know it is not very fancy, but would the kids want that?"

Carla laughed and yelled to the kids, "Do you want some Happy Meals tonight?"

The news that they were getting McDonald's for dinner sent the kids screaming. Sara laughed on the other end of the phone. A half-hour later, she delivered the bags of food that the kids loved—maybe not for the food itself, but for the prize inside. She also brought two meals for Mona and Carla who, after trying to eat healthfully for the entire last month, enthusiastically dug in.

This angel college student had just dropped twenty bucks on people she barely knew. It was probably the equivalent of two to three hours of work for her. Most likely, she was broke. Yet she chose to spend money on us, strangers in a community she had not really lived in for years. Incredible.

One group of ladies within the church optimized the efforts to help. They met multiple times each week to make quilts and shawls for the sick, those leaving for college, the newly baptized, and those entering military service. These quilts were given so that each individual would have something to wrap themselves in when they felt lonely or depressed. They symbolized the love of Jesus and the community wrapped around them and offered an amazing amount of comfort. As a quilt is hand-stitched, these women pray for the person for whom it is intended, asking God to keep them safe or to heal them. These wonderful ladies made a quilt for each member of our family, customized to us as individuals. Mona's, of course, had horses, mine had fishing and hunting, the girls' had various animals, and Chase's had cars and sports.

The strange thing was that each of us used the quilts every night without really thinking or talking about it. We all had plenty of blankets to keep us warm, but each one of us, acting independently, wrapped ourselves in those handmade quilts instead. It was something that brought great comfort knowing we had a community of people thinking of us. We all automatically held them close, absorbing the prayer and love put into them. It was another one of those "God moments" we needed to survive. It felt like His arms were wrapping around us with those quilts. In fact, they were.

The veterinary community also came to help. The veterinary field is a relatively small profession and so we get to know each other pretty well. Dr. Mike Aushwitz was one who had graduated with Mona; he was also one of my best friends since my second year in undergrad. I was in charge of his floor as a Resident Assistant and lived right next to him. We had followed similar paths to veterinary school, both spending three years in undergrad before getting into vet school at Wisconsin. He was even the best man in my wedding. When he found out about the crash, he came to visit and soon realized we would not be able to work for months. Knowing how hard it is on veterinary practices when one, much less two, veterinarians are out, he decided to do what he could do: He came to work at our office. Mike had every Thursday off, so every week he drove the hour down to our place and worked for us. He would accept no pay; it was just his way of helping out. The clients and staff loved him because of his upbeat attitude and his hard work. He took on every task without complaint so our other two vets could take a lunch or simply slow down for a while. We never asked him to do this; he took it upon himself.

Mona's classmates, Dr. Chris Holder and his wife, Dr. Tracy Kusik, sent their little girl to stay with her grandparents and came down to help us for three days. They lived over two hours away, and both ran their own busy practices. Chris was a solo practitioner, which meant he had to close his office, while Tracy had to pay a part-time vet to work extra hours—all because they wanted to do their part. Like the other angels, neither one would accept any payment from us.

Dr. Jeff Korosec, a veterinarian from a neighboring practice, scheduled himself to come to our office and perform some surgeries that simply could not wait. This was in spite of the fact that these clients probably would have traveled to his practice for the surgery since he was just a few miles away. He came to our facility anyway—sacrificing the thousands of dollars he could have made had these clients come to him instead. He also refused any compensation for his good deeds.

Every single one of these people was an angel, stepping in when they were needed to help us survive. We could not have made it without them.

Of course, our office staff had also been plunged into a huge mess because suddenly we were two doctors short in a four-doctor practice. For months, the other vets, Doctors Chris Welch and Kay Stratton, would be asked to work a boatload of hours, including every Saturday. They would be on call every other day and every other weekend. Between vets, receptionists, and technicians, we still had a staff of about fifteen people to support and did not want to lay anyone off. Appointments and surgeries would have to continue.

Dr. Welch, a one-third partner in the business, now had to run the whole show. He also had a wife, Kelly (also a veterinarian), and three very small children including a newborn. He would work all day nonstop, run home to see the wife and kids for a few hours, then run back to the office, fill out records, and call clients after the kids were in bed. Mona and I had done this during our start-up years, and I knew how exhausting the pace could be. Yet Dr. Welch soldiered on, keeping the business afloat and paying the bills.

Dr. Kay Stratton was our associate veterinarian working part time. A level-headed woman, she takes all things in stride. Kay had been working for us and for another practice forty miles away, where she lived. In the aftermath of the accident, she decided to quit her other part-time practice in order to work full time for us. We had been considering offering her a full-time position anyway but had been waiting to do so until spring when our caseload usually got busier. However, the crash had accelerated this process: We needed her *now*.

But moving closer would be no small task for Kay and her family. It required selling their house and transferring the kids to a new school. Any parent who has ever had to do this knows just how disruptive it can be, so the family decided to wait until the school year ended in seven months. In the meantime, Kay commuted two hours round trip to our office daily. By joining us full time, she took a huge burden off Chris. Together, their hard work enabled the practice to continue employing all staff members and keep up with payroll.

We were fortunate to have very well-trained and dedicated people working for us. Our office manager, Karen, had been with us from the start. She had been our first employee, coming with the practice when we bought it from the original owner. Karen is one of the few people I have ever met who is always happy; she has an attitude such that she can handle anything with a smile. Life has not always been easy for her, but our clients and staff love her. When we first took over the practice, we had no idea what a blessing she would be. In the very beginning, Karen was the liaison between suspicious clients who still wanted the original owner and the two new young vets in town, Mona and me. Although we were strangers to these clients, they trusted Karen; if she said we were okay, then we were okay. Now she faced this latest challenge with her usual smile and upbeat attitude. She was the one clients called for updates on our condition; she dealt with ordering the myriad of supplies needed each week; she handled the staff issues that invariably arise with fifteen women and one man working together suddenly, under the stress of fewer doctors and a cloud of uncertainty. Karen smiled through it all, drinking lots of coffee along the way.

The rest of our staff took it upon themselves to do as much as they could so Chris and Kay could tend to their next appointments. Everyone was forced to become more efficient and take on more duties—and each one did without complaint. In the end, it forced the hospital to run much more smoothly and efficiently; ultimately, we would continue the changes they had instituted. In the end, the extra stress and work had forced the staff to grow and improve to the point of transforming themselves into some of the best veterinary workers I have ever been around.

Our staff was a truly great group of people. More angels among us.

Every one of these angels provided a big lesson for us. When others are down and out, they need more than words of support—they need actions. Cards and letters are great, and I read them over and over as I lay in the hospital bed, but the wonderful actions of these people truly spoke louder than words. Not having to cook dinner, do laundry, or shovel a walk when we were physically unable was incredibly helpful, especially since we never had to ask. They just did it. For the first time in our lives, we simply could not physically do things on our own; we needed help.

Yet we were reluctant to accept it. One day, Mona called to tell me we were getting a donation from the local Boy Scouts. They had sold pizzas downtown on a terribly cold winter day to raise money for us. How do two professionals who had made a good living accept money from a group of young boys who could use it themselves? A few months ago, they probably would have been coming to *us* asking for a donation; now they were raising funds on our behalf.

Mona wanted to know about sending the money back. I wasn't sure what to do so I told her I would think about it and follow up with her the next day.

Pastor Mark walked in a short time later to check on me, and I mentioned our dilemma. He, of course, had a great story to share in response.

Mark began, "There was a man who had great faith in God. He was stranded on his roof during a flood. With his great faith, he prayed for God to deliver him and save his life as the water got higher. A boat drifted by, but he did not jump in, telling them, 'I don't need your boat; God will save me.' In a little while, a group of firemen came by in another boat and told him to jump in, but he again refused, saying, 'God will save me.' Next, a helicopter hovered overhead with the water now nearly up to the man's feet, yet he still refused to leave, stating, 'I have faith that God will save me.' Finally, the water got too high and swept the man away. When he reached heaven and saw God he said, 'God, I prayed to you to save me and you let me drown. Why didn't you save me?' God replied, 'You prayed, and I sent a boat, a team of firemen, and a helicopter, yet each time you refused my help. You died because you expected something different and failed to see me in the people I sent to you. I was working *through* the people I sent. You were arrogant and thought you knew what I would do to save you. You did not know my ways; nobody does.'"

His story made perfect sense. These people were sent by God to help us like the firemen sent to save the man trapped in the flood. Turning the Boy Scouts away, refusing to accept their gift—or the gifts of others—is turning away God's help. As hard as it was for us to take charity, turning it away would have been pure arrogance. For now, we needed help and people were willing to assist any way they could. We would use the charity for its intended purpose: to get us back on our feet. There was no shame in that.

After Pastor Mark left, I called Mona and advised her to accept the gift from the Scouts: "It would be a slap in the face to those boys to refuse their generosity. We have helped them before, and now it's their opportunity to help us. Accept the money and the help. We will pay it back somewhere down the road."

Indeed, in the aftermath of tragedy, there were angels all around us.

For Reflection

For he will command his angels concerning you to guard you in all your ways. (Psalms 91:11)

Then the devil left him, and behold, angels came and were ministering to him. (Matthew 4:11)

1. Have you had angels in your life who have been there only temporarily? Do you have angels who have stayed in your life?
2. Have you had angels come into your life whom you did not know? What role did they play?
3. Have you ever encountered an angel who would normally *not* be considered one? How did he or she become an angel for you?
4. When is accepting charity right? How or when could it be wrong?

CHAPTER 22

A LONG ROAD TO NORMAL

With my sister Julie's help, I was transferred from the intensive care ward in Madison to the rehabilitation floor in Julie's hospital eighty miles away in Fond du Lac, our hometown. My parents still lived in the area, along with my sisters Julie and Kim. Since I was in no shape to return home and Mona was in no shape to care for me, it was decided that I would go to the rehab unit. There, my family could take care of me while Mona's family took care of her and the kids at home.

I was excited to finally be starting the process of learning to walk again. Although I wouldn't be able to put any weight on my left leg for another month, I could start rehabbing the rest of my body as soon as I recovered from the move.

As they wheeled me into my new room after the hour-and-a-half ambulance trip, a nurse walked in.

"Scot, do you remember me? It's Renee. We grew up a few houses apart from each other."

Indeed we had. Renee and I had known each other since kindergarten but lost touch after graduating from high school. I had no idea she was even a nurse—much less worked on the floor I'd be residing on for the foreseeable future.

Renee got me settled in and told me she'd get me into a wheelchair and out of the room the next day.

Having been in bed for three weeks and sick of being confined to a room, I was excited to get into a wheelchair; visions of racing down the hallway and popping wheelies danced in my head. I settled into my new room, snuggled into the warmth of my bedding, and thought about Renee. I hadn't seen her since we were teenagers, and now she was yet another angel sent to guide me through all of this.

The next day's rehab started pretty simply. The first goal was to get me out of bed and into a wheelchair. Renee came in with another nurse and a board used to slide from the bed to the chair.

Piece of cake, I thought. *I just need to slide down the board.*

Renee put the board between the bed and the wheelchair and told me to move up onto the ramp. I struggled to get myself up, raising the bed as much as possible to get to an upright position. I pushed and fought to hoist myself onto the board to slide into the wheelchair but could not do it. My arms were still too weak to shift my butt even half an inch to get onto the board. It was unbelievable how much strength I'd lost and how far I needed to go. But having accepted this devastating injury as something I might not have wanted but something God said I needed, I could laugh it off rather than do the "this sucks" thing. At this point, I was so weak, there was nowhere to go but up.

The nurses helped, but they did not want to do too much for me; they knew I had to get stronger. After three tries, I was finally able to get onto the board. By then, my arms were shaking and I was starting to sweat. I slid down to the wheelchair, nurses on each side to keep me from collapsing. With a lot of effort, I got myself into the chair. My arms were now exhausted. I had no chance of cruising around the hospital and popping wheelies—not yet, anyway.

As I sat in the chair trying to get my strength back, Renee wheeled me over to the sink and helped me take off my shirt. Part of rehab was learning how to live at home with my new body, and they wanted to show me how to do a sponge bath in the sink. (I wouldn't be showering for a while.) When I looked in the mirror for the first time since the crash, I was shocked at what I saw: I had lost about thirty-five pounds and my face was gaunt and hollow. My body looked like that of a twelve-year-old: skinny, with no muscle at all. I had bony legs with knobby knees and arms so thin I could almost encircle my biceps with my fingers, something I hadn't been able to do for nearly thirty years. Although I was never a huge guy, I had worked out hard from high school through college to develop some muscle, and now it had all disappeared. All those years of trying to stay in shape, and it had vanished in a few weeks. I had gone from a healthy, vibrant, hard-charging man to a skinny, weak invalid who couldn't even get out of bed without help. I felt my will starting to fade. I had so far to go; it looked like an impossible mountain to climb. Running between three exam rooms and doing ten surgeries in a day seemed a distant memory.

Renee helped me do a quick sponge bath, and I was freezing afterward. The side effect of losing this much weight was that I had no fat to hold in the heat. Even though the water was warm, my wet skin quickly got cold. Once I told Renee I'd had enough, she immediately put on my shirt, noticing that I was starting to shiver and my teeth were chattering. She helped put me back into bed.

Once there, I pulled the covers up tight while my teeth continued to chatter and the rest of my body shivered uncontrollably. I hadn't been this chilled for a long time; it was nearly impossible for me to stay warm. This was something I had not expected, but here it was, another battle to fight.

After shedding a few more tears and rededicating myself to rehab, I drifted off to sleep. I put myself in God's hands and thanked him again for all of us surviving. I would put up with the pain and struggle: It would make me stronger, and I would be thankful for any little advance. It had started to make sense. If I wanted to get my stamina back, I would have to do the conditioning and push my body. If I wanted my muscles back, I would have to work them and work them hard. Nothing would come back by me lying in the hospital bed feeling sorry for myself. It would not be easy or fun, but I would have to put in the work if I wanted to have a better life than this. I would have to get the strength to be on my feet all day if I wanted to do my job—the job God had designed me seemingly since birth to do. I knew it would be hard—*really* hard.

I had done the "long struggle" thing before; becoming a veterinarian took a tremendous amount of work and study. I'd put an incredible amount of effort into my chosen profession, spending countless hours studying and practicing techniques until I got them down. I would read veterinary articles until I fell asleep at night instead of relaxing and watching TV. In school, I would be looking through a microscope alone in the lab after everyone else was gone, because I wanted to be the best. It has been estimated that you must put in about ten thousand hours to master anything, from music to business to medicine, whatever. It had taken about that much effort, but I had become very good at my job and had reaped the rewards of the hard work. I thought I was far beyond this kind of struggle and could live the rest of my life on cruise control. Of course, I was wrong again, but my past struggle had prepared me for my current one: I would push my recovery just like I had pushed in vet school.

Getting better would take major effort, but so what? I wasn't going anywhere for a while, so I had the time. Reaching the finish line with an even stronger mental and spiritual outlook was more important to me than the physical aspects of my recovery. Looking back, I couldn't think of much in my life that was both valuable and easy. My kids were my greatest blessings, but parenting was tough and I needed to keep working at it to improve as a father. Being a veterinarian was tough but offered great rewards. Maintaining a healthy marriage took a lot of effort but was well worth it.

I was done whining. I had survived; time to be grateful. Anything from here would be a blessing.

The next day I woke up ready to hit rehab with everything I had. My sister had lined up a physical therapist named Jeff to take on my case. I would soon discover he was another one of my angels. It wouldn't be easy and it would be painful, but I was ready.

Unfortunately, though I could now sit up, all I could do was some minor range-of-motion exercises. My arms were still splinted and my leg was too weak to support weight. Learning to stand or walk was still out of the question.

Rehab at that point consisted of sitting up in a chair and stretching. I had done this routine for the last week at the other hospital, and it was all I could do. My mind was ready for more, but my body wasn't. I had to be patient.

At the start of the second week in Fond du Lac and a month after the crash, the doctors removed the splints on my arms and the casts on my feet, replacing them with lighter, more flexible wraps. I was instructed to take it easy, but I could start using them. My left leg was not splinted, but I was instructed that I could not bear weight on it. I was now ready, physically and mentally, to start rehab.

About twenty minutes into my forty-minute session with Jeff, after stretching and doing range-of-motion exercises, I stopped.

"What's wrong?" Jeff asked.

"We need to start pushing it. I'm ready. It's time to get me up and going. I want you to push me every day. Don't be nice. I don't need you to be my buddy. I don't even need to like you. I need you to get me back to where I was before this happened, and I don't care how you do it. I will take anything you can dish out; just push me so I get better. I won't walk again by just stretching; my muscles need to work. I have made my peace with what happened. I have made my peace with Jacobs. I understand that this is just some mountain I have to climb, so let's get going."

Jeff replied, "Julie told me you had the drive, but I wasn't sure. Now I see it. Some of this stuff may hurt and you may not like it. By the way, I can still be your friend. You don't have to hate me."

"I have a ton of pain medication so I can handle the hurt, but I will only be your friend if you get me walking." Of course, that was a lie; Jeff was hard not to like.

The next four weeks were grueling as Jeff pushed me harder and harder. We did some stretching at first, but even that was painful. Jeff wanted me to get better range of motion in my joints. Having been broken and splinted for weeks, all the joints had started to freeze up due to scar tissue. If I wanted to use them again, that scar tissue would have to be broken down.

We also were working on other things. I couldn't do much with my legs yet, but Jeff wanted me to start strengthening my upper body. I would need to be able to push the wheelchair and eventually use crutches, but my arms were so weak I could do neither.

We used weights—two pounds to start—just lifting them off the bed. These were the puny weights that I used to move out of my way to get to the *real* weights when I was working out. Now, lifting them was a struggle and a bit humiliating. Humility was another lesson I was learning, but after having to defecate where I slept for weeks, this humiliation was minor. My elbows and shoulder were still healing so I was very limited in what I could do. Still, I could do something, and that felt great. The stretching was necessary, but I wanted to get strong. Unfortunately, the doctors did not want me even to stand on my plated leg or lift much with my plated elbows and shoulder for another month or two. The "girly" weights would have to do.

Jeff was in a real predicament. How do you strengthen a man who can't bear weight on his legs or lift more than two pounds?

His solution was to start with what he *could* rehab. At first, this entailed just getting up from lying flat on my back, if that was all I could do. Soon it transitioned into a modified sit-up with my back on a raised mat and my feet on the floor. Then Jeff added balance exercises and more core work.

Slowly, day by day, I got stronger. At the end of the first week, I could sit all the way up from a lying position. Even though I could only do it once and it hurt like hell, a single sit-up was progress.

Though I couldn't stand on my leg, Jeff got permission from Dr. Lang to try to bend it. It had been immobilized for weeks to allow the torn muscle and broken bone to heal and was now stuck in the slightly bent position it had been in when I was lying in my bed. He sat me on a chair and grabbed my ankle. Before he could push, I stopped him.

"You aren't going to break this thing, are you?"

"Guess we'll see."

"Real funny."

He pushed down to flex the knee and my foot moved an inch before it stopped dead; the knee was frozen. Jeff pulled a goniometer out of his pocket. This tool—basically a couple of plastic legs joined at one end—is used to measure angles. He placed one side of it along my thigh, the other along my shin. "Fifteen degrees," he observed. "A knee can normally bend about a hundred."

"Wow, really? I have a long way to go."

"We figure that if we can get ninety degrees of bend, you will be functionally normal."

"So, how do we get it to bend?"

"We'll do some stretching exercises and some other tricks I have."

"You are going to just push on it until the scar tissue breaks up, aren't you?"

"Yeah, you got it."

"I bet that's going to hurt like hell."

"Remember, it was your own sister who asked me to help you."

"I don't remember ever being *that* awful to her growing up."

"Well, you must have done something to her. Unfortunately, that is what we need to do if that leg is ever going to bend again."

"I figured brute force was the only way to tear down the scar tissue."

"There is no other way that I know of, and the sooner we start, the better."

"Are we starting now?"

"Tomorrow. I want you to take some extra pain meds before our session, okay?"

"That bad, huh?"

"I will get more done if you are a bit doped up."

"Deal. I don't think I want to feel this anyway."

"Don't worry. You'll feel it."

The leg muscle of the thigh, the quadriceps, had been torn apart during the crash. Muscle is nearly impossible to suture back together, so it was basically left to form a big scar. Unfortunately, the scar grabs on to anything in the area and starts tying it all together. Because the bone was broken and I was not allowed to bend my knee for the first three weeks, the scar got stronger and stronger. By now it was a solid band of immobile scar tissue keeping my knee from bending.

As part of the healing, it had even started to calcify (laying down new bone in addition to scar tissue), but the new bone was in the muscle a few inches away from the thighbone. This happens frequently in major trauma, and I had developed some more of it in my chest muscle also. The tendon to the shoulder from the chest had been stretched and damaged when my shoulder was dislocated. Now there was a perfect outline of the calcified tendon on my shoulder X-ray as well as what looked like a second thighbone in my leg muscle. Both of these I could feel as rock-hard masses where the tendon or muscle should be.

Of course, calcified tissue (bone) doesn't stretch, so if I wanted to move those joints, I would have to work to free them up. A surgeon could not remove it, since they would have to do more damage, so with rehab I would try to limit how much formed.

I did not have a choice but to try to stretch my knee, because a knee that doesn't bend is worse than useless—it is in the way. Even getting into a car is impossible without bending your legs; you can't get your foot in the door. If I couldn't get it to bend, then I would be better off having it amputated. A "frozen shoulder" from that calcified tendon made even getting a coat on difficult. Both needed to gain mobility if I was to get anywhere near back to normal. I would have to break down a lot of scar tissue, and I realized this would involve an incredible amount of pain. When I got back to the room, I contemplated the long road ahead.

I was staring down my pathway *through* while hoping that at some point I would find a way *out*. All I could see was the long road ahead of me, without a finish line in sight. I could not see an end to this pain, this suffering, this hell.

"God, I asked you to help me through this. Please help me through the pain and get my leg moving again. I told you that I would put in the work, and now it is time. I just ask for Your help getting through the pain. I am scared. Please help me if You see fit. Your will be done."

With that, I felt peace. The pain would really suck, but my desire to be active again compelled me to soldier on. The ensuing sense of peace I felt after my prayer assured me God was with me. It would be all right. Not fun, but all right.

The next day, I arrived at my therapy session psyched up and ready to hit it. I had taken some extra OxyContin to help with the pain and I was raring to go. Jeff began with some upper-body work to strengthen my chest and arms and some simple stretching of my leg. When he tried bending it, it would stop at fifteen degrees. There was no give; it just stopped. Jeff looked at me soberly and asked, "Are you ready?"

"Go ahead" I replied.

I sat on the bench and gripped the sides. Jeff put his shoulder into my shin and pushed. I just about flew off the table as the pain shot through my leg. Early scar tissue is composed of many nerves, and mine had all just gone nuts. The pain was horrific as Jeff bore down.

After ten seconds, he stopped; I was already sweating. He simply stated, "Let me know when you are ready to do it again."

Again? I thought. *I don't think I could possibly do this again!* Yet I also understood that every day we waited, the scar tissue would only become stronger and better organized. If it was going to get broken down, it would have to be now.

"God help me."

After a minute, I was ready again. "Let's go," I told him. Jeff grabbed hold again and pushed. Again, the pain shot through my leg as the scar tissue let me know I was going to pay for disturbing it. I screamed and Jeff stopped.

"No," I ordered. "Keep going!"

Again, he pushed down and held for a count of ten. After a minute, he repeated it for a third time. The pain was greater than any I had ever experienced, since I didn't remember the crash. Now I would be enduring it daily for the foreseeable future.

We did this exercise every day for the rest of the week: stretch and work on upper-body strength, then try to bend the leg. Little by little, the scar tissue began to release. At the end of the week, we measured the angle again. "Twenty degrees," Jeff declared.

All that pain and agony had moved the leg an additional five degrees. To get back to useful, the leg would have to bend to ninety degrees. I did the math: five degrees a week, seventy more degrees to go. That would be fourteen weeks. Three and a half months of this agony just to return to "functional"—not "normal"—just "functional." That is when I knew I had a very painful road ahead.

Again, my spirit started to sag. I never realized the rehab would be this painful and take so long. I had expected to be rehabbing for weeks, and now it looked like it would take months or even years. I also knew that the first week was probably the easiest since the scar tissue had not fully matured yet. The stretching would probably get harder as time went on, so it was likely to take much longer than the three and a half months I'd figured. I wasn't sure I could handle that amount of pain for four or five more months.

The next day, I asked Jeff if he could push harder and get this over with.

"Relax," he said. "Your bones are not strong enough to push any more than we're doing. If we push too hard, the bone will break."

I knew he was right. The bone in my thigh would take another two to three months to fully heal. If Jeff applied too much pressure, it would snap. This would be a very long and painful road. I started feeling the sadness and depression returning as I realized just how tough the next six months to a year would be. I had just learned to slide into the wheelchair; how would I ever run with my kids again? I hadn't even started yet on my shoulder and elbows. How much pain would that take? I didn't know if I could do it.

Again, I asked God for the strength to keep going and got no answer. I would just have to *believe* He was listening. I would have to have faith.

For Reflection

Therefore, my beloved brothers, be steadfast, immovable, always abounding in the work of the Lord, knowing that in the Lord your labor is not in vain. (1 Corinthians 15:58)

1. Have you ever had people from your childhood reenter your life? What impact did they make on you?

2. Describe some events in your life that were long struggles but ultimately very worth it.

3. How does it help to ask for God's support in getting through struggle?

These photos taken by the Dane County Sheriff Department show Madison first responders working with the Jaws of Life to free me from our family's crumpled van. I was carefully extricated from the vehicle and rushed to a waiting helicopter, which airlifted me to a hospital.

While first responders tried to free me, true angels sat on the guard-rail, comforting the kids. We didn't know these people, but they treated our battered and terrified children as they would their own. Off to the left, our little dog, Olivia, lay under a sheet, presumed dead after being thrown through one of the windows of the van.

In Mike Jacobs' car, an open can of beer tells the story of the drunk driver who nearly killed me and my family.

In the hospital in Madison, Mona lay in a full-body brace, healing from a broken back and traumatic brain injury.

Meanwhile, I was in a coma following numerous surgeries. No one knew whether I would survive or, if I did, whether I would recover completely.

Here I am on Day 4 in the hospital, held together by braces, bandages, pins, and the miraculous work of dedicated doctors and nurses.

Awake and out of my coma, I'd surely seen better days, but I was grateful to be alive! I had no idea yet how God was about to work in, on, and through me in the months and years to come.

Just before the crash, our family enjoyed a Disney vacation, not knowing our world was about to be turned upside down. With Mona and me are Victoria (left), Chase, and Alexa.

Our little terrier, Olivia, needed time to recover from her head injury. We're forever grateful to the vets and veterinary staff who gave of their time, talent, and resources to ensure she survived.

A year after the crash, the kids were doing great, as were our resilient dogs, Olivia and Annabelle. We even added a puppy to the mix!

And here we are—Chase, Mona, Alexa, Victoria, and I—twelve years post-crash, thankful and blessed!

CHAPTER 23

ROCKY ROAD AHEAD

Everyone has his own mountain to climb. Mine was a hundred-foot ramp connecting the rehab floor with the main hospital. I was spending time in my wheelchair every day but was still very weak in spite of doing rehab twice a day—once with Jeff and a second time with an occupational therapist who worked on me while in bed. The rest of the day, I either slept or watched TV. I couldn't read since I was still on a lot of drugs and concentrating was impossible. With all the exposure to inane television programming, my brain would need some rehab, too, once I was off all the drugs.

One night I decided to take a spin in the wheelchair since my arms needed the work. I got into the chair and headed down the hall, advising the nurses as I wheeled by that I would be right back (like I could go anywhere). I headed for the ramp.

From the bottom, I rested as I gazed up at it: one hundred or so feet with a gradual climb. *No big deal.* I started up with confidence, but within ten feet, my arms gave out and I could go no further. Already in a sweat, I locked the wheels and rested. After a minute, I tried again. This time I only made it about five feet and had to stop; the ramp was too long. I turned and headed back down. At the bottom, I turned back around in the direction of my room. This ramp would be my mountain. If I climbed it every day, I could judge if I was getting stronger. Tomorrow I would try again.

Week after week, Jeff and I continued to work. Through forgiveness for Jacobs and faith that God wanted me to go through this, I had beaten back depression and anger; I would still cry, but only about every third night instead of every night. I did not hold back—if I needed to cry, I cried. This wasn't a lack of faith in God's plan or a show of weakness but justifiable sadness over my predicament. As long as I didn't allow it to consume me and push me off my path, the path God had chosen for me, I would be fine. Unwavering faith that I was following *His* path now, not my own, allowed me to accept the pain and boredom of being in bed for twenty-three hours a day; it made me accept the reality of being far away from my family and my job. Knowing that there was an intended purpose, that He was making me stronger for another reason, enabled me to accept what had happened as my mental and spiritual workout. I needed spiritual rehab as well as physical.

I was also learning how to fend for myself in a wheelchair, developing a decent ability to move from the bed to the chair and back again. Soon, I could do it on my own without a board to slide on.

Again, a nurse moved me to the bathroom to take a sponge bath. Every time I took my shirt off, I confronted the complete loss of muscle. As I removed my pants, I noticed my legs were just knobby knees crisscrossed with long scars. Frankly the scars did not bother me; as I mentioned before, being a guy, scars were a badge of courage. What bothered me was the muscle loss. I had expected some loss, but this was amazing. Because I had been down so long, there was literally no muscle left on my frame.

However, this time as I looked in the mirror, I laughed (I was learning to do that again). This was just my starting point, and I would work the muscle back from here. It helped that I had seen this in animals that had been starved. They'd come in with no muscle and protruding bones, but with some exercise and good food, these animals would rebuild their muscle mass. Within six months, they'd be healthy and vibrant—forgetting the past and wagging their tails in their joy to simply be alive. I would learn from them. This time I thanked God for being with me and smiled. At some point, I would be wagging my tail too.

The sponge bath felt great. I experienced that clean and cool feeling that comes after washing up. Within moments, though, that cool feeling became a *cold* feeling, necessitating a return to bed to snuggle under the covers, my teeth chattering. Soon, I learned to ask a nurse to preheat the bathroom in preparation for bathing and have my clothes ready the second I came out. My clothes were all modified with Velcro sides so I could put them on myself, but the minute it took to dry off and dress left me exhausted and shivering under the bed linens and blankets. Handling the cold requires fat and muscle. It would be a while before I had any of that.

I had reached the point where all I wanted was to go home. I missed my kids, I missed Mona, and I missed my life. Yes, this hospital was located in the town in which I grew up, the same place where most of my family still lived, but I had left twenty years earlier. This was no longer my hometown; I knew very few people anymore, and it had changed greatly. Prior to the crash, I still liked to drive around during visits to Fond du Lac and pass by my high school and junior high. However, both the town and I had moved on. I needed to get back to the area that I now called home, the area where my own family was living. Lake Geneva was my new hometown.

But the hospital had a rule: It would not discharge me until I could function in a home environment. This meant being able to feed myself, clean myself, and get to the toilet myself. I also had to prove I could get in and out of bed, up and down stairs, and in and out of a car. All these everyday tasks I'd been doing since I was four years old had to be relearned with the reality of my new body.

Eating wasn't a problem since my right hand was working fine. My stomach was still terribly shrunken, but even though I could not eat much, it was getting better. I was so sick of ice cream after having it with every meal that I had to stop eating it entirely. I could still hear God laughing about that.

The other tasks I needed to master would either require crutches or be made a lot easier with crutches. The problem with crutches is that they require stable shoulders and arms. My arms were just starting to get there; I had been strengthening them in rehab and with my nightly trips to the ramp. Although they were definitely stronger, the thought of supporting all my weight on arms that were smashed just a month and a half ago was pretty scary—especially when I knew I could not allow myself to fall down.

But I had to learn to use them and get out of the wheelchair if I wanted to leave the hospital. I asked Jeff to teach me.

Jeff was ready with a set of crutches waiting. He placed a belt around my waist to help lift me and had me sit up on the edge of the bed. "On three," he announced before counting. On the count of three, he pulled as I pushed up, trying to get the crutches into my armpits. Jeff did not want to help too much; I needed to do this mostly on my own. Like riding a bike, there was a certain amount of "feel" to it. Since I didn't have it, I fell backward onto the bed.

"Try again?" he asked.

"You bet," I replied, getting excited about the prospect of being on my feet. We counted again; this time I got up and almost fell forward on my face. The adrenaline rushed through me as I envisioned doing a face-plant onto the linoleum floor and re-breaking my arms and nose. Jeff caught me and pulled me back onto the bed again.

"Not quite so fast," he said. "On three."

This time I got it. I had never been on crutches before, and this was all new, but soon I was starting to get the hang of it. I took a few minutes to get my balance, and then, tentatively, I started to take little baby steps forward. The thought of falling still terrified me and I made sure Jeff was continuing to hold my belt.

"Don't let go," I reminded him.

"I don't let my patients fall," he answered, as I started to wonder if I should apologize for doubting him.

My shoulders and armpits were aching almost immediately. Even though the crutches were well padded, the muscles and tendons were screaming in protest at having to carry my weight. At this time, I probably weighed only one hundred fifty pounds—twenty pounds less than my normal weight—but it was more than my muscles could handle. I ignored the pain (the oxycodone I'd taken prior to rehab didn't hurt) and started moving forward. This was freedom from the bed, freedom from the chair, and the first time I'd been off my butt since the crash. I had expected some discomfort as the muscles got used to their new task, but this involved so much more. This was screaming pain from joints and bones that had been stretched and shattered, now protesting at having to hold together.

I'd become accustomed to the fact that nearly everything I did now had an element of pain associated with it, but I'd had worse. Still, pain is never easy. After I was back in the room and the staff was gone, I broke down again. Not only was this pain unbearable, it was inescapable. Every move was a struggle; every task involved planning how to do it. Rolling over in bed required thinking about exactly what arm or leg to move first, then next, to accomplish the task and minimize the pain. With every task, I debated whether it was worth the effort. Often, I decided it was not and I reached for the oxycodone that made it go away. I knew I was walking a dangerous line with this stuff, but after all the pain that I had been through and the long road ahead, I just needed a break. I popped a few more pills and closed my eyes for a rest.

Day after day, we kept working on the crutches. I no longer wanted the wheelchair; I knew that using the crutches would eventually be a lot easier and would get me home. They just hurt...a lot.

I still used the chair to go around the hospital. It was a great workout for the arms and chest and didn't put the strain on my joints like the crutches did. Yet I knew the crutches would provide more freedom, which was my main focus.

After a week, I was getting pretty confident on them and using them more and more without any help. One night, I got up to use the bathroom and grabbed my crutches. About five feet from the bed, I make a mistake by moving a little too fast. I felt my weight shift from forward to back as I started to lose my balance and fall. With so many broken bones, falling had been my absolute worst fear: It could re-break my bones and hurt like hell. Now I knew I was going to hit the floor and there was nothing I could do about it. I let out a yell hoping a nurse would happen to be near, but no such luck.

As my weight shifted backward, I tried to minimize the damage. I would be landing on my butt with its broken pelvis, catching myself with my arms—and their broken elbows—jarring all my weight on to a shoulder that had popped out not too long ago. I rolled a bit to the right to use my best arm to cushion the fall, the one that had broken at the elbow but had *not* dislocated at the shoulder. Even that was not a great option, but it was the best one I had.

I needed to get the crutches out of the way; otherwise they'd catch me halfway down and put all the force into my armpits. They clattered across the floor as I threw them to the side. This noise, along with my yell, was enough to bring the nurses and a doctor running. I hit the ground with a thud and the pain shot through me. I took most of the fall on my right but primarily landed on my butt.

The nurses and doctor arrived a few seconds after I had hit the floor as I lay there feeling the full effects of the fall. My butt was throbbing and my right arm felt like it had been hit with a baseball bat. Reverting to my veterinary training, I evaluated the situation. I had not re-broken anything to the best of my knowledge; I had not heard anything crack, nor did I feel anything shift. I would be okay; I would just hurt for a while, again.

The staff looked at me in horror. I could see the expressions on their faces, that "Oh shit!" look when something goes wrong. (In the medical profession, it is also the "Oh shit, we are going to get sued!" look.)

I tried to put their minds to rest. "I'm okay," I assured them. "This was my fault; I thought I was better at the crutches than I am. Just give me a second and then help me up."

I sat there for about thirty more seconds as the pain started to subside. This was why I'd feared falling: I was *really* hurt and *really* embarrassed for needing three people to pick me up. The nurses and doctor each grabbed something to pull on and, on three, lifted me back to the bed. I lay back down exhausted. They left the room and I reached for the Oxy again. I deserved some more; I had just hit the floor and my whole body now ached. As the meds kicked in, the pain stopped and I started to drift off to sleep again. I remembered that I had never made it to the bathroom but decided it wasn't worth the effort. I could pee in my sheets like a baby if necessary. It was just too painful to move.

The next day, I crutched down the hall for physical therapy, moving very slowly and concentrating on each step. I wanted to do it myself, the proverbial getting-back-on-the-horse-that-just-kicked-you-off idea, but I was scared.

Jeff met me at the door with a big smile on his face. "How is your butt?" he asked with a grin.

"Pretty sore," I replied.

"I guess I had better teach you how to get up from the floor."

"I never thought about it, but you're right. I can't get up like I used to, and I may not have help around if I fall at home."

"Before you are released, we have to know you won't be stuck on the floor waiting for someone to come home and find you. Let me show you how you can get to your feet if this happens again."

The next hour was spent on and off a two-foot-high mat working on ways to get up. They included using a chair, the crutch, and nothing. The biggest problem was my inability to bend my left leg. It was like trying to get your butt off the ground with a three-foot stick attached to your hip. It was virtually impossible without something to grab onto. A heavy chair was the easiest, since I could pull myself up to seat height, rest, and then use the crutch to get to my feet. Jeff taught me three or four ways to get off the floor depending on what was around me. Now I could do it—one more hurdle down. I was just very careful when I got to my feet that I didn't shift my weight backward again and end up on my can.

The second thing Jeff had to teach me was how to get into the car. They actually had a small car mock-up to practice getting in and out without going to the parking lot. It sounds easy, but that long left leg made it nearly impossible to get my foot in and close the door. I could slide over on the seat, but eventually I had to turn my body and get my foot in front of me. There simply was not enough room if I couldn't bend at the knee.

"We need to get your leg to bend before you can go home," Jeff declared.

"That sounds painful."

"You should be getting used to it by now."

"You seem to be really enjoying it. Do you like to kick puppies in your spare time?"

"No, just rehab patients."

I still had a long way to go before I could get my leg in the car; I was bending only at about thirty degrees and probably needed forty degrees more before I could get in. Hopelessness washed over me again. There seemed to be no way to get that much bend out of this knee. Jeff pressing on it had nearly killed me. *How was I supposed to get this to stretch all the way to seventy so I could get in the car and go home? How would I ever get back to near normal at one hundred degrees?* It just didn't seem possible. I couldn't wait to get back to the room and take more OxyContin.

Later that night, I woke up and thought again about the long road ahead. The ramp that I once perceived as a challenge now seemed like nothing; I'd believed the worst pain was behind me and it would lessen as time went on. Now I realized it was just beginning and that the rehab would get much worse before it got better. I had slept through the initial pain after the crash and then been on a morphine drip. Now all I had was the Oxy.

This sucked. I didn't do anything to deserve this. The jerk who hit us wasn't getting his leg bent until the muscles ripped. He had gotten a few bruises that were probably gone in a week. What an asshole.

The anger washed over me like a flood. I stewed for twenty minutes unable to sleep, getting more and more upset. I should be at home with my kids or at work fixing broken bones on dogs and cats, not waiting for my own bones to heal. I reached for the OxyContin, assuring myself that I needed it to sleep. There was no way I would be able to nod off with the pain—in my leg, in my arm, in my other arm, take your pick. The pain would keep me awake and prevent me from doing my rehab in the morning. I deserved more Oxy.

In reality, I wanted the Oxy because I was mad—mad at where I was, mad at the man who put me there, mad that I would need to suffer every day if I ever wanted to bend my knee again, mad that I would have to endure so much pain just to get back to anywhere near normal. Just a few weeks ago, I'd been normal; I just didn't deserve to go through this hardship.

Though I normally took thirty milligrams of Oxy, tonight I took fifty. The nurse had advised me I could take up to eighty, so fifty was not a big deal, right? At least it wasn't *twice* the amount I had taken before, and thirty milligrams just wasn't cutting it at this point. Anyway, I was taking fifty milligrams only just this once; tomorrow I would cut back down to thirty.

I downed the pills as the anger boiled within. I had tried to do everything right, and *this* is what I got.

Again, I heard the words inside my head: *It is not your plan.*

"What does that mean?!" I shouted out. "Why do I need to go through all this? I just want to know why."

Silence.

"Figures," I retorted. "No answers, just more pain."

I had no idea how right I was.

For Reflection

The LORD is my shepherd; I shall not want. He makes me lie down in green pastures. He leads me beside still waters. He restores my soul. He leads me in paths of righteousness for his name›s sake. Even though I walk through the valley of the shadow of death, I will fear no evil, for you are with me; your rod and your staff, they comfort me. You prepare a table before me in the presence of my enemies; you anoint my head with oil; my cup overflows.... (Psalms 23:1–5)

1. Have you ever had a mountain to climb or a goal to reach that took a lot of time and persistence? How did faith help you attain your goal?

A time to weep, and a time to laugh; a time to mourn, and a time to dance. (Ecclesiastes 3:4)

2. Is crying a good thing, or should we hold it in? Does crying help to deal with tragedy?

CHAPTER 24

MY LIFE IS THE WORST

Jeff started physical therapy the next day with a lot of stretching and strength exercises. I had worked for almost an hour before he decided it was time to stretch the leg.

I was still pissed from the previous night, doubtful that I could go through all this pain. If I didn't have the guts to make the effort, I would have to quit my career as a vet. Yes, I could collect disability to keep us from going broke, but we would have to sell the house and downsize. I also knew I would hate not working and be bored to death.

I knew I was wallowing in self-pity, as did Jeff, who noticed my lack of enthusiasm. After our normal rehab routine, he set me on the chair to try to bend my knee, noting, "Like my dad used to say, 'This is going to hurt you more than it's going to hurt me.'"

I told myself to relax but tightened up as soon as he touched my leg. As he pressed, I fought to suppress a scream. Jeff counted down from ten, applying pressure to the foot with his shoulder in a downward motion. As he released, I tried to catch my breath. Before I could, he pressed again.

"Ten, nine, eight..." he counted down again.

After the third time, we were done. I lay flat on the mat waiting for the pain to subside. Jeff waited for my eyes to open and bent down to help me up. I got to my wheelchair; he had suggested I use it today since my leg would be killing me. He was right. There was no way I could use crutches after this latest grueling session.

"See you tomorrow and we'll do it again."

I nodded but remained silent; the pain was still too fresh in my mind. I thought about having to go through this again: *Was it even worth it?* The thought of repeating this daily pattern of rehab was draining my will. This amount of pain was more than I thought I could stand. I got to bed and popped some more Oxy—sixty milligrams since my leg was killing me. *This is temporary*, I told myself. *Just until I get through this leg thing.* I drifted off to sleep, thoroughly unconvinced I could do this much longer.

The next day, Jeff met me with a smile. "Ready to go?" he asked.

"Sure," I replied half-heartedly, "I'm ready to scream again."

"I could go easy, but your sister told me to push you hard. You must have really been an awful baby brother to her."

"Payback is a bitch," I said.

I smiled but was rapidly losing my drive. The pain was wearing me down and the drugs were sapping my will power. Although I told myself I needed them to get through the day, they robbed me of my strength and clouded my mind. I had taken eighty milligrams of Oxy this morning knowing that this day was going to be hard, reasoning that without the drugs, I would not be able to do the therapy. In order to get flexibility back into my legs, eighty milligrams were necessary. It was temporary, just until the leg could stretch farther, and then I would drop it down.

On this particular day, though, Jeff wanted to take me to the stairs because the ability to go up and down stairs was one of the skills I needed to develop to get back home. Though our house was a single story, navigating stairs was part of life and very scary. If falling to the floor was painful, I couldn't imagine what falling down the stairs would be like, especially if I were halfway up and fell backward. My right foot was no longer immobilized, and they had taken the cast off my left foot, replacing it with a boot. The nurse had cut it off the day before while I slept. I didn't even remember them doing it; I was out cold on the Oxy.

"Let's first see what your ankle can do," Jeff announced as he pulled out another one of his exercise devices. It was a flat board with a half-ball on the bottom. "This will force you to use your ankle to keep balance," he explained as he brought me over to the parallel bars.

Using the bars for support and with Jeff holding my waist, I put my right foot onto the platform. Immediately the foot bent to the left and I was unable to straighten it because my ankle was too weak. I pushed my weight off that foot and tried again. This time my foot bent to the right; there was just no strength left in it after being in a cast for five weeks.

"Let's try this sitting down," Jeff suggested. We moved to a seat and tried again. This time I could at least start to keep my foot stable until I put some weight on it; then it would fall to one side or the other.

"Don't worry," Jeff encouraged, "it will take about a week for you to get some strength back."

"A week?! This looks like it will take a month."

"You'll be surprised."

After working on the ball-board for twenty minutes, we continued with more upper-body stretching and exercises. At the end of the session, I knew it was time to try to bend my leg again. I got over to the chair, and Jeff asked if I was ready.

"As ready as I'll ever be."

"Here we go," he said while I braced. He pushed my shin and my knee started to bend. The pain ripped through my thigh again as he bore down, counting down from ten. I clenched my teeth and tried desperately to think about something other than the pain tearing through my leg.

"Three...two...one."

He let off my leg and the pain eased up—not entirely, since the muscle still throbbed, but it did ease up.

Thirty seconds went by in what seemed like two. Jeff was ready again. "Here we go," he warned as he pushed once more. Again, the pain ripped through my leg for the ten seconds he kept it there. By now there were tears in my eyes.

He let off as I fought to keep myself from crying like a baby. Men were not supposed to bawl like that, especially not in front of other men.

"I know this is tough," he offered, "but it is the only way to get you home."

"I know. It just sucks," I replied, wiping away the tears and feeling ashamed for crying.

"One more time and we will check your angle."

"Okay, one more."

Jeff pushed and the pain hit me again. He counted back from ten for what seemed like an hour.

"Three...two...one." He let off and I collapsed back on the chair, my leg screaming at me.

"Let's measure," Jeff suggested as he grabbed his goniometer and carefully adjusted it to my leg. Once satisfied, he read the number: "Thirty degrees. That's better."

Four degrees' difference with all that agony!

I would probably need another thirty to get in the car and sixty before I got a functional knee. How could I withstand this much pain for that long?

Jeff read the disappointment on my face. "Four degrees is great," he assured me. "We only worked at it for a little over a week and it got better, but I should warn you, it may not improve every time. You will have setbacks and days where it stays the same."

"Great," I retorted, "if I can't get a degree a day, this will take a hundred sessions, a hundred times having my leg scream at me. I just don't know if I can do this. Maybe I just need to go on disability and forget about ever bending this leg again. I had a horrific injury. Most people would just go on disability and collect a check, wouldn't they?"

"Your sister says you're not like most people. I've seen people like you before. You would be bored out of your mind in a month and wishing you had done the rehab right away. Now is the best time to get that leg functioning; it only gets harder if you wait."

I knew he was right. I had told myself that I would do whatever it takes. I should not have been surprised that it would not be easy.

"I just never expected it would be *this* hard," I confessed.

I was too exhausted to crutch back to the room, so Jeff called Renee to bring a wheelchair, and she pushed me along the way. I was mentally and physically shot. She helped me into bed and I stared at the ceiling for a while contemplating whether this was worth it. Undecided, I took another eighty milligrams of Oxy. I still could not roll onto either side due to the boot on my left leg and the pain in my shoulder. I could roll about halfway to the right, but it was so much work to stay in that position that I could not sleep. I was stuck on my back like a turtle for the foreseeable future.

My life was upside down. The Oxy kicked in and I began to drift into sleep as the pain subsided. I thought about how life would be if I were on Oxy for the remainder of it. The Oxy sure made the pain better, so maybe I would just stay on it forever. People would understand. Anyway, I figured I could stop it at any time. Now, I just needed it.

I was going through my personal hell—terrible pain, drugs, uncertainty, and fear. I had always been in control of my life and now I couldn't even roll over in bed. The Oxy had constipated me to the point that even going to the bathroom was an agonizing struggle. I was a shell of the man I had been before. I knew I couldn't work with my body like this and certainly not with my mind clouded with drugs. It seemed like my world had ended. I was lost.

I cried again, this time for a long time. I had never been so depressed and scared. It seemed like my hell would go on for eternity.

The next day, Jeff arrived an hour ahead of schedule. "Hope you don't mind. I wanted to do your session a little early."

"No problem. I didn't have any plans."

Jeff handed me the crutches.

"I think I need the chair today. My leg is too sore for the crutches."

"Okay, let's get you rolling." Jeff could sense the lack of energy in my voice. He could tell I had realized the length of the road ahead of me. I wasn't Superman who would be back to work in a month as if nothing had ever happened.

We rolled into therapy and I started to move to the chair to work on the ball-board. I needed to strengthen my ankle before I could do much else. As I started to work, the other therapist called Jeff over to help her.

"Be right back," he told me.

Since we had started early, there were a number of patients in the rehab room I had never seen before. Over by the other door was a younger man; just a kid really. He looked about eighteen, roughly half my age. He was a good-looking kid but very thin like me. Although he was in a wheelchair, he did not have casts or bandages like mine. He smiled at the two nurses and the two physical therapists who were helping him. I noticed a slight tick as his head moved back and forth between the two nurses, who started to place his feet into position on the floor as he gazed at them. With his feet set, they pulled him out of his chair. Jeff and the other therapist stood on either side behind him, bearing most of his weight. His knees buckled and his hips swayed hard to the left. Jeff caught him and pushed his hips back under him. He continued to smile and look back and forth at the nurses.

"Okay, take a step," a nurse told him. He gazed at her with a smile, but his foot didn't move.

"Come on, Jimmy, take a step," she repeated.

He smiled.

She pulled his foot forward and placed it about six inches in front of him. The physical therapists and nurses moved him forward placing his feet and congratulating him on his progress the whole time. Jimmy just smiled as his eyes moved back and forth. They repeated this for about five feet and moved the chair back behind him. They lowered him into it and again congratulated him on a great job. Jimmy smiled.

By now it was obvious that this young man had a severe brain injury. He was not comprehending much; just how much was anybody's guess. His body was thin and atrophied; obviously he had been in a bed for a prolonged period of time. His mind was atrophied too.

Jeff returned and began to move me over to start my next exercise. As I got up, I noticed a face in the hallway window. She was about my age or maybe a little older. She smiled at the nurses and therapists as they waved and gave her a thumbs-up. She nodded weakly, but her smile was noticeably forced now. I could only assume that this woman was Jimmy's mother. As she started to move to the doorway, I could see she had a tear running down her face. She walked over to Jimmy, who was smiling at her—the exact smile he'd offered the nurses. He just continually grinned like that with his head swaying back and forth. His mother was just another face to him; he didn't recognize her.

"Jeff, what happened to him?" I asked.

"I can't tell you due to confidentiality issues, but let me just say that if you ride a motorcycle, wear a helmet. Now, let's get to your therapy."

We spent the next hour stretching, doing weights, walking with crutches, and starting to walk without them at the parallel bars. The entire time, Jeff supported me to keep me from falling. At the end of the session, I sat on the chair and he pushed on my leg, trying to get it to flex. Once again, the pain was intense and I had tears in my eyes when he was done.

"Let's measure the angle," I said.

"It probably won't change every day," he warned.

"I know. Let's measure it anyway. I want to keep track."

He grabbed the goniometer and measured again.

"This can vary day to day and I will try to measure it the same each time, but this is not exact."

"I understand, but I want to see anyway."

He lined up one leg of the goniometer down my thigh and the other leg down my shin.

"Try to flex your knee as much as possible," Jeff suggested. "We will measure it the same way each time, so try to flex it as much as you can on your own."

I bore down and flexed the knee. I could tell the knee didn't move much. The foot still stuck out almost straight.

"Thirty-six degrees," Jeff announced.

"By the end of the week, I break forty," I said.

"You can't expect progress every day. There will be ups and downs."

"Then I guess I will just get a new therapist."

"I'm more worried about your sister than you."

"I don't blame you. I've been afraid of her as long as I can remember. She used to beat the snot out of me," I said. "Thanks for bringing me in early. I was feeling sorry for myself."

"Look, I see bad injuries every day. Yours are extreme and you have a lot of work to do, but you have a shot at getting back to close to where you were. Many of my patients don't. Therapy may help, but we won't get Jimmy anywhere close to where he was before his accident. You *can*."

As he got me in the chair and started to roll me out into the hall, I told him I would make it myself. I had gotten the hint and was sick of being sad and depressed. It was time to be thankful that I had a chance. I didn't know how close to normal I could get, but my brain was intact. Any of the things I went through should have killed parts or all of my brain, leaving me smiling in a wheelchair with my head swaying back and forth for the rest of my life. I still had a long road in front of me, but long roads had never stopped me before. What was I complaining about? Six months was nothing; college had been seven years. We had been building a business for eight. Nothing I had ever done that was worth anything had happened quickly. This would be no different, and I shouldn't expect it to be.

Jimmy did not seem to fully comprehend his surroundings, thankfully for him. Knowing what he had been before and comparing it to what he was now would be the worst part—at least for me, anyway. He did not have to deal with his "old" reality; that life, he had forgotten. He was living in the new one. Good for him that he didn't know what he had lost.

Of course his mom knew.

I knew what my life had *been*; now I had to get it back. I knew that my chance was now. I was fighting the daze of the oxycodone, but I realized that I was in a pretty good place. My doctors had saved me and my limbs. All in all, I had a good chance to get back close to normal. Jimmy, I figured, would never be close to what he had been. My mother had hope; Jimmy's mom did not. I had a path out of my own hell. Jimmy—or I should say Jimmy's mom—had no easy way out. I needed to quit whining and be thankful.

That day I prayed for my newest angel, Jimmy.

For Reflection

Have I not commanded you? Be strong and courageous. Do not be frightened, and do not be dismayed, for the Lord *your God is with you wherever you go. (Joshua 1:9)*

1. Have you ever faced a long struggle when you wanted to give up? Why did you decide to give up or to keep going?

For I consider that the sufferings of this present time are not worth comparing with the glory that is to be revealed to us. (Romans 8:18)

2. How does it feel to see someone else struggling when you're dealing with major issues? Does seeing someone else's battles make dealing with your own tragedy harder or easier?

No temptation has overtaken you that is not common to man. God is faithful, and he will not let you be tempted beyond your ability, but with the temptation he will also provide the way of escape, that you may be able to endure it. (1 Corinthians 10:13)

3. How can faith help us deal with addiction?
4. Can we be faithful in service to God and still be addicted?

CHAPTER 25

One Hurdle at a Time

Renee entered my room one morning with her perpetual smile and asked, "Do you want to try the shower this morning?"

They had taught me to take a sponge bath, but if I wanted to go home, I had to learn to shower. I did not have a wheelchair-accessible shower at home, so I had to develop the ability to move myself in and out. Fortunately, my home shower did have a bench, enabling me to sit down once inside; however, the doorway to it had a raised lip that the chair could not cross. I would have to crutch in and out.

"You bet," I replied as I started to sit up in the bed. The casts were all off, but I still sported a walking boot and a brace on my left arm. The bones were healing, but I was not ready to trust it yet. Because I had broken my elbow where the muscle attaches, bearing weight would put a huge amount of strain on the fracture. At this time, there was still a good chance that bone might be unable to handle it and come apart. This was especially true if I fell backward and tried to catch myself with my left arm. For these reasons, it was splinted to keep it in position, but both the splint and the walking boot were attached with Velcro to make it easy to remove them before showering. Renee slid the chair over to the bed and gestured her assistance in getting me in.

"That's okay," I countered. "I can do this myself."

I struggled to get in position at the side of the bed and had to grab the far arm of the chair to slide my butt into the seat. As I did, the chair started to roll away from the bed, inciting a huge adrenaline rush as I envisioned the chair rolling out from under me. Although I caught myself, the adrenaline made me nauseous. Renee gave me that "wife look," indicating I had screwed up.

"You always want to make sure the wheels are locked before you try to get in, or you will end up on the floor."

"Do you do that to everyone, or did I do something to you growing up that made you want to scare the crap out of me?"

"No, I do this to everyone. Don't worry; my foot was an inch behind the wheel in case you didn't stop in time. I wanted you to learn your lesson. You will never make that mistake again."

I thanked her and tried again. This time after locking the wheels, I slid into the chair with little effort. In fact, I was getting good at it, and as a result, my arms were getting stronger every day. Of course, it didn't hurt that I was still twenty pounds lighter than before the crash. God was probably still laughing at me for my inability to gorge myself on all the fatty, high-calorie foods I was now permitted to eat, thanks to my shrunken stomach and newly developed hatred for ice cream.

We rolled to the shower with Renee carrying my crutches. It was much like the one at home with the exception that there was no lip going in and the chair could roll right up to the bench. I locked the wheels and slid onto my perch.

"Next time, we'll work on getting over a lip, but today you can just get the shower done."

With that, Renee stepped out and pulled the curtain closed. "Just hand me your clothes when you're ready," she stated.

I was not wearing the usual hospital garb. Another couple of angels had taken care of that; the wife and the mother-in-law of one of my best friends had made me three sets of hospital clothes. These were made of a thick flannel to keep me warm. They had split them down the outside seams and stitched in strips of Velcro. This allowed me to fully open the pants down the outside of each leg. I could get them on and off by simply sliding them out from under my butt instead of pulling them off over my feet. Without the seams split like this, there would be no way to get them on and off by myself with a leg that didn't bend. They also had made matching shirts that split down the seam under the arm, allowing me to take it on and off with one hand like a poncho.

Having been a nurse herself who had witnessed the struggles of patients with my type of injury, my friend's wife knew this would help greatly. I had only met this woman once at a baptism for my friend's child, but she, in a great act of kindness, had spent hours making these special garments for me. Just being able to get out of hospital clothes with their thin material and terrible fit had done me a world of good. It created a little bit of normality to be in pajamas instead of the hospital gowns. And they felt great. I thanked God for sending yet another pair of angels.

As I sat on the bench, I tore the Velcro seams open on my shirt and pants and slipped them off. Now I remembered why they were made out of flannel; it was freezing in here. I handed Renee the clothes from behind the curtain as fast as I could and cranked the shower on hot. It seemed like forever until the water warmed up. I just let it run onto the floor for a while to heat up the shower stall. I had it so hot I could not be under the water myself; I just sat in the steam and waited for the shivering to stop.

This was the first shower I had been able to take for five weeks. Never one to take long showers, today I indulged. Yes, it took me much longer to get everything washed with one working hand and being forced to sit down, but I was really enjoying the process of cleansing my body. Sponge baths are okay but not the same as a good, hot shower. For the first time in years, I simply sat under the spray and allowed the water to wash over me. I was starting to feel human again. This was a major step toward going home, and I was fully enjoying it.

"Everything okay?"

I had forgotten about Renee waiting outside the curtain.

"Just finishing up," I yelled, somewhat embarrassed. I grabbed the razor in the shower and quickly removed a few days of stubble. Previously, my sisters had been shaving me, which prevented a beard, but now I could perform the task myself.

I turned off the shower and Renee handed me the towel. I got a blast of cold air as the curtain opened a few inches, and I immediately began to shiver. I quickly toweled off and asked for my clothes, dressing as fast as I could and going "commando" since it was too hard to get underwear over my feet. The Velcro pajamas would be just fine. Renee pushed in the chair and I moved myself into it, this time checking to make sure the wheels were locked.

"You remembered," she enthused with a wise smile on her face.

"The feeling of that chair starting to roll as I tried to get in it scared the crap out of me. I hadn't felt that since the time I fell learning to use crutches, and I remember how much that one hurt."

"You were always a pretty fast learner, even as a kid," she replied.

"Pain is a pretty good teacher."

Showering was just one requirement before earning the right to go home, and now I could check it off the list. Only two tasks remained: doing stairs and getting into the car. Those I would work on next.

At rehab, I asked Jeff if I could try getting into the car.

"Maybe next week. You're not quite there yet."

"I think I can do it. Let me try," I insisted, pushing him just a little past where he thought I should be.

"You are not going to stop pestering me until I let you try, so let's give it a whirl."

We went over to the car cab mock-up; it was complete with a door and steering wheel. They kept it very realistic in order to determine patients' readiness and ability to truly get in and out on their own.

We rolled over to the car, and Jeff stepped back. I opened the door with some difficulty as I tried to swing it open while in a wheelchair.

The door hit the wheels twice before I figured out how to pull it open with one hand and turn the wheelchair out of the way with the other. I could use my leg in the boot to push the door open all the way. Jeff just laughed at my use of my broken leg to move a thirty-pound door.

Having accomplished this, I sat and stared at the car seat. "Now what?" I asked looking over my shoulder at Jeff.

"The trick here is to shift your butt in first and then swing in the legs."

Getting into a car would seem to be a very simple task. We all do it multiple times a day, though not with weak, injured arms and an unbendable leg. I tried to rotate in but soon realized my foot could not even get past the door, much less get into the body of the car. I tried to bend my knee and move my left foot—still encased in a walking boot—past the door. Unable to bend it, I tried to slide farther into the car. But sliding was painful and difficult due to the weakness of my arms. Instead, I had to "walk" my butt back across the car seat shifting side to side, using my arms to lift some of the weight. I got my body almost halfway across the bench seat before trying to swing my feet into the car. My right leg could bend, so this one was not a problem. The left leg could now swing past the door, but it soon became apparent that there was no way it could get inside the car body. I tried to slide farther into the car and swing again, but again the leg wouldn't fit; it was just too straight to fit under the dash. My heart sank. I was exhausted from the effort and sweating.

I knew I would not be able to go home until I could get in the car, and for that, it looked like I needed at least another twenty degrees of bend. Now I could appreciate just how critical the ability to bend the knee would be. Of course, the only way to bend it more would be to continue Jeff's incredibly painful daily torture sessions; there was simply no way around that.

I looked at Jeff, and he smiled. "Ready to get back to work? We will get you in there eventually."

I knew I'd been expecting too much; no matter how much I wanted to go home, I just wasn't physically ready. I'd made good progress over the few weeks I'd been at the rehab hospital, but I still had a long way to go. Like most people, I had never dreamed that the ability to get into a car would be lost after a crash; now this was the one thing preventing me from going home. I got back into the chair, again checking to make sure the wheels were locked, and rolled back into the physical therapy section.

After doing the stretching exercises, Jeff told me to grab my crutches and follow him. I was getting pretty good with them because my upper body, though still weak, was getting stronger. I followed him as we crossed the rehab unit expecting him to stop any second at one of the therapy contraptions that were scattered everywhere. Jeff just kept walking. Finally, I saw where he was headed: The far end had a door with a word that scared the hell out of me: STAIRS.

Oh damn! I thought.

It made perfect sense that I would have to learn how to do stairs, but the thought of navigating them on crutches with a foot in a boot and non-bending elbows brought back memories of falling backward in the hospital. Falling this time would be much, much worse. I envisioned getting my weight too far back and tumbling down eight or ten stairs at a time; I still did not trust my broken leg. Though I knew it was healing, it wasn't healed. There was still a gap in the bone where I had lost the piece, and a fall would re-break it. Jeff opened the door as my anxiety level shot up again. These were concrete steps, with no padding whatsoever.

Jeff saw my thoughts reflected in my facial expression.

"Still don't trust me not to drop you?"

I sighed. "Yeah, I trust you. If you drop me, I'll kick your ass."

"Julie never told you I have a black belt, did she?"

"In that case, if you drop me, I'll give you a really nasty look."

"I'm not going to drop you, so it's not a problem. Now, let me tell you how to do this."

As I was learning, there's a trick to everything when you have a disability. Nothing is done normally. Here, I had to get up or down the stairs with both crutches under one arm and the other holding on to the stair rail. Jeff had me put the two crutches under my left arm (the one with the bad elbow and shoulder), which freed my right arm to use the handrail. With Jeff holding me, I moved the crutches down a step and stopped.

"Now, just lower yourself down," Jeff instructed.

I was frozen. Taking a single step like that while I looked at the next five concrete steps was akin to jumping off a cliff. I did not trust my leg to hold, I didn't know that my arms would not give out, and I feared the crutch would slip on the concrete. Jeff waited a few seconds and encouraged, "I got you; go ahead."

I literally closed my eyes and stepped off my six-inch cliff. Everything was okay; no pain, everything held. I prepared for the next step and took the leap. Okay again. With each step, I gained confidence; only the first one was hard. Soon I had it; I could go all the way down the flight, with Jeff letting go on the final two steps. I turned around and repeated the procedure on the way up, with Jeff behind me but no longer holding my belt. Check this one off the list: I had the stair thing down.

"Good job. Now when we get you in the car, you may be able to get home."

"Well, I guess it's time to stretch the leg."

"Sorry, but this is the only way to get it to bend."

"I know. This is what will get me home and get me closer to normal, so go ahead and torture me."

We went over to the dreaded chair and did the same routine. Three times, Jeff pushed on my foot trying to flex my knee as far as he could. The pain was not getting better. I figured it wouldn't. Scar tissue is full of nerves and doesn't really "stretch;" the fibers have to "tear." And that hurts—there's just no way around it. It just really sucked.

Back in bed after the therapy session, I laid my head back and sighed. I felt my spirits sink again as I contemplated the daily agony awaiting me for months.

I prayed: "God, just help me get through this. I don't know what you have in store for me yet, but I know you have a reason for this. I see now that the plan is yours and I am just along for the ride. That's okay, since I realized I was never really in control anyway. I just ask for the strength to endure it and that it works. I really want to play with the kids again and not be the dad just sitting on the sidelines. But, God, if that is the best I can do, then I will accept it. Just please help me get through this."

I was hoping again for some voice answering my prayers but heard nothing. Discouraged, I reached for some more Oxy. I didn't really hurt now, but I figured it would make me feel better—just a few more pills.

For Reflection

When I am afraid, I put my trust in you. In God, whose word I praise, in God I trust; I shall not be afraid. What can flesh do to me? (Psalms 56:3–4)

1. Is it good to let people make mistakes? How can mistakes be an important part of learning?

2. Describe an experience when you had to take a leap and trust that it would be okay.

He saved us, not because of works done by us in righteousness, but according to his own mercy, by the washing of regeneration and renewal of the Holy Spirit. (Titus 3:5)

3. Being able to take a hot shower for the first time in a month marked an important step in my recovery. Compare this to baptism and the washing away of sin.

CHAPTER 26

TIME TO GIVE THANKS

Thanksgiving was coming. This was the day the kids would finally come see me. We had kept them away until I was in better shape to protect them from the sight of me lying there with feeding tubes and IVs running in and out of my body. By now, the bruising in my face had mostly healed, and the only remaining casts were on one foot and one arm. My foot had a big, nasty, open wound that was still healing, but it was invisible to the kids since it was under wraps. At last, I was no longer at risk of giving them too many nightmares based on my appearance. It was a good time for a reunion.

My sisters came also, including Bonnie, my middle sister who lived with her husband and daughter in Chicago. Bonnie had felt bad since she could not really help with my care due to geographical distance, but now she had a few days off and drove up for the holiday. They all came in with loads of food—something my Polish family never skimped on. They had made the traditional Thanksgiving turkey dinner. I had been looking forward to this for a week, dreaming about the turkey and stuffing I loved.

Mona and the kids were the last to arrive. The kids nervously hung out against the far wall, obviously unsure if they could touch me, lest I just fall apart. "It's okay," I soothed. "They have me pretty well back together, so you can hug me now."

With that, they all ran over. They didn't know quite how to do it since I was all bandaged on my left side and could barely lift my right arm, but we managed. It was one of the best hugs I had ever received.

Mona came over next and gave me a kiss on the cheek. It had been now about five weeks since I had seen the kids and about two weeks since I had seen Mona. When they inquired as to how I was doing, I told them everything was going well, neglecting to inform them about the grueling physical therapy—my daily torture session. I figured they didn't need to know everything.

My mother, in her infinite optimism, kept repeating how well I was doing and how I would be home in no time, blissfully unaware that I was now getting by on eighty milligrams of oxycodone three times a day to control my pain, both physical and otherwise.

We all headed down to a larger break room the nurses had set up for our use. They had rolled in a TV and DVD player at my father's request.

"I have a DVD of the news report out of Madison. Thought you may want to see it," my dad said.

"Sounds great. I haven't seen any pictures or anything yet."

He started the DVD and the reporter began the story.

"Six people, including three children, were injured in a two-car accident on Highway 94 today," a voice said as the camera showed our wrecked minivan with exploded airbags and the doors pried off by the Jaws of Life.

"The victims were identified as Doctors Scot and Mona Hodkiewicz, veterinarians from the Lake Geneva area, and their three children. They were all taken to the University of Wisconsin Hospital and both parents are listed in critical condition with severe, life-threatening injuries. Also injured was the driver of the other vehicle, identified as Mike Jacobs, who currently has seven drunken-driving arrests on his record. Police report that Mr. Jacobs fled the scene and was arrested a short time later. He was taken to the hospital and released to the police with minor injuries. He is currently in jail on suspicion of his eighth drunken-driving charge."

As the report continued, I could feel the emotions welling up inside of me. I fought back tears but soon was crying. My father ran to stop the recording and apologized for showing it, but I told him to continue. I needed to see the truth of what had happened: the mangled vehicle, the caved-in front end, and the collapsed dashboard that had shattered my leg. This was all part of the healing process—confronting what had happened—so I could appreciate the miracle that we were all still alive.

As I looked at the devastated car and contemplated the force of the impact, it became very apparent that I never should have made it. Again I thought, *There is just no reason for any of us to have survived this.*

Then I heard the words again in my mind: *It is not your plan.* It was the first time I had heard them in weeks.

The report continued: "Two of the family's pet dogs were in the car also. One is at the Emergency Veterinary Hospital while the other is missing." The reporter made no attempt to hide the disgust in her voice as she ended with, "Police report Mr. Jacobs had registered 0.22 on the Breathalyzer, nearly three times the legal limit."

By now I was sobbing. Mona had her arm around me and her face pressed down against the top of my shoulder. I could feel her body brace under her clothes. Everyone was quiet, and the silence in the room was awkward. I wasn't crying in anger, nor was I sad that something bad had happened to us, since I was sure there was a purpose for it. They were mostly tears of relief and gratitude. I could not believe anyone had survived this crash much less that *everyone* survived, even the dogs. God had protected us, though he had allowed some pain into our lives. I thought about the twelve disciples who had followed Jesus, most of whom died in all sorts of terrible ways. I remembered the words of my pastor, "God never promised our lives would be free of pain, just that He would be with us as we went through it."

I wiped away the tears and regained my composure, more convinced than ever that God had more for me to do, that I just wasn't seeing the whole picture yet.

I also realized that God had not miraculously prevented me from being injured. He had let me feel the pain because this was part of the lesson. It was so terrible, I'd never forget it. I would remember the hard work of the tortuous rehab. And that was the point: I was getting stronger *because* it wasn't easy.

The pain was necessary for me to change, to refocus on what was right. The pain was transforming me, both physically and spiritually, teaching me forgiveness and how to deal with real adversity—lessons I had never had to learn in almost forty years.

I would not have changed on my own. Why would I? I thought I was doing everything right. But now I knew I could do better. I was beginning to see that all this hardship might be worth it.

I remembered a card one of my clients had sent with a Bible verse. I could never remember Bible verses or recite them like some others, but this one had stuck in my head:

Consider it pure joy, my brothers and sisters, when you face trials of many kinds, because you know that the testing of your faith develops perseverance. And let perseverance have its full effect, that you may be perfect and complete, lacking nothing.

I was being tested, and as a result, I was developing great perseverance. I was getting stronger than I had ever been spiritually and mentally at a time when I was at my weakest physically.

I looked at my family surrounding me with all their love and support and knew I would be better. Maybe not perfect but better than this. I was convinced that there was just more to this whole thing and that it was leading somewhere and I would know when it happened. Somewhere, sometime, somehow, it would all make sense. I still had my family. With time, I would be spiritually perfect and complete, lacking nothing.

"All right," I announced, "let's eat."

That night, I wanted to try getting up the ramp. The nurses had gotten to know my schedule, though I never mentioned the ramp to them. After dinner and a rest, I would get in the chair and wheel myself down the hall. The halls were empty of visitors and most patients were asleep. I would roll myself over to my mountain, my hundred-foot ramp. I would try to get up it, fail, and turn back toward my room. I would then take three, then four, then five laps around the hallway, pushing my arms to get stronger.

I thought: *Today is the day. I'm getting to the top of that ramp.*

I had been close before but had always had to stop. I psyched myself up and started to push. As I reached seventy-five feet, I was sweating and puffing; my arms ached, but I felt great. A few weeks ago, I had stopped at ten feet; now I was at seventy-five. I was getting stronger, and the sweat and the pain told me this work was starting to pay off. A few more last pushes and I crested the top. I yelled in triumph, dropping my aching arms to my side, feeling like Rocky. I would have shadowboxed if I could have.

Behind me, I heard more shouts and applause. I had not known it, but the entire nursing staff had been following me out for the last week, secretly watching to see if I would make it. Now they were jumping up and down and whooping like high school cheerleaders.

For a moment I was embarrassed, but that feeling was soon replaced by a flood of joy. I realized my triumph was their triumph. Their work changing my bandages (as well as my dirty sheets), bringing me food, and getting me in and out of bed had gotten me to the top of the ramp—the top of my mountain—and we all rejoiced. I turned and headed back down at full speed. The nurses lined up for high fives as I sped past, slapping their hands as they cheered. Today was a good day.

FOR REFLECTION

The LORD is near to the brokenhearted and saves the crushed in spirit. (Psalms 34:18)

1. Does God want us to confront unpleasant memories and feelings or simply focus on God and forget about the tough days in our lives? Explain your thinking.

2. Is it good for God to allow us to feel pain? Would it be better if God prevented us from feeling pain? How might hardship lead us to permanent change and greater strength?

CHAPTER 27

ONE STEP FORWARD, TWO STEPS BACK

During the last two months of rehab, I had progressed from barely alive, to struggling to sit up, to a wheelchair, to walking on crutches. By now I was even pretty good at the whole crutch thing and could get around very well.

At first I had been unable to brush my teeth or take care of any personal hygiene, but now I was able to shower (though I had to sit) and mostly care for myself. I had gained back about twenty of the thirty-five pounds I had lost and was now able to eat small meals (my stomach still did not allow me to eat a lot at one time). I still lacked stamina, but my broken bones were getting stronger every day.

At last, I was getting ready to go home. I thought I could do it, though I conceded I'd need some help from Mona and the kids. No matter—I wanted to get out. Because I was still working on the ability to simply get into a car, I definitely would not be driving for a while. But I didn't think I would be a huge burden either.

Deluding myself that I was ready to be home was just wishful thinking. In truth, I still needed a lot of assistance. Yes, I could get out of bed, but it was a huge effort. It was also an enormous risk; one fall could set me back a month, so I was actively avoiding getting in and out of bed. I called for a nurse to get my food or drink and limited my trips to the bathroom. If I went home, I wouldn't be able to help with laundry or dishes, nor would I be able to drive or make a meal. I couldn't do anything with the kids.

I wasn't thinking this through but somehow was convinced I was ready; I just needed to get my leg in the car. This was progressing with Jeff pushing on it to bend every day. It still just about killed me every time he did it, but it was working. I was getting about two or three degrees of additional bend every day or two. Now it was just a matter of time until that foot could make it into the car. Well, time and pain.

At least I had the Oxy. I still needed about eighty milligrams three times a day. By now, I had developed a tolerance, which meant I needed a whopping-high dose. I told myself the Oxy was just a vehicle to enable me to do my physical therapy and get home. If I took some extra medicine for the purpose of getting home sooner, then it was all good.

The reality? I was addicted because it made me feel good.

Mona didn't think I was anywhere close to being ready to live at home again. She was still in the back brace but had returned to work out of fear of losing the business. Alexa still had to help her bathe and dress in the morning, but they managed. Due to the lingering effects of the concussion, Mona would still forget things and mix up words.

The staff did not let her lift any dogs, and a technician was always with her in the room to prevent a dog from jumping on her or knocking her over. Still, even with the extra help, work was exhausting. A day for a vet might include seeing twenty to thirty appointments in an eight- or nine-hour period. There was usually little time for breaks because there was always another client waiting, another phone call to make, or another surgery to perform, especially being short one doctor. It included a six-day workweek and emergency calls after hours. Mona also had to run the house and take care of three young kids, plus we owned three rental homes as a side business. She was dragging through every day. When she got home, she would feed the kids (luckily, we still had meals being delivered every night from our church), help them finish homework, and then collapse.

I was oblivious to all this—exclusively focused on getting home to the point that I didn't see the added stress my presence would cause. I'd be just one more thing for Mona to deal with and worry about. My wife may have said she wanted me back in the house, but she didn't think my homecoming would take place anytime soon. She had been told I would be in the hospital for four to six months; we were only two months in. Although Mona could easily tell I wasn't close to being independent, I couldn't. She kept dropping not-so-subtle hints that I should not rush my return and instead take advantage of the care I had in the hospital.

Every male knows (and every woman eventually learns) that "subtle" hints go right over a guy's head. Mona's implications did not register with me. I was in mission mode to get back. All I could see was that if I just got my leg to bend some more, I could get in a car and head back to Lake Geneva.

Finally, about a week before Christmas, I succeeded. It was an arduous struggle, and bending my leg sufficiently to enter a car hurt like hell, but I got it in. Jeff congratulated me and advised that if I could do it every day for three days, he would sign off on the release. Subsequently, I did it with no problem. I was going home.

I had a great idea (again, I was oblivious); I asked my dad to drive me home so I could surprise Mona. *And surprise her I did!* She looked absolutely shocked to see me as the kids ran out screaming with glee that their dad was home. Later, Mona told me she wasn't shocked but highly pissed that I had left the hospital, fully expecting I would stay for at least another month or two. By then, she would have healed a little more and I would have needed less nursing care.

She kept her feelings to herself, though, and hugged me. My father helped get me into the house. A friend, another angel, had stopped by the day before to install a wheelchair ramp he had made. He also had installed a new showerhead for me and some grab bars around the toilet. The house was ready, but now I had to learn how to do these things on my own.

I stopped my father as he motioned to wheel me up the ramp into the house. "No, Dad, let me do this." I knew his intentions were good, but I was sick of everyone helping me so I pushed myself up the ramp. This was steeper than the ramp at the hospital, but I wanted to show everyone, including myself, that I could do it. I pushed and struggled getting up the steeper incline and reaching the top, out of breath but smiling. I was home. It would be a hardship for a while yet, but I was healing and knew I just needed time.

I set up in the living room on my favorite recliner. Mona always hated this chair because it didn't match anything else in the house, but it was the most comfortable and I really didn't care what it looked like. I could get in and out relatively easily and would spend a lot of time in that spot.

The Wisconsin winter had settled in. I had come in from the cold, but it took a good half-hour under a blanket to warm up my skinny body. Once the excitement of being home started to wear off, I became very tired. Then the doorbell rang, and my aunt and uncle came in for a visit from out of town; I could not sleep yet. Mona had made me some food, which I was just finishing as the visitors arrived. I would not be able to sleep for the next six hours as I recounted to my relatives all I could remember about the last eight weeks. I had told the story many times and could recite it well. I kept quiet about hearing God's voice and His lesson to me about "His plan," because I still wasn't quite sure about how people would react. If I'm honest about it, I couldn't even be sure I hadn't made the whole thing up in an attempt to discover a "why" for all our pain. I kept it to myself while I wrapped my head around what had happened. I had learned not to guess; it was out of my hands, and I would not have been right anyway.

Still, I wondered if there was some greater good I had not seen yet. My best guess was that God wanted me to work on changing the drunk-driving laws in a state that sorely needed it. Wisconsin had some of the laxest laws in the country. First-time drunk driving wasn't even a crime, it was a traffic violation. This had to change, so I figured that was the purpose behind the accident.

As I conversed with my visitors, I remained cold in spite of wearing a sweatshirt and pants and huddling under a thick blanket. I simply could not warm up; I was chilled to the bone. My joints ached and I needed to take a higher dose of OxyContin to control the pain, especially in my left elbow, which was starting to throb.

The move was tougher than I had anticipated, but I was thrilled to be back home again. I had closed the door on the hospital phase of my recovery. I had found a great physical therapist in town whom a client had recommended, and starting in a few days, I would go to see him. I was mentally ready to hit it hard and heal. Yes, once again I had a great plan.

By the next day, I wasn't feeling too well. I could not stay warm and would shiver for twenty minutes any time I got out from under the covers. I figured it was from my weight loss and the previous day's drive. I just needed time.

I made the not-so-wise decision to go to church that Sunday. Mona told me I should stay home, but I loved my church and wanted to show people that I was back in town and on the mend. After bundling up in full Wisconsin winter garb, I made my way out to the van. Mona and the kids had to help me get in and put my wheelchair in the back. Mona was still wearing a back brace, so Alexa helped her get the chair in the car.

We made it to church, where I was mobbed by well-wishers. My pastors came over and hugged Mona and me. Everyone was thrilled to see us after almost two months away. The pastors addressed the rest of the congregation, and everyone cheered as it was announced that we were there. I basked in the glory of all the attention, exactly what I should *not* have been doing in God's house. Again, I needed to be reminded that it was His plan and His glory, not mine.

When I got home, I was freezing. It was about five below outside, and the trip home had left me shivering and my teeth chattering. The car had been warmed up before I got in, but it didn't make a difference. Mona helped me change into sweats and get into bed. After an hour, my teeth were still chattering. Something was wrong. I felt weak and simply could not get warm. My left elbow was pounding in pain and swollen. Mona saw it when she helped me change and immediately noticed a problem. "Was your elbow always this big?" she asked. I looked down and noticed it also.

"No, I guess not."

"I'm getting a thermometer," she announced.

She soon returned and stuck the thermometer under my tongue. When she touched my elbow, I winced: it was much more painful than yesterday. I knew before she checked the thermometer what she would say.

"One hundred and three. I'm taking you in."

With that, she quickly got on the phone to call a neighbor to watch the kids while she drove me to the local hospital's emergency room. As soon as she rolled me in, the staff took one look and rushed over: I was bundled up in layers of clothing—white as a sheet—with eyes barely open and body shivering. Mona tried to explain the situation and her suspicions about an infection in my elbow.

We were scared. Mona explained to the attending nurse: "There is a plate in that elbow. If it gets infected, they will have to take it all out. It's not healed yet, and removing the plate could let the whole thing fall apart. He could lose his arm."

A nurse took my temperature: 103.5 degrees. I was getting worse.

They called for a doctor as they changed me into a hospital gown and got me into a room. Mona started to explain everything that was broken or injured. The nurse looked at her in disbelief: "Seventy miles an hour, head-on, and you all survived? I have never heard of that. People just don't survive that kind of collision."

"Yeah," she replied, knowing the nurse was right, "we were really blessed."

I looked at her and smiled. A broken back and major head injury, kids scared and injured, a husband in a wheelchair with a fever, and "we were really blessed." We sure weren't looking blessed right then!

When the doctor came in to evaluate me, he confirmed what we suspected. "I think you have an infected elbow. We are going to X-ray it to see if anything is out of place. Then we will stick a needle in it to get a sample of the pus and culture to see what is growing. In the meantime, we will set an IV and start antibiotics. Tomorrow, you are getting sent back to Madison. You should be back there with your history. In fact, I am a little surprised you were back home already."

Mona gave me the "wife look," agreeing with the doctor's statement.

"You don't want me to stay here? I'm offended." I protested with a smile.

"I don't want to even touch you," the doctor replied. "The doctors that put the plate in can deal with you now. If you were in better shape, I would send you tonight. Let's get the antibiotics started immediately and I will send you when the fever is a little better. Right now, you look like crap—no offense."

The X-rays showed that nothing had moved or let loose. A nurse prepped my elbow and the doctor stuck a long needle into it. I clenched my teeth as the needle slid in. He pulled back on the syringe and removed some thick, yellow pus.

"We will see what grows," he declared, "and start the antibiotics. Get some rest, and we are sending you to Madison as soon as we can."

By now, I just wanted to sleep. I was exhausted and still freezing. I had gotten "toxic" from the infection in my elbow. I was absorbing all the bad chemicals formed by the bacteria, and it had caused my temperature to spike and my blood pressure to drop. This had given me the chills that I could not shake. If it didn't respond to medication, my blood pressure would drop further and I could go into shock. I was again at risk of systemic infection, organ failure, and death. The bacteria from my elbow could spread infection to other areas, including any or all of the other five fracture sites and any of the hardware, the screws, and plates. All I wanted to do was sleep, but I knew I was in trouble; bacteria on the loose in the bloodstream can quickly be fatal.

I stopped and prayed, asking God to help me one more time. I kicked myself for going out to church that morning, not because of the weather, but because of my reasons: I had gone as much for the attention, the words of encouragement, and the praise for being such a strong fighter. I had gone into the Lord's house for selfish reasons, and now I knew I had screwed up. I asked God for forgiveness. I understood that church and prayer were not about me; it was about talking with Him. I had gone to church my entire life but was only now learning what prayer and God were really about.

I asked that He help me through this infection and that I keep my arm. In the past, I would have bartered with Him, stating that in exchange for His help I would do something in return. I would be nicer, never miss church, read the Bible from start to finish, any of those favors that I had tried to trade with Him in the past and promptly forgotten as soon as the crisis ended. This time, I didn't barter. I knew He would do His will whether I did my horse trading or not. I just prayed for His help healing, but I would accept His plan no matter what.

With this, the tears began to flow. Mona had left to get back to the kids so she never saw me crying, but I knew the next twenty-four hours could change my life again. I was helpless and my life was out of my hands—another lesson about who was really in control.

The fever burned hotter and hotter as I shivered under the blankets. Even though I was drenched with sweat, I could not get warm.

I knew I was in trouble; this infection was serious. If the infection didn't respond to the medicine, I would probably lose my arm (or at least the ability to move it at the elbow) and my career.

I also knew I had no control over any of this. It was God's plan, not mine, and I accepted that. I had given control of my life over to Him. In the face of all that was going on, I felt strangely calm. There was simply nothing I could do to change my fate. All the doctors could do tonight was administer the antibiotics; all I could do was pray.

I asked for help. "God, I pray that I heal and can keep use of my arm. I accept Your plan may not be what I want, but I will accept whatever You give me. If I die, I pray then for Mona and the kids, that they heal and are happy. If I live, then I pray that I can continue to do my job since that is what I love to do and I feel I can help a lot of Your creatures. I pray for Your help to get me through tonight."

This was all I could do, knowing the outcome was out of my hands. I might live; I might die. I might lose my arm, or the joint might be trashed and only partially usable. Knowing I had done all I could and resolved to stop worrying about things I couldn't control, I felt peace.

I gave myself up to God and fell into a wonderfully deep sleep—the deepest, most peaceful sleep I'd had in months, possibly years. All my cares were gone, even though the stakes were high.

The morning came quickly. I had slept through the night but had a quick flash of panic as I checked to see if my arm was still there. I had to make sure they hadn't amputated it. With a sigh of relief, I reached over and felt my hand. Whew!

I could feel that the fever was gone. I felt warm under the blanket, no more chills. I knew the infection was responding. I would survive. I realized I could still lose my arm if the plates or joint got infected and that the inflammation could create so much scar tissue that I might not ever bend it again, but I could still work with an immobile elbow. To do my work, I needed two good hands. An elbow that doesn't bend would make work difficult but not impossible. Now the worst-case scenario could be managed. My elbow still throbbed, but not as much as the previous night.

Once Mona arrived, we headed for Madison. The hospital had called ahead and the staff was waiting for us.

I spent the next week there to ensure that the infection was under control. They had stopped my physical therapy and would not restart it until I was home. I was disappointed that I was not working at it, since I knew how quickly the gains I had made in stamina and strength could disappear. I was still too weak to handle any strenuous work, but I was also too anxious to not do anything. I began pushing myself in the wheelchair again to get some use of my arms. This hospital did not have a ramp to scale, but I was able to cruise the halls for long periods of time. Mainly, I just wanted to get home and start my real physical therapy; I had had enough of lying around.

The day before I left for home again, Dr. Lang came in, dragging a third-year resident by the arm. He said, "See, see, this is the one I told you about. This is the one that survived a factor VIII shot." Looking at me he added, "Dr. Johansen doesn't believe anyone survives a factor VIII injection. I had to have him meet you so he could see that someone did."

"Everyone I had ever seen given the shot died within an hour," Dr. Johansen explained. "Obviously, they were all in terrible shape to begin with, but I had never seen it work before."

I was a bit shocked but laughed. "Dr. Lang did a lot right that day. Stick with him and do what he does and you will be okay."

Again, I thanked God for saving me by working through all the angels who had made it possible. (This conversation reminded me how close I had been to death.)

A week later, I was back home, with the infection under control.

By now I was starting to see that it would take me another four or five months to get back to work, and I was starting to get antsy. I had never been away from work that long and did not know how to handle it. Though I was starting to receive disability payments, I wanted to be seeing patients again. Our business relied on me doing the more complicated surgeries. If I was not there, we had to refer these patients elsewhere. It was inconvenient for the owners and delayed care for the patient. If an animal had a broken leg and I wasn't there to fix it, we had to move it thirty or forty miles to a hospital that could handle the surgery. I needed to get back so we could treat those animals here.

In the past, part of my drive to do these procedures was financial: These were expensive surgeries that brought in thousands of dollars—much of which went directly into my pocket. Every time we sent a patient to another hospital, we lost the money.

After what I had been through, my drive to make money had changed. It was no longer about making money for *me*. If I was not there, forcing the practice to send patients to a specialist, the cost to the client would be double what we charge, putting many procedures out of reach. A good portion of these patients would simply be euthanized instead. I could save them, but only if I was there.

Second, lower income for the business put the employees at risk of layoffs. These employees were like my family, and they were darn good at what they did; I did not want them to lose their jobs.

Making money was no longer just about me but also about them. I figured God was telling me—no, forcing me—to wake up and put my priorities back in order. I had started my career as an idealistic young doctor who did not care about the business side of veterinary medicine. Over time, that had transitioned into concern about *me*, not *them*. I had begun to use the gifts He had given me to better my life and to acquire more stuff, not help animals. This was going to change.

I remembered the story of Jesus turning over the tables of the money changers in the temple. He had become enraged that *business* was taking over a house of worship. I had done the same; my business had taken over my life.

The crash, that one-in-a-million chance that Mike Jacobs would cross the median and hit us, was my wake-up call. It was like Jesus turning over my money-changing table and scattering what I thought was important all over the ground. I had told myself I would change my priorities. I would make God, family, and patients my reason for doing my job. I would make the money I needed by doing this, but it was no longer the driving factor. Now I wanted to get back to work because veterinary medicine was my calling; it was the gift God had given me, and I needed to use this gift in the right way. Maybe that was why He put us in the crash; maybe He needed me to refocus.

At last, I had it all figured out—I had a plan for my life and knew where it was going.

I should have known I didn't know squat.

For Reflection

Beware of practicing your righteousness before other people in order to be seen by them, for then you will have no reward from your Father who is in heaven. Thus, when you give to the needy, sound no trumpet before you, as the hypocrites do in the synagogues and in the streets, that they may be praised by others. Truly, I say to you, they have received their reward. But when you give to the needy, do not let your left hand know what your right hand is doing, so that your giving may be in secret. And your Father who sees in secret will reward you. (Matthew 6:1–4)

1. Is it ever okay to attend church for reasons other than praising God? Give examples of when it might be right vs. when it might be wrong.

And when you pray, do not heap up empty phrases as the Gentiles do, for they think that they will be heard for their many words. (Matthew 6:7)

2. Have you tried to barter with God to have a prayer answered? What did you promise to do if you got what you wanted? Did it work? How do you feel as you look back on that experience?

Every good gift and every perfect gift is from above, coming down from the Father of lights, with whom there is no variation or shadow due to change. (James 1:17)

3. Do you believe God gives everyone a gift? Why or why not?
4. How does God expect us to use the gifts we've been given?
5. Have you ever experienced a job taking over your life? How did this affect you, for better or worse?

CHAPTER 28

SHE HAD SEEN IT COMING

A few weeks later, Mona had a recheck back at Madison, per her doctors' recommendation. They needed to examine her back, head, and elbow to determine if they'd healed as anticipated. Thankfully she hadn't had much pain recently, other than the usual soreness that comes with being in a brace for so long. By now, Mona hated it and was in a hurry to get it off; she just needed the okay from her doctors. This checkup would confirm that everything was back to normal and she could close this angst-filled chapter over the state of her health. Her medical team treated this checkup as an afterthought, too, completely confident that all would be well. I was not worried either and stayed home.

Mona's doctor had given her the option of doing the CT or regular X-rays since there were pluses and minuses to both. They could simply X-ray the spine, but that test could be less sensitive than a CT and not show things as well. In cases like Mona's, often fracture lines become blurred and overlapping at this point in the treatment process; therefore, X-rays might not detect whether the bones had completely healed. If the bones were not healed, getting out of the brace could allow them to shift and cause paralysis. The CT scans the bones and surrounding tissues in much greater detail and can detect subtle changes in the fracture; it would also peruse the abdomen where she had bruised her pancreas and suffered internal bleeding. A bruise would certainly be gone by now and the internal bleeding long since resolved. The downside of the CT was that it was much more radiation, equivalent to hundreds of X-rays rather than just two spinal radiographs. They expected everything to be healed so they did not push strongly for the CT. Mona could choose.

She considered having the X-rays instead of the CT because of the increased exposure to radiation. Radiation, and the cancer it can produce, had always scared her. She had gotten more radiation exposure than most people because of all the X-rays we took in our profession. In addition, we had both gotten loads of radiation from all the CTs and X-rays we'd endured over the past two months. For these reasons, she didn't want a ton more radiation and told the doctors to just do the plain X-rays. They would shoot her back and elbow to ensure they were both healed, then take off the brace. It was scheduled for the following week.

That night, Mona was uneasy and did not sleep well. The next morning, even through my haze of OxyContin, I could see she was troubled. She just seemed off, as if her mind were elsewhere. By evening, her mood had not improved at all, and she seemed very distracted. In response, I did the "good husband" thing and assured her it was all routine; we both knew the fracture should be healed. Mona agreed that it should be, but still something bothered her.

We both had learned in our profession that you always trust a gut feeling. I also had learned by now that a gut feeling is often God's voice and you had better listen up. We'd discussed changing the X-rays to a CT if it would make her feel better. I thought she was being a little paranoid, but I also knew the CT provided much better images. I left it to her discretion but encouraged her to follow her gut.

The next morning, she had made her decision: She would risk the radiation of the CT. Her gut just kept telling her this was the right way to go, and she would follow that.

By now, I felt the same way. There was a reason why she felt so uneasy about not doing the more sensitive test. Maybe, as we'd witnessed countless times before, these were God's messages to us to take one path or the other—one of those forks in the road. When we chose not to heed His voice, things generally went terribly wrong. How many times did we end up saying, "I had a feeling this would happen. I should have listened to my gut"? Of course, this statement fails to credit the true source of "gut feelings," but He is used to us turning a deaf ear to what He is trying to say and then forgetting to thank Him. It is just the way we all are.

Today, Mona would listen. When we called to reschedule for a CT, the nurse informed us it would be another week before Mona could get in. It didn't matter. My wife was now adamant, in spite of having to wear the hated brace for another week, that she would do the CT. That night, she slept well for the first time in two days, finally at peace as if God had smiled on her. Mona knew she had made the right decision but still did not know why. After all, there was no reason to believe her back would not be completely healed.

The following week, I did not go with her to the CT because I wasn't worried about it. Besides, loading me into a car for an hour-long drive was a real project since I still needed the wheelchair instead of crutches, due to my infected elbow. I was also starting rehab that day and felt Mona was just being paranoid. So Mona drove herself to the hospital, knowing they would not sedate her. She was fully aware she would not get the results back for a week, yet she was strangely nervous about the CT. I knew her fractures were pretty stable and unlikely to have had any problems healing. Mona couldn't pinpoint the cause of her concern either, but we both attributed it to trepidation about returning to Madison and reliving the worst day of her life.

The CT came and went without a hitch. Afterward, they told her to expect a call in a week with the results. But as she waited for the valet to bring her car around, her cellphone rang and displayed an unknown number from Madison. Her heart sank as she guessed it was the hospital. There was only one reason they would be calling so soon; they had found something wrong.

Mona answered to her doctor's urgent voice advising her to come back in immediately. Fear overwhelmed her. This could not be good news. Had the back not healed? Would she need to have surgery and have it plated? She turned around and headed back to the doctor's office careful how she walked, expecting some major problem with her back. By now, her adrenaline was pumping. She was scared but not surprised because she had seen it coming—that gut feeling to do the CT was about to be validated. She had heard God's voice in her ear and listened.

Once Mona got to the doctor's office, the receptionist escorted her into a room right away. Mona was no longer smiling or making small talk. The nurses wore troubled expressions also; they looked at her as she came in, then quickly went back to what they were doing. *Something* was very wrong.

The doctor walked into the room after just a few minutes, accompanied by another older doctor (a bad sign), and a nurse. He sat down on his stool in front of Mona with a very serious look on his face.

"What is wrong?" she asked. "Did the vertebrae not heal?"

He shook his head. "No, your back is fine. You don't need the brace anymore. The radiologist looked at your CT as it was being processed. The problem isn't your back. That mass on your pancreas that was seen on the first CT is still there. We thought it was a bruise, but it should have resolved by now. Mona, we no longer believe it's a bruise."

My wife felt like her world was collapsing again. She knew there were only a few other choices when there is a mass on the pancreas.

The doctor continued, "It is a mass of some sort. You will need some additional tests." The nurse began getting needles and tubes ready for a blood draw. "We can test for some of the pancreatic markers and repeat the previous blood work, but I want you to have an ultrasound. This is Dr. Wilson; he is a specialist in pancreatic disease and surgery."

Mona sat in disbelief. Though he'd been careful not to say the word *tumor*, she knew "pancreatic markers" meant that was what they were looking for. "Markers" are proteins given off by specific tumors in the blood, an indication not just of cancer but also of the specific type.

Could this really be pancreatic cancer? This was supposed to be a simple recheck to confirm that everything had healed and the worst was over—the day she was supposed to be allowed to get back to her life and put this nightmare behind her. She thought she was done with her hell. Now she was finding out that not only was she still traveling through it, it was about to get ten times worse. At this point, her very survival was in question. Pancreatic cancer can be fatal in weeks. *What if it had spread? How would she tell the kids she was dying?* The thought of months of chemo and radiation terrified her as she sat there stunned.

Dr. Wilson took over as he sat down in front of Mona and calmly explained the tests. They would draw blood today and set up an ultrasound to look at the spot more closely. If they suspected a tumor, she would need surgery to remove it.

She fought to catch her breath but couldn't; it was coming short and fast. *Could she die before her fortieth birthday? Could she miss her kids graduating from high school? Had she survived the wreck and all this pain only to die a few months later of something completely unrelated?* She slowly formed the words to ask, "Is this pancreatic cancer?"

"I think it is going to be a pancreatic tumor of some type. I just don't know which one. The tests may help, but it is very likely I will have to take it out. Set up the ultrasound as soon as possible and I will wait for the results."

"How likely is it that it is cancer?"

"I can't tell yet, but I will say that over 90 percent are removed surgically whether they are cancerous or not. We rarely can leave them alone. Let me tell you: This is what I do. I am very good at it, but pancreatic surgery is rarely easy. You are a veterinarian, so you already know this. Let's get the tests done before we jump to any conclusions."

With that, he left the room and the nurse prepared to draw blood. Mona just sat there not knowing what to do, unable to move. The thought of cancer had stopped her in her tracks. There are few words in the English language that strike fear so quickly in people's hearts as *cancer*. Today she had heard it in connection to "pancreatic cancer," one of the most aggressive and deadly forms of the disease. The father of a good friend had died in his fifties of pancreatic cancer, and we'd witnessed his rapid, terrible decline and death. Mona knew pancreatic cancer was one of the most aggressive forms and came with a terrible prognosis; people just do not survive it. But she also knew there are multiple types of pancreatic cancer—the aggressive type that usually takes the patient in a matter of months, and less aggressive types that are deadly but take years to end a life. There are also benign (noncancerous) tumors that can be removed and cured, but these are rare. The blood tests and ultrasound could help determine Mona's particular brand of pancreatic cancer and, ultimately, whether she would live or die.

As the nurse moved forward for the blood draw, the room suddenly felt cold; Mona tried to hold back the feeling that her world was caving in. A few months ago, her world had been smashed to smithereens, but it had been slowly returning to normal. Now she felt it happening again just as quickly as that Jeep had crossed the median. Last time, she had been wheeled up to say goodbye to me before I died; now, I soon might be doing the same for her. The nurse applied a tourniquet to her arm; Mona didn't move. The nurse tried to make small talk; Mona didn't hear a word. The nurse put the needle into her arm; Mona didn't flinch. She was numb.

Dr. Wilson returned and briefly stuck his head in the door, oblivious to the ton of bricks now sitting on Mona's lap. "Set up the ultrasound at the desk, and we will call in a few days with the lab results," he said.

Then, grasping the terror on Mona's face, he stepped in and placed a hand on her knee. "Don't panic," he said. "We don't know what it is yet."

It is simply impossible not to panic in this situation; the mere thought of a cancer diagnosis and impending death naturally will cause any human being to lose control of his or her emotions. It doesn't matter if you are thirty-eight or eighty. We have all seen the effects of cancer, and most people have lost loved ones to this menace. But watching someone else deal with cancer is very different from having to cope with it yourself. In a daze on the way out, Mona stopped at the front desk, where the receptionist put down what she was doing and inquired as to when Mona could come back. She responded by asking if she could do the ultrasound near home, much to the receptionist's surprise. Most patients facing this diagnosis opt for the ultrasound as soon as possible, but Mona wanted to be close to home. The receptionist nodded and assured her that would be fine; the doctors here just needed the report.

Although still shaking, Mona knew exactly what she wanted to do. Dr. George Fueredi had been a client of ours for years, starting in the early days when we were just getting our practice going. He had three big Labs that were always getting into trouble, so we had gotten to know each other well. Most medical doctors get along well with veterinarians, as there is a lot of mutual respect.

Dr. Fueredi was an interventional radiologist. His job was to use ultrasound, CT, and radiology to diagnose and fix problems. I had called him once to help me find an abnormal liver vessel on a two-pound Yorkie. I'd suspected the vessel was there but could not seem to locate it. Dr. Fueredi found it within minutes. He excelled at his profession and would perform the ultrasound for Mona. As soon as she arrived home, she'd call him—right now, she just needed to leave ASAP.

She walked out of the hospital without even noticing the world around her. Once the valet brought the car, she got in and held the steering wheel, unable to put it into drive. As she fought to summon the strength to move, she just held on to the wheel as she began to cry uncontrollably. The overwhelming fear of cancer flooded out in waves. Her hands were shaking, her breathing was shallow, and she gasped in between sobs. Then the questions came hard and fast.

Why me? What did I do wrong? I don't deserve cancer; I didn't do anything to deserve this. How much pain am I going to go through? What about the kids? How will they deal with their mom having cancer? How will they deal with it if I die?

She didn't want to miss the rest of their lives and she didn't want to miss the rest of *her* life, either. Like any mom, Mona wanted to watch her kids grow into adulthood. Now there was a very real chance she might not live to see our oldest even get to high school, much less graduate. All she could think was, *This CAN'T be happening to ME.*

After she let it all out, she started to gather herself with the admonition that she would fight with everything she had and that she needed to be strong. But this wasn't going to happen today. Mona had just faced her mortality in a very palpable sense—not just this theoretical knowledge that we will all die *someday*. True, there was a chance it was not cancer, but she had to face the fact that cancer was a very likely outcome that could rob her of all the plans she had ever made.

Throughout her battle, she'd also have to watch her children and husband cry every day as she endured chemo, surgery, and radiation. This prospect was simply terrifying. Mona had gone through hell for the past three months and was supposed to be through the worst of it. Life was supposed to get back to normal. But in one instant, she realized her trip through hell had just begun. She started to pray, asking God the questions we all ask: *Why me, God? What did I do?*

She waited for an answer that never came. *God, aren't you listening?*

Then she started to get angry. *Damn it! Why don't You answer me? Tell me what I did wrong!*

Of course, she was too scared to realize that God had been with her the entire time. That "bad feeling" she'd experienced when she was scheduled for a simple X-ray was His warning to get the CT. Listening to Him had enabled her to find the tumor and given her options that most people don't get. Usually, pancreatic cancers aren't even detected until they have already spread, after it's too late to do anything to save the patient's life. In Mona's case, she was finding the cancer before it caused any symptoms. She was finding it *because* of the crash.

God had been with her during the accident and would be with her now also. We all think God should save us from pain and hardship, but we were learning that was not His will. God is always with us *through* the pain, but He never promised a life *without* pain. We all need trials and tribulations to teach us how to cope and to force us to re-examine ourselves. God is there to guide us through to the other side.

Mona's thoughts began to shift from *Why?* to *Please help.* She knew this would be the hardest six months of her life, that she would endure more pain, more sickness, more trips to the hospital, and more doctors than ever before, even including the crash. Fear would be her constant companion as she went through all the treatment, with no guarantee she would live in the end. Worse yet, she had absolutely no control over where her life was headed.

All she could do was ask God for help. She told herself she should prepare for the fight—an easy thing to say. The first step was to just get home.

For Reflection

I will instruct you and teach you in the way you should go; I will counsel you with my eye upon you. (Psalms 32:8)

1. How does faith help you cope with bad news?
2. When someone is sick, is God punishing that person? What are some other possible explanations for why bad things happen?
3. God does not promise us life without pain. God promises to be with us to help us endure pain. Is this enough?

CHAPTER 29

HERE WE GO AGAIN

Mona hadn't called me to tell me the bad news. Instead, she drove home crying the whole way. Before walking into the house, she gathered herself so as not to scare the kids, but I noticed her deep red eyes and shiny, tear-stained face immediately. As she hung up her coat, the kids met her at the door while I rolled in on my wheelchair to inquire about her checkup. But the look on her face told me all I needed to know before I could even ask the question; now it was my turn to be shocked and confused. This was just supposed to be a recheck. I could see that her brace was off—why wasn't she happy? Instead of joy, her expression resonated utter devastation. Something was very wrong.

She quickly greeted the kids before we both headed to the bedroom for some privacy. The second the door closed behind us, I braced for the news, reaching for her hand as she sat down on the edge of the bed.

"They found a mass on my pancreas," she began. "They don't know what it is, but they are checking for a pancreatic tumor." In spite of her best efforts, she burst into tears. I just sat there in shock and fear as the tears began to stream down my face.

What could I say? *"Don't worry, it will be all right"?*

Give me a break! She had the absolute right to worry. There was no way I could tell her, "It will be all right," when she could die in a few months. Should I suggest, "Maybe they are wrong and it is nothing"? Being doctors ourselves, we had both diagnosed hundreds of animals with cancer and seen many, many tumors, fully aware that little else looks like a tumor—a round, solid mass that shouldn't be there. It is almost never just a normal structure that someone misinterpreted, and it was highly unlikely the doctors would be wrong about this. In that moment, there was simply not much I could say or do. Stuck in my wheelchair, I couldn't even hold my wife, so I just held her hands as we both sobbed.

After about ten minutes, the kids started knocking on the door. Even though they were young, they knew something was wrong. It was time to tell them. Our policy was to never lie to our kids, and we weren't about to start now. Yet we were also uncertain as to what we were dealing with and wouldn't have confirmation for a while.

Mona walked over and opened the door.

"Dad and I were just talking," she began. They could all tell we'd been crying; they knew there was trouble.

Never shy about asking questions, Alexa spoke up first, "What's wrong? Why are you both crying?"

"Mom will need some more tests from the doctor. She has something in her tummy that isn't supposed to be there." I hoped that would be the end of her questions, but of course that wasn't the case.

"What's in your tummy? Did you eat something you weren't supposed to?" Chase asked with the typical innocence of a four-year-old.

"No, it isn't anything I ate. We don't really know what it is yet. That is what the doctors will find out."

There was a brief pause during which I hoped this was the end of the conversation, but Alexa was not one to give up easily. The next question was the one I feared the most.

"Mommy, are you going to die?"

Now what to say? We honestly didn't know if Mona was going to live or die. I gazed over at my wife and noticed the tears beginning to flow again. Instantly, I felt my own eyes welling up once more as I struggled to speak without choking up. "Mom is going to have some more testing and the doctors will deal with it. This is what they are good at, so we will have to trust them."

I didn't really answer the question, but I didn't lie to them either. From the beginning, I always taught my kids to tell the truth; I surely was not going to lie to them about something as serious as this. They already knew something was up. The truth would emerge in the end anyway, and I didn't want to betray their trust. They were small, not stupid.

However, at their age, they did not have the capacity to deal with the thought of their mom dying, especially after they'd come so close to losing both of us a few months ago. Telling them that we did not know *was* the truth, and they deserved that.

The kids ran in and hugged their mother; the only thing they knew for certain was that they wanted to be with their mom and dad. All five of us just stood there holding each other because it was what we all needed. I realized then just how much we had relied on one another since the crash; in the aftermath of this dire prognosis, we would need one another even more.

Mona and I fully understood the gravity of what could happen and felt the overwhelming horror. Even though we didn't yet know much about the mass, we did know it was not good and was going to be a real bitch to remove. We were both aware that pancreatic surgery is one of the most technically difficult procedures to do and fraught with problems. The pancreas does not like anything or anyone messing with it, and it gets inflamed easily—a terribly painful problem with limited treatments. An inflamed or damaged pancreas can leak digestive enzymes into the surrounding tissues. Since these enzymes are designed to digest our foods, they have no trouble digesting any surrounding tissue. In our profession, we'd both seen animals suffering incredible pain from inflammation of the pancreas. Often, even our morphine drips were not enough to ease their discomfort. In Mona's case, because the surgeons would have to cut out the diseased pancreas and leave the rest, we both knew what was coming. It would be indescribably awful.

As I sat there motionless in my wheelchair, anger flared inside of me, along with a thought most would have in this situation: *God, why are we going through this? We can't handle anymore. Our family has been beaten and battered for months, and I thought this was over. I thanked you every day for saving me and now we're getting kicked again, facing possible—no, probable—cancer and quite possibly the death of my kids' mother and my wife. How much more can anyone face?*

We were both exhausted from our ordeal and now we realized the worst was yet to come. I wanted to face this with an upbeat and positive attitude, but we had both hit a wall of emotional and physical exhaustion that made it very easy to get angry. We needed rest and time together to heal from our injuries, but now we were about to start a new journey, one none of us wanted to take. We really had nowhere to go but down. Fear and anger flooded me in waves, worse than I had ever felt before.

We were simply worn out from fighting. This was the low point of all this, the point where we just wanted to give up.

Again, we had lost control, and that was the scariest part. As a dad, I was expected to protect the family, both my wife and kids. Now, I had no way to do this, no way to change the course of the next few months.

As I looked up, the kids were still huddled around looking at us; they hadn't said another word. I gazed over at Mona, who looked tired and scared. Nobody really knew what to say anymore. The thought of my great plan for my life flashed through my head again. It was all unraveling. I figured the mass would certainly need surgery and, if it was pancreatic cancer, it would kill Mona. Yes, I would continue to hope and pray it was all benign, that it would all turn out to be nothing, but the chances of that were slim. Our fate was completely out of our hands. I just didn't think we could do this.

Then that voice was back. *Yes, you can. You have done it before.*

Was that God speaking to me again? I can't say for sure. Once again, there was no burning bush in the desert. Yet as I looked at our family, I knew one thing: We had been through hell once, we had the support structures of family and community in place, and we knew all about hospitals and recovery from major surgery. We were ready for this. Yes, we *could* do it again.

The only thing we could really control was our attitude and behavior—the way in which we faced this new challenge. We had a choice: We could remain paralyzed in fear and anger, or we could take it on, no matter how tired we were or how difficult the struggle. We were going to go through it and I could not change that, but we could control *how* we went through it.

After two months of being cared for as a patient—of being a victim—it was time for me to take charge again. I was still in a wheelchair and had a splint on my left arm, and I was still close to twenty pounds underweight. Due to the pain meds I was still taking, I could not even drive, but I could set the tone. Mona was an incredibly strong woman who had kept it all together through what seemed to be the worst possible time we could imagine, but she was too close to this to carry the kids and me anymore. It was time for me to lead.

I also knew this was more than I could do by myself. We would have to support one another, but we would need help again from our families and friends. Even though we'd asked so much from them already, we would have to ask again, knowing we could rely on our families, church, and community to help pull us through as they had done the first time. The crash had helped to get everything into place in time for us to deal with this next obstacle. It had been a practice run, a warm-up for the real struggle coming down the road.

I released the hug for a second and announced, "We are going to fight this. We have been through a lot already, but that made us stronger for the fight we are now in. Getting through the last few months allowed us to put the people and faith in place to take this on. It will be tough, but we are tough already. This family can do this; we have done it before."

While I talked a good game, I still didn't think our determination would be enough. I did not start this journey as a person who let God into his life very much. Like most people, I had talked to God only when I needed help; I wanted him to hear me when I needed something or when I didn't get what I wanted. Rarely did I even stop to thank God when things went right.

Up until the crash, I really hadn't needed God's assistance for anything major in my life. I had prayed to get into veterinary school after I had applied, but I had earned excellent grades and done all the things required for admittance. It had never really occurred to me that I would *not* get in; I was still in control. When I asked Mona to marry me, I had prayed she would say "yes," but because I was pretty sure she would, I had control there too (obviously, Mona had control also, but I asked only when I was confident in the answer). I had prayed for healthy kids each time Mona was pregnant, but most children are born healthy in this part of the world and our family histories had few medical problems. For most of my life, I had simply never thought I needed God's help with anything. Even in the aftermath of the crash, I was not able to ask God for help since I was unconscious. Our collision with Jacobs's Jeep was the first time I had not been in control of the major changes in my life, and as my recovery progressed, I expected to get back in control very soon.

But once again, control had vanished. We would pray for help but acknowledge that it would be God's plan for the outcome, not ours. We would put ourselves into His hands, surrendering completely to Him and His will.

Mona was going to endure this hardship with the rest of us along for the ride. The kids and I would have to face the thought of losing a mother and wife we loved dearly, the woman who ran and organized our lives for us; a mother who loved and cared for me and the kids, tending to all of the mundane details. She was the "snuggler" for the kids, curling up with them under a blanket when they needed that kind of comfort. I saw myself as the provider and protector, though I wasn't even sure I could do that anymore. Our roles in the family were very different but complemented each other well. Now I faced the fact that I might be raising these kids alone—possibly without any way to provide for them.

We hugged and cried and held each other for a long time. The kids did not really understand the threat of pancreatic cancer; they didn't need to know the details, which was fine with me because I had none to give them anyway. Either the tumor was benign with no cause for worry, or their mother could be dead in months. As we consoled one another in silence, there was simply no way to know.

FOR REFLECTION

For the sake of Christ, then, I am content with weaknesses, insults, hardships, persecutions, and calamities. For when I am weak, then I am strong. (2 Corinthians 12:10)

1. How do you feel about telling children the truth about difficult situations? Is honesty always the best policy?
2. What do you think of the expression, "God won't give you more than you can handle"?
3. Have you ever been put through a hardship to prepare you for something more? What do such hardships teach us about ourselves?

Trust in the LORD with all your heart, and do not lean on your own understanding. In all your ways acknowledge him, and he will make straight your paths. (Proverbs 3:5–6)

4. Why do we pray for certain things when in the end everything is God's will? What use is praying?

CHAPTER 30

Good Things Happen
to Good People

The first step was to call Dr. George Fueredi to get an ultrasound. Mona had the CT images on a disk in her hand, but she was too shaken to speak to him. I had his number on my cell and dialed him as soon as I felt I could get through the call.

When he answered, I identified myself, prompting him to cheerfully inquire as to my well-being. I told him I was getting better but we had a problem with Mona and I needed his help.

"Anything you need. Shoot."

I filled him in on her latest news, requesting that he please take a look at the CT and offer his opinion.

"Do you have the images?" he asked. "I could get access through the network, but that may take a while."

"I have the CD in my hand."

George replied, "I'm on my way over. Should I meet you at the clinic or your house?"

"We are at the house right now and I am in no condition to drive, so could you come over here?"

"I'll be there in a half-hour."

This was above and beyond the call of duty. Physicians and vets have great respect for each other; they also understand the busyness of our professions and thus will call for favors only when absolutely necessary.

George had brought in his hunting dogs to our practice a few times on emergency—usually needing stitches. But he had also nursed them through the night a few times to avoid having to call after hours. Nonetheless, he had three big Labs I'd examined more than once in the middle of the night. I had given him my cell number so he could call me any time and not have to take his dogs to someone he didn't know.

Now he was returning the favor. He could have stopped by on his way home from work, but that would have left us hanging for hours. He dropped everything with the intention of arriving on our doorstep as soon as possible.

Within twenty minutes, George was knocking at our front entrance, where I met him in my wheelchair, welcomed him into our home, and led him to the computer. Although I'd already loaded the images, I had not looked at them. Doing CTs on dogs and cats was very new when I was in vet school and I had not been trained to read them; I had no idea what I was looking at. I needed expert advice, so George began scrolling through.

"There it is," he said, pointing to the screen.

As he continued to scroll down, the mass was clear. It was about the size of a quarter, round and solid. I could see large vessels all around it. I knew it would be in a really tough spot to remove. If I had found this in a dog, it would have been nonresectable. This was not good.

George continued: "Let me show this to a colleague and get the blood work. They probably checked some tumor markers and I want to see the results. I should be able to get the results today; I will put my assistant on it as soon as I get back to the hospital. I have a friend I'd like to take a look at this, but I may not get the opinion until tomorrow. I will have him check it out right away. Regardless, Mona will need an ultrasound. We'll do it as soon as I see the blood results."

"Thanks, George," I replied gratefully. "I really appreciate your help and getting over here so quickly."

"No problem. You both have met me more than once with my boys. I'm glad you called."

With that he left, CD in hand. I returned to Mona and announced we'd have another opinion by tomorrow.

"I just can't believe I have cancer," she sighed, tears flowing and voice cracking. "I never felt sick; I just don't know why this is happening to me. What did I do wrong?"

These were the same questions I'd asked during my recovery. *Why me? What did I do wrong?* They're the questions everyone asks when they're embarking on a trip through hell.

"Mona," I began, "I can't believe it either. We've been through a lot already, but we learned in the crash that we do not see the big picture, His big plan for us. We were both angry that we had gotten into the crash and that it wasn't fair, but the crash enabled us to find this thing on your pancreas. Maybe God put us in the crash that day just for that purpose. Maybe *that* was the reason all along. Maybe He put us in Jacobs's path to *save* us, not to hurt us. Now that we found it, we can deal with it. This is another hurdle to get over. We will face it the same way we faced the others. We will bear down and do it together. We have done it before, so we can do it again."

With that, we both just cried together for a long time, knowing that the next few months would be the hardest yet.

For Reflection

And let us not grow weary of doing good, for in due season we will reap, if we do not give up. (Galatians 6:9)

1. Think about favors. How do you feel if someone does you a favor and you can't pay it back? How do you feel about the idea of paying something forward?

2. How can we use our faith and the angels in our lives to cope with shocking news?

CHAPTER 31

A GLIMMER OF HOPE

The next day, Mona drove me to rehab as usual, and I spent over an hour working on my body while my mind focused exclusively on her. Pancreatic cancer: I still couldn't believe it. More bad news, more struggles. Now I could lose my wife in the next six months. Could I raise the kids on my own? It was a struggle before the crash to balance work and the kids with both of us healthy. How could I do it with just me, especially when I was nowhere close to the physical condition I enjoyed before the crash? My youngest was just about to turn five—big enough to get himself dressed and into the car seat, but he still needed a father who could keep up with him, playing and roughhousing. I still needed to carry groceries and do yard work. Various things around the house would still need fixing, but crawling under a sink was impossible with arms and legs that still did not bend.

What if I could no longer work? I had some disability insurance but not enough to maintain the lifestyle we had had before the crash, especially if I was the sole parent. Mona had some life insurance, but we had never taken out a huge amount since we were both relatively young and healthy. Most likely, we would have to sell the house and downsize. I had never been emotionally attached to any house, including this one, but I also hated moving with a passion, and the kids had never lived in town. This would be all new when what they needed was normality.

John, my new physical therapist, could tell my mind was racing. He didn't ask any questions, however, knowing I would tell him if I wanted to. At this point, I was nowhere near ready to talk about it. Any mention of Mona's pancreatic cancer incited immediate tears.

Since I could not drive on my own, John's assistant gave me a ride. This was a wonderful service John offered to clients who were unable to operate a vehicle. Mona, in an amazing show of toughness, went into work that day. We were still dependent on the business to generate our income so she put in a full day at the office. The staff did not even know anything was wrong.

About two o'clock, my cell phone rang. It was George.

"Scot, I tried to call Mona, but she didn't answer."

"Yeah, she's at work."

"Really? Wow. Anyway, I showed the CT to Dr. Jackson. He is a leading specialist in arteriovenous fistulas. He thinks this may be one, not a tumor."

I couldn't believe it. An arteriovenous fistula is an abnormal connection between an artery and a vein. Arteries carry oxygenated blood into the tissues, and veins carry the deoxygenated blood back to the heart. The blood then goes back through the arteries and the process starts all over again.

An arteriovenous fistula (called an AV fistula) bypasses the tissues and allows arterial blood, under high pressure, to flow directly into the vein, which is under very low pressure. This subjects the vein to high arterial blood pressure it was never designed to handle, making its thin walls bulge and give the appearance of a mass. In this scenario, a vein wall often ruptures, leading to a potentially fatal hemorrhage.

These AV fistulas often develop after injury when the artery and vein are torn and fuse together during the healing process. This fit with what had happened to Mona during the crash when they suspected internal bleeding and a "bruise" (a torn blood vessel) on her pancreas. It was a dangerous thing and it would have to be fixed, but it wasn't cancer.

"Can Mona come in tomorrow at seven? She can meet with Dr. Jackson and I will do the ultrasound. If it shows what we expect, maybe I can try to fix this thing tomorrow afternoon. I already cleared my schedule so I'll have time to do it. It should not involve major surgery, but I want to get on it before it tears. Mona may even go home that night if it goes well."

I was thrilled. This was great news! *Not cancer—just an AV fistula that a friend can cure without major surgery?* That was the best news in the world. God was smiling on us again. All those good things we had done in our lives were paying off.

"George, I can't thank you enough. We will be there at seven."

I hung up and called Mona right away. My hands were shaking with excitement. Things had always worked out for us in the past, and now I thought the luck, good karma, whatever you want to call it, was returning. We had dodged a bullet and were not going to have to deal with cancer after all.

Of course, I forgot to thank God.

"Hello," Mona answered.

"Mona, I just got off the phone with George; that buddy of his looked at the CT. He thinks the mass is an AV fistula, not a tumor. They want to try to fix it tomorrow. This is great news."

There was a pause. I expected her to be jumping and screaming with joy, but there was nothing on the other end of the line but silence.

"Did you hear me?"

"Yeah, I did. I'm not going to get too excited."

"Not too excited? They don't think this is cancer anymore."

"They don't know for sure. I have to hope they are right, but I will not be convinced until they are sure. I have an appointment waiting."

I hung up the phone a bit deflated. She was right in that they did not know for sure what this was and they would be unlikely to find out for sure tomorrow, even after the procedure. They would guide a catheter up from Mona's groin and feed it into the vessels surrounding the mass. Once in the right vessel, they would deposit a "coil," basically a small spring that expands once released that wedges itself into the vessel. This foreign substance quickly becomes covered with a blood clot that fills the vessel, cutting off the blood supply. Eventually, if the inflow to the AV fistula is cut off, the whole thing scars up and is gone forever.

Mona decided to inform Dr. Wilson and left a message explaining Dr. Jackson's diagnosis and her impending procedure the next day. In less than an hour, Dr. Wilson called back.

"Hi, Mona. I had the radiologist look again at the CT. They still think it is a mass."

"I know, Dr. Wilson, and I hate to second-guess you, but Dr. Jackson disagrees."

"I would love to be wrong, but I've been doing this for forty years now, and I think it's clearly a mass."

"If I have this done and it ends up being a tumor, would that change the surgery if you end up having to do it later?"

"Maybe. The coils may change the blood supply and I may have to adapt. I hope I can, but it complicates an already complicated surgery."

This was not very consoling; Mona could hear some irritation in Dr. Wilson's voice as much as he was trying to hide it.

Dr. Wilson was convinced she had a tumor that needed to be removed immediately. Nobody likes to be told he's wrong, especially a doctor, but it was Mona's call, and this was the decision she had made.

"Good luck tomorrow. Let me know how it turns out."

She hung up with the thought that she had ticked off the man she might ask to save her life down the road.

We showed up for her procedure the next day. While I beamed with excitement that this would cure her, she remained cautious.

"Mona, things have always gone well for us. This will also," I stated confidently. We were good people, and I was positive God would look after us.

When we met with Dr. Jackson, he painstakingly went through the CT, pointing out what he saw and his findings. When he was done, he asked if we had any questions,

"Dr. Wilson in Milwaukee thinks this is a tumor. He said that this is what he does and this should come out."

"I understand, but this is what *I* do and *I* think it is an AV fistula. We should be able to coil this without major surgery."

"When will we know if it worked?" Mona asked.

"In about a month, we will recheck a CT to see if the mass is gone. If it is, we are done. If not, we will re-evaluate."

Re-evaluate?

Such an event would mean it was really a tumor and we'd lost valuable time by waiting an extra month to have it removed. It was a risk, but it just made better sense that this was anything but a tumor. Mona was only thirty-eight; she could not really have cancer. It just couldn't be; enough bad things had happened to us, and we were not bad people. We deserved this to be something other than cancer. Unlike the procedure Dr. Wilson suggested, this one was minimally invasive. It just *had* to work.

After Mona shook her head to indicate she had no more questions, Dr. Jackson left. That's when I gripped her hand and assured her, "This is the right thing. They will find out that this is just an AV fistula from the crash and we will go home tonight cured. Dr. Wilson was a good doctor, but he was wrong here. He saw every mass as a tumor, not something like this. He also didn't really know us; our families don't get cancer."

Sure, some of our family members had dealt with cancer, but all had been at least sixty years old and/or smokers. By contrast, we were still young, had never smoked, and had kept ourselves in pretty good shape by being active and eating relatively healthy. Cancer did not happen to people like us; it happened to bad people or smokers or people who did not take care of themselves. "We have always been lucky," I told Mona. "Today we get lucky again."

Mona smiled and nodded. Still, there was doubt and fear in her eyes. I was a little offended that she didn't see the simple logic that this was an AV fistula from vessels tearing during the crash, because it just made perfect sense.

"We'll see what happens," she replied.

In about an hour, the nurse came in and administered some morphine to sedate Mona. "Take this and we'll call you when she is done," the nurse informed me, handing me a pager similar to the ones they use in restaurants. In a few minutes, the morphine kicked in and they wheeled Mona into the prep room. I kissed her goodbye and told her that we just had to clear this one hurdle and we would both be through the worst.

She nodded but, again, did not look very confident. "We'll see," she muttered, half-dazed from the sedative.

Two hours went by before they paged me that the procedure was done. I crutched over to Mona's room to see her, still heavily sedated with her head back and her mouth slightly open. She turned to me as I said her name.

"Did they get it?" she asked.

"I haven't spoken to anyone yet," I answered. Mona did not smile; she just turned her head.

A few minutes later, Dr. Jackson walked in. "How did it go?" I blurted out.

"The procedure went fine," he answered. "It was more vascular than we had hoped, but we coiled and injected everything we could see."

"Great," I replied. "When can she go home?"

"Tomorrow. I want to watch her incision tonight in case there are any problems."

"Okay, thank you for all you have done. This was much better than the invasive procedure Dr. Wilson wanted to do."

"I will order a CT in a month and see how everything looks. We can't tell much before then."

With that, Dr. Jackson left and I turned to Mona. "The procedure went well; they said they got it. You are over the last hurdle."

"He said the procedure went well, but he didn't say they cured it. They got all the vessels they could see, but he did not say he was sure it was an AV fistula."

Even through the haze of morphine, Mona had heard every word. She was right; the doctor did not say she was cured. I had heard what I wanted to hear, what I had *expected* to hear. An AV fistula would fit perfectly into my perceptions of how this should go, as well as my new plan for our lives, but the doctor had not definitively stated one way or another what we were confronting.

The next day, Mona left the hospital. She was sore in her groin where they had made the incision and located her femoral artery but was otherwise doing well. She was only sent home on ibuprofen for pain and some OxyContin if needed. She took the Oxy the first day and slept but was off it by the second day. While she felt good physically, emotionally she was on pins and needles. It would be a month before she would know if we'd made the right decision. In the meantime, Mona's life hung in the balance.

The fact was, in medicine this happens all the time. Most diagnoses are educated guesses based on formal training and real-life experience. No one is 100 percent accurate, and all doctors—no matter how brilliant—will be wrong at times. The problem is that a doctor's "wrong" analysis has the potential to end your life. If Dr. Jackson was wrong and this really was a tumor, would a month's delay make a difference? Would the coils he put in make removing the tumor more difficult? We didn't know, but it could mean the difference between life and death.

Now we were expected to go back to our lives as if nothing were happening while we waited for confirmation. I remained optimistic.

Up until the crash, we had always avoided major bumps in the road; I expected this to be no different.

I was reformulating the *plan* for the rest of our lives. Sure, the first plan had been changed when the crash happened, but now we were back on course and I figured I could see the road ahead. Mona would heal up and get good news in a month; the AV fistula would be gone. I would continue rehab and my body would heal. I had a long road but was making progress and was not going to die from my injuries. I could see that I would be back to work in a few months. Though I still needed a lot of OxyContin to get through the day's activities— especially rehab—that was okay. It wasn't like I was addicted. The Oxy was necessary with the injuries I had. I could stop anytime once the pain was gone.

The next month was spent trying to get better. Mona took three days off after surgery and went back to work. She put on a happy face, telling each client who asked that I was healing well and she was fine. This was getting a little old since she repeated the story about twenty times a day.

Being on her feet all day was very tough. The clinic has a tile floor that holds up great against dogs but is incredibly hard on your feet. Now she was asked to stand on it all day with a sore back and groin. With her characteristic toughness, Mona made it through, but at the end of the day, she was completely exhausted. Thankfully, we were still getting food delivered from the church, which was what we all lived on for the next month. Each delivery was like manna from heaven for Moses in the desert.

I figured we had beaten the odds. I was more and more upbeat as I thanked God for helping us through this latest scare. Mona was much less optimistic, saying she would believe it when she saw the next CT.

I was confident that things had worked out for us again. We had been basically good people and helped countless animals and owners with our skills. We would be rewarded for our good works by avoiding cancer. It all made perfect sense. My view of how God worked would be confirmed: Good things happen to good people. That was what I expected. That was my new plan.

FOR REFLECTION

And after you have suffered a little while, the God of all grace, who has called you to his eternal glory in Christ, will himself restore, confirm, strengthen, and establish you. (1 Peter 5:10)

"Let not your hearts be troubled. Believe in God; believe also in me. In my Father's house are many rooms. If it were not so, would I have told you that I go to prepare a place for you? And if I go and prepare a place for you, I will come again and will take you to myself, that where I am you may be also. And you know the way to where I am going." Thomas said to him, "Lord, we do not know where you are going. How can we know the way?" (John 14:1–5)

1. Why does God let bad things happen to good people?
2. Mona had lingering suspicions that her mass was cancer. Do you think that was God talking to her? Why or why not?
3. Have you ever felt apprehension even when others were telling you everything would be fine? Were you right or wrong? How do you feel now when you look back on that experience?

CHAPTER 32

Now I Get It

A month after surgery, Mona returned to the hospital for another CT. I didn't go along since I was still extremely immobile and the results would not be read for a few days. She scheduled a meeting with Dr. Jackson for two days later to discuss the findings.

The delay was terrible: two days of pure stress and anxiety while waiting to find out if you've been cured and can close an awful chapter in your life, or if you have cancer, will need major surgery, chemo, and still might die, regardless of your medical team's best efforts.

In this kind of scenario, there's very little you can do to ease your mind and live life normally. Mona tried to go back to work, but her every thought focused upon her upcoming meeting about her test results. Putting on a brave face, she went through the motions of her life—working, tending to my needs, taking care of the kids, sharing my latest health updates with every client (most clients assumed she was all better since she was back at work)—all while coping with overwhelming anxiety. Two days seemed like a year.

The morning of the second day, her phone rang while she was at work. It was George. Mona's heart seemed to stop beating as she picked up the phone, knowing she would finally have her answer one way or another.

"Hi, George," she answered as she sprinted to get to the break room and away from everyone.

Dispensing with the formalities, he got right to it. "Hi, Mona, I have your results." His voice was clinical; he was speaking as a doctor, not as a friend.

"Mona, the mass is still there."

Immediately, she knew what that meant. This was a tumor, not an AV fistula as we had hoped, but more like what *she* had expected. Her lingering pessimism had been accurate. That voice in her head was right again.

George continued, "I spoke with Dr. Jackson and he agrees, you need to have this removed surgically. We could try the procedure again, but I don't think it is an AV fistula."

Her hands were shaking as she collapsed onto a couch.

"Thank you for the call, George. I guess I will call Dr. Wilson and beg him to take me on again."

"Dr. Wilson is a good man and you are in the best of hands. Good luck. Mona, I am truly sorry that we were wrong here."

"We both know medicine is not an exact science, George. I'll call Dr. Wilson. Tell Dr. Jackson I appreciate his efforts."

With that, she hung up the phone. A flood of fear washed over her as she sat there alone in the break room. Meanwhile, the busy practice was humming along while her next appointments awaited her. My wife had to process the news of her having pancreatic cancer all alone in an employee lounge. A wave of nausea compelled her to run for the bathroom while she broke out in a sweat, her heart racing. Then the tears came—an unstoppable torrent of sobs. Her world had crashed yet again.

After a few minutes, our office manager and good friend, Karen, knocked on the door.

"Mona, are you all right?"

When she opened the door, Karen immediately knew what had happened.

"Did the doctor call?"

Mona nodded.

That was all it took. Mona and Karen had always been very close, in part because Karen had been our first employee. She knew immediately that it had been confirmed by the doctor that Mona had pancreatic cancer. Karen encircled Mona in her arms as she cried along with her, without another word spoken. These two had been through a lot over the years, but this was entirely different; this was life and death, not an irate client or someone wanting to return half-used medicine. It was Mona's mortality and it was downright terrifying.

After a few minutes of holding her close, Karen pulled away and told her, "I will cancel your appointments; Chris and Kay can handle the rest of today. Give me a minute and I will drive you home."

When Mona arrived, I was in bed resting from my physical therapy session. She made a beeline for the closet as she walked into our bedroom, yet I didn't really notice in my oxycodone-induced stupor. "You're home early," I observed, oblivious to anything being wrong. There was no answer.

A minute later, she emerged from the closet dressed in pajamas in an effort to just get comfortable. By now, I saw her face and noticed she had been crying.

"Did you get the results?"

"George called," she replied, and immediately I knew what it was.

"It's still there?"

"Yeah, I knew it was a tumor," she declared.

"I'll call Dr. Wilson."

"I don't know if he will see me after I doubted him."

"Of course he'll see you. I can't see him putting his pride in front of your health. We've had enough people going and getting a second opinion and then coming back to us that we know how it is. You don't turn them away; if anything, you welcome them back since now they trust you completely. It's the same for us; we believe him now and will trust what he says. If he turns you away, then he was not the man we thought he was and we don't want him as our doctor anyway."

I realized this was another lesson from our first stay in the hospital. We'd gotten good at picking the right doctors for us. Having to pick and choose among various physicians throughout our ordeal taught us what to look for: confidence without arrogance. We wanted someone we could talk to, who would spend the time answering our questions, someone who could put our needs ahead of his wounded pride and ego. We wanted a doctor whom the nurses liked and recommended. I had found it with Dr. Lang and thought I knew Dr. Wilson well enough to expect the same qualities in him. I did not think he would let us down.

Mona's eyes filled with tears, as did mine. At this point, we had no idea which type of pancreatic cancer Mona would be facing, but we knew we needed a biopsy to find out. The surgery would be grueling, and Mona would end up with a large scar. Facing a fatal disease consumed her with fear and dread.

Again, there was no booming voice nor any burning bush in the desert, but I knew God was telling me something loud and clear: Neither I nor Mona was going to be in charge. The only one in control of any of this was God. In the end, it was all part of a larger plan. It could not have been more perfect: The breaks in Mona's back were the first and second lumbar vertebrae (the mid-back just below the last rib) and just "happened" to be directly over the pancreas. Of all the places and bones that could have been broken, she broke the ones inches away from a silent but potentially deadly tumor. The radiologists *had* to focus on this area and would no doubt see it. This was more than a coincidence; I could not believe this was just plain luck. This was God's plan; it was Him in control. This was the reason for all we had endured in the last few months. The crash, my survival, and Mona's injuries were all about getting Mona a CT of her pancreas. The whole ordeal was about finding her tumor. I had been looking for the reason God had put *me* through this when it really had nothing to do with *me* at all.

I also realized once again that I was not, nor had I ever been, in control of anything. My life had been directed for me, and the crash was just part of God's plan. I thought back about the day at the cabin. My last memory had been of going to check the door to make sure it was locked. I remember sitting in the car ready to head out and *needing* to recheck. I walked up knowing I had locked the door and uncertain as to why I was checking it again. I had just had this feeling to do it and had learned to trust that gut feeling when I got it. I remember walking back to the car muttering to myself about wasting time checking something I already knew was OK. That half-minute delay had ultimately put us in line with Jacobs. Had I not obeyed my gut feeling, we would have been a half-mile ahead and evaded the crash. In that case, we would not have found Mona's tumor. That voice in my head was God's, telling me to do as He said; it had nothing to do with a locked door.

I also thought about the other warning I had been given the night before the crash as I was preparing for bed, the one that told me, "If a car comes across the median, your job is to protect the kids in back." There had been something about it that forced me to pay attention. Somehow it had seemed a very important thought, though I didn't understand why. But there had been no mention of protecting Mona. I had just assumed she was included among the people I was told to safeguard. But the voice had mentioned only the kids. God did not want me to protect Mona, just the kids. Mona *needed* to break her back if we were going to find the tumor that was inside of her. That night in the cabin before all of this had started, I hadn't fully understood the meaning of this apparently random thought, but now it stopped me in my tracks. I had not seen the entire picture and could not possibly foresee where our lives were heading, but now I did. Nearly six months later, it finally made sense.

Now I understood that Mona *had* to break her back to ensure they found the tumor. God was telling me He would take care of *us*, not just *me*; just do *exactly* as He says. Don't ask why. This is true faith: not asking why, not understanding why, but trusting Him nonetheless.

I thought about my survival with the clotting problem that should have killed me, the one-in-a-hundred chance that the factor VIII shot would save my life. I thought about how Dr. Lang had kept me alive with his quick thinking and superior skills. I thought about how he wasn't supposed to even be there that day, how he had changed his schedule due to coaching his son's football game, which placed him at the scene that Sunday instead of Saturday. How he was supposed to be gone at noon but was stuck filling out paperwork after his shift when the call came that we were on our way. His subsequent decision to help rather than go home. How the man who would make all the right decisions in his effort to preserve my life had not even been scheduled to work a shift at the hospital that day.

Too many things had gone right; too many things had fallen into place to attribute it to just random luck. As I sat there and pondered everything, I was amazed that a collision that had nearly killed us had ultimately saved us.

Though I could not tell for sure, I simply couldn't believe God would take us through this horrific ordeal only for us to lose Mona in the end. It just could *not* be. We had become a very close and strong family, tempered by pain and fear. We were now focused on what was right, not money or business or popularity, but on being better people. We had grown spiritually and emotionally. We were better in so many ways that it couldn't end with Mona dying. *It just couldn't.* Still, I knew that only God was the final decision-maker and I could easily lose my wife.

I really did not know the details of His plan, but I had to believe that the discovery of this tumor represented the good that comes from the bad. Some refer to it as the silver lining; I call it our spiritual workout. Like one of those ninety-day programs advertised on infomercials, the crash was an intense training program that pushed us to our limits and made us stronger than we ever thought we could be. As with the physical workouts, it takes great drive, dedication, and discipline to achieve the desired results. There were many times when we wanted to just quit, but we kept going. Now we saw the benefits. We had a long way to go physically, but mentally and spiritually we'd changed for the better. It had been arduous work to get to this point—a long, hard slog—but we were truly ready to confront this next challenge.

Our spiritual and emotional workout had prepared us to go the distance. It was the hardest thing we had ever done, but the result was strength. There was no easy way; we had to put in the work if we wanted to be fortified beyond anything we'd experienced before.

In the end, it forced me to re-examine who I was as a person and my relationship with God. Before the crash, I had thought I could handle anything; now I knew I could not. My spiritual growth had been achieved as I worked through my pain and fear of what lay ahead. Yes, I had definitely needed to become a better person, but before I could, I had to invest the time and energy. Otherwise, I would revert to the arrogant S.O.B. I was before the crash. I would receive nothing in return for all of this pain and work and be just like the person who faithfully does the workout for three months, gets in great shape, and then goes back to his old, unhealthy lifestyle—the one he'd sought to change in the first place.

However, I was ready to change permanently, having understood the extent to which my life was beyond my control and how God wanted me to take a different course. We humans are naturally resistant to change; it usually takes a major cuff upside the head (figuratively speaking, or in my case, a literal whack of my face against the airbag) for a person to realize he is doing something wrong. Of course, if all had continued to go well, with no pain in my life, I would not have had a reason to change. And that is why God had to give us a wake-up call to get our attention and force a spiritual transformation—we hadn't been listening.

I remembered something I had once been told: "People only change when the pain of what they are doing is greater than the pain of change." That is why drug addicts or alcoholics can stop using and become sober only after they finally hit rock bottom. They will change when the pain of their addiction is greater than the pain of quitting. Now I was forced to see that the crash had changed me; it just wasn't an easy realization.

Previously, I'd thought we were pretty good people. Now I knew God thought I could do better. Therefore, like many other fathers when their son steps out of line and isn't paying attention, He gave me a good whack in order to wake me up.

Yes, God, you have my attention now.

Strangely, I felt a real peace, a peace that came from knowing He was in control and we were just along for the ride wherever it took us. We had been through it once; we could do it again.

Our family had made it through hospitals and recovery; this time around, we were seasoned veterans, not rookies. All the pieces were in place to support us. Our families were together and strong. They knew their roles and what to do to help us; they would take care of the kids while Mona had surgery, they would transport us to and from the hospital, and they would feed the animals and keep the house clean.

Once the community found out about this latest health scare, it would rally around us. The church would deliver meals and keep prayer chains going. Our pastors would visit the hospital. Our partner and employees could run the business until we returned, with no bickering or complaints.

This struggle would be a terrible one, but we had confidence going in that at least we could handle it. We were simply better prepared for dealing with this than we had been just a few months back. We were ready.

I was still terrified by the cancer and the prospect of losing Mona. The thought of our young son and daughters having to witness their mother wasting away to her ultimate death was unbearable. Yet there was also hope that we could remove the tumor and cure her—all because we had found the cancer early, thanks to an eight-time drunk driver named Mike Jacobs.

FOR REFLECTION

But rejoice insofar as you share Christ's sufferings, that you may also rejoice and be glad when his glory is revealed. (1 Peter 4:13)

1. Over what things do you believe humans have control, if any? If all is God's plan, how do our actions play into that plan?

2. Do you believe the crash was God's way of making sure Mona's pancreatic tumor was found? Why didn't God simply help the doctors find it some other way?

3. I ultimately realized that the crash that nearly killed my family is actually what saved us. How do you feel about that statement? Do you agree?

4. What are some of the ways that God changes us throughout our lives?

5. Can we change and grow strong without struggle?

6. Do you believe God always answers our prayers? Do you think God can ever answer us without our knowing? Explain your thinking.

7. Describe a time when God has used an unlikely person to make a positive impact in your life.

CHAPTER 33

THIS AIN'T GOING TO BE EASY

We called Dr. Wilson immediately. I don't know if he's a Christian, but he certainly acted like one: He was kind, gracious, and forgiving. He never held a grudge against us for doubting his judgment the first time; instead he scheduled Mona for surgery a week later. She would have a Whipple procedure to remove a large part of her pancreas. They would also remove dozens of lymph nodes to look for evidence of spread.

This surgery is very risky—one of the most technically difficult performed on a routine basis. Dr. Wilson would have to cut out the section of pancreas with the tumor and leave the rest. This is fraught with potentially deadly problems.

Because Mona's tumor was smack in the middle of her pancreas, Dr. Wilson would have to cut on each side of it, creating two separate cuts into the organ. These cuts would then release enzymes every time Mona ate anything. These enzymes would leak into the surrounding tissue and do just what they are designed to do: digest any tissue they touch. This "self-digestion" inflicts widespread damage and inflammation in the tissues surrounding the pancreas.

There is no magic drug to stop it. The treatment is to simply abstain from eating to prevent the release of digestive enzymes while waiting for the inflammation to subside. The hope was that the cut ends of the pancreas, sewn together by Dr. Wilson, would heal—a process that could require days or weeks of pain and vomiting before Mona could even attempt to eat again. In the meantime, the hospital staff tending to her would fight dehydration and muscle degeneration.

Mona understood all the ramifications. She knew the recovery from this surgery would be tough and would involve the administration of morphine for several days to ease excruciating pain. She also knew the morphine would make her nauseated, constipated, and paranoid, but she'd have no choice but to take it.

She would spend days to weeks wanting to vomit at the sight or smell of food. Of course, vomiting with a fresh, long abdominal incision just compounded her fears. She knew this would be hell.

The incision itself would run from her ribs to below her belly button. There was no minimally invasive way to do a Whipple; she would inevitably be left with a huge scar. Such a visible sign on her body would oppose her natural tendency to eliminate bad memories by suppressing them. The constant presence of this scar would ensure that she'd never forget her battle with cancer.

Though most pancreatic cancers are very aggressive, Dr. Wilson suspected Mona's was less so, a neuroendocrine tumor. Mona's tumor's characteristics and the extent of its spread within her body would determine whether she lived or died. The Whipple, with all its risks, was our only real option. Chemo, radiation, and even holistic treatments weren't the best choices. Most pancreatic masses do not respond well to chemo; radiation would blast the tumor trying to kill it but would not arrest or contain any spread; and holistic treatments sound good but rarely work.

The only course of action was to get this thing out for further examination and diagnosis. After consulting with Dr. Wilson again, I humbly asked him to save Mona.

God had taught us another lesson: humility.

While elated that Dr. Wilson would do the surgery, we were also very aware that we were headed right back into hell.

For Reflection
When pride comes, then comes disgrace, but with the humble is wisdom. (Proverbs 11:2)

Pride goes before destruction, and a haughty spirit before a fall. (Proverbs 16:18)

1. What does God say about pride and forgiveness? How does Dr. Wilson exemplify humility and compassion?

Whoever believes in the Son has eternal life; whoever does not obey the Son shall not see life, but the wrath of God remains on him. (John 3:36)

2. Mona and I knew we were going back into hell when we had to deal with the pancreatic tumor. How can you prepare yourself spiritually to go through hell? Is this the meaning of faith?

CHAPTER 34

A FORK IN THE ROAD

The days leading to surgery were characterized by pure, relentless stress as we attempted to live as if nothing was wrong. It was completely insane. How could we go back to our old routine when in a matter of days, Mona would find out she had a cancer that could kill her in a few months, a few years, or never?

I wasn't much help because I was still pretty immobile and dealing with my own never-ending pain. Due to the drugs, driving was forbidden, and I could walk only with the aid of crutches. No matter how much I wanted to, I couldn't console Mona or assure her everything would be all right since she knew things might not be.

In preparation for her possible death, Mona wrote letters to all the kids and me to be opened if God called her home. She wanted each of us to know the exact nature and scope of her immense pride and love for us all, focusing only on the positive—not on the fact that if we were reading her letters, she would be gone.

Ultimately, we decided that all we could do was pray. And pray we did—alone, together, and with our pastors. Our church set up another prayer chain that enlisted hundreds, if not thousands, to pray for Mona much like they had done for us after the crash. We had to rely on our faith now more than ever. Even after everything we'd been through, it was still incredibly difficult to face the fact that the outcome of this new challenge was completely out of our hands. We longed to have control of our lives back.

One night, I awoke to the sound of Mona sobbing in another room because she was just so incredibly scared. She told me the thought of the pain that comes with aggressive pancreatic cancer was terrifying her more than the thought of death itself. We had both seen what cancer can do to animals and the torture it inflicts upon them. As veterinarians, we could end their suffering with a shot. A few times a week, animals would come into our practice clearly in need of euthanasia. Invariably, we'd experience great relief as we ended their pain. Now Mona faced the fact there was a strong chance she would have aggressive pancreatic cancer that would subject her to indescribable misery over the next few months before robbing her of her life. Since there was no way to humanely euthanize people, humans were left to suffer in excruciating pain for days or weeks—much longer than we would ever allow an animal to go on.

Mona and I both had great reservations about doctor-assisted suicide, but when you are the one facing this terrible possibility, those reservations go out the window. Having been raised Catholic, she was worried she would go to hell if she took her own life, but the thought of a slow death from pancreatic cancer frightened her even more. For now, she prayed that if God were to take her, He would not allow her to suffer too much. Privately, she had a syringe full of euthanasia solution that she used on dogs in an IV that she could place if she needed to kill herself. Yes, at thirty-nine years old, my wife had to plan how to end her life if circumstances demanded it.

Amazingly she continued to go to work, trying to act concerned about a dog's itchy ear or a cat's diarrhea. Mona confessed that being at the practice made time go faster and took her mind off her upcoming date with destiny while the kids were in school and I was lying in bed. But the thought of her having cancer never left our minds. It is easy to say, "We are all going to die someday," but when that day could be a few days or months away, it is in a whole new realm. Logically, we might accept that we are all going to die, but we assume that we have plenty of time. When that time is short, when it has a definite endpoint, the thought of death reverberates through your head every three seconds. It is nearly impossible to think of anything else. Life just kind of stops.

Day after day, we kept going in a daze. Nothing could really progress until we had a full understanding and knowledge of the cancer. Time dragged on as we both counted the hours. We should have been doing all the fun and crazy things we had always dreamed of, but we were simply too scared. Should Mona jump out of an airplane when the possibility of cancer would steal the joy from what would normally be an exhilarating adventure? Awareness that impending death was the only reason for skydiving at this time in our lives would kind of take the thrill out of it.

On the day of the surgery, we arrived at the hospital at five o'clock in the morning. We could have arrived at two since neither one of us slept that night anyway. They wanted her there early so she could be ready for surgery at any time. Mona walked and I was on crutches as we approached the check-in desk, where after looking us both up and down, the receptionist asked what *I* was having done that day. I then explained that my wife was the patient, not me, and that she was here for a Whipple—the complex operation that would remove the head of the pancreas, the first part of the small intestine, the gallbladder, and the bile duct.

A bit embarrassed by the mistake, the receptionist apologized. I also noticed a change in her expression when we mentioned the word *Whipple*. First, surprise that a young woman needed this risky surgery, followed by a noticeable sadness as she helped us fill out the necessary forms. Although she made a gallant effort to stay upbeat and positive, we both sensed the change. This woman appeared to be the same age as Mona and no doubt knew that this procedure was done only for pancreatic cancers, which seldom turn out well.

We went up to the third-floor surgery ward, already bustling with the day's activity. Nurses walked quickly back and forth in the halls setting IVs, filling out forms, and going through checklists to ensure each patient was identified and could recite which surgery they were having done. Mona was told to change into a surgery gown they had laid out on the bed. Luckily, the new gowns had a second layer that covered the opening in the back—no more walking down the hall holding the gown closed over your butt.

When a nurse came in to set the IV, it really hit home that our lives were going to change radically in the next few hours. The gravity of what was happening was in full force, and we spoke very little. All I could think to tell Mona was that this was another step closer to being healed. I was convinced this was all part of God's plan from the start, yet Mona remained unconvinced, preferring to wait and see what happened, not getting too high or too low. She had been through too many ups and downs already.

Before the surgery, Dr. Wilson came in to check on her. Although he was always upbeat, he was also realistic. He would not tell Mona everything was going to be fine, because he had seen too many patients found to have inoperable cancer that had been undetected until surgery. Dr. Wilson was optimistic about Mona's chances but refused to give odds on the outcome. When asked, he would smile gently and say he would find out more when he got in there.

About an hour later, they came in to administer a sedative with some valium in the IV line. Mona's eyes started to glaze over as the drug kicked in. I worked myself over to her bed, struggling to get close. Finally, I arrived at her bedside and lowered myself to kiss her forehead. A few weeks ago, my arms would have been too weak to do this, but those trips up the ramp in the rehab unit had paid off. Mona was already out of it, and it hit me that this may be the last time I saw her as she'd always been. After the surgery, she might never be the same.

The nurses came in and started to wheel her out; Dr. Wilson was ready and the time had come. Life was at one of those forks in the road. We were either going to cure her or find out she was going to die soon. There wasn't much in between.

The hospital had given me a pager to allow me to travel around the hospital while waiting for word. Mona's parents had arrived with her sister Carla. The wait was excruciating. What would I do if she only had six months to live? How would I raise the kids and run the business without her? I thought about all the nights and weekends we had spent on call seeing animals instead of spending time as a family, all the times one of us left a birthday party because of an emergency or missed a school play due to work. Our plan had been to work hard when the kids were young so Mona could go part time and be home when the kids were teenagers. Now she might be dead before our oldest was even eleven.

Pancreatic cancer had the power to kill Mona and destroy everything we'd worked so hard to build. Professionally, we could hire another vet, but nobody had the bedside manner of Mona. The clients absolutely loved her. She also kept track of all the paperwork of a million-dollar business—taxes, payroll, staff benefits. All of those were her areas of expertise and things I had never done.

Mona also dealt with all the staff issues, and I couldn't possibly replace that. My business partner or I would have to take that over if she couldn't do it anymore, but I knew that neither of us would be any good at it.

More important than the business, how would these kids handle the death of their mother? She was the cuddler. I was more about just dealing with whatever came up and not getting emotional. I was the rational one, the fixer. The crash and the cancer had changed this some; the kids had seen me cry a lot and were getting used to my sensitive side. But they still needed their mother. Alexa and Victoria were going to be teenagers soon. They would want to go shopping, pick out clothes, and discuss boyfriends. Who would teach them how to apply make-up or talk to them about boys?

Chase would be easier for me to raise, but he still loved to lie down with his mom. He would crawl into bed before school to be with her "just for ten minutes" before we all got going in the morning. They both always loved this time. I was usually already out of bed and "getting something done," but those two would just lie together and talk before starting their day.

It terrified me to think about the kids watching their mother die. Pancreatic cancer could be so aggressive. It meant months of watching a strong, beautiful woman waste away to nothing. She might recover from the Whipple in about two weeks but then start chemotherapy or radiation and basically spend the next six months to a year visiting hospitals and going to doctors' appointments, all the while getting thinner and weaker. In the end, she would be reduced to a shell of her former self, fed through tubes and suffering from excruciating pain. We would have to keep her on morphine, which would put her in a fog, unable to interact with the people who loved her until her body finally succumbed to the cancer.

We would try to enjoy life, to do all those things that were on her bucket list, but Mona would not take much pleasure in them. She hated traveling; it was always stressful with three little kids. She wasn't one to be jumping out of airplanes or riding a bull. She probably would want to just go home and be with her family and horses. But I couldn't imagine enjoying anything knowing that you were going to die an agonizing death in a few months. Fully savoring her remaining days on earth would be impossible. A diagnosis of cancer is something that just doesn't leave your head. Every thought is interrupted by *I have cancer and I will die soon.*

Then, I thought about myself. If I lost Mona, I would have to start dating again. I did not want to be alone all my life, but bringing a new "mom" into my kids' lives was something I had never thought about. At four, eight, and ten, they were at a bad age for this. I could not think of a worse time in a person's life to watch your mother waste away and die and then your dad start to "replace" her with someone else. They would need a mother in their lives, but this would be occurring as Alexa and Victoria hit the young teen years, a time when girls can be very emotional anyway. The natural resentment the girls would feel at that age would be compounded by witnessing their dad dating. It would just be another devastating blow.

The thought of getting back into the dating scene again scared me also. How do I even ask a woman to go on a date? The women I met were clients or employees; when the date goes bad or the relationship doesn't work, how do I see them around town? What if women don't find me attractive anymore? What if I don't find any of them attractive? I would be constantly comparing them to Mona, which was unfair. What if they didn't like horses or dogs?

The horses were another dilemma. I was never a horse guy. They were fun to have around, but I didn't *love* horses. They were Mona's, and *she* loved them. I couldn't sell them because I would be selling something that was part of her. The kids could help with their care, but the horses would become a constant reminder of losing their mom.

My head swam with all the "what-ifs," but I kept repeating the words I had heard so often after the crash: *It is not your plan.* I remembered what I had learned, that we couldn't control our future. If Mona was to die in four hours, four months, or forty years was simply not up to me. If the kids had to deal with the loss of their mother, it would be that spiritual workout that would make them stronger than ever before. The loss would be terrible, but it would bring us closer together and force all of us to grow from it in some way. God had a plan, and I needed to accept that.

My tension level started to drop as I stopped trying to plan the rest of my life. Mona, the kids, and I would just have to accept what God brought and deal with it. As we faced the disease, I didn't know what the result would be, but I prayed that this was all about *curing* the cancer, not just finding it. I prayed that God's plan was to have Mona here for a long time and that was why He put us in the path of a drunk driver careening across the interstate.

I prayed that this was the case but ended it with "Thy will be done," the phrase from the Lord's Prayer that I had repeated almost every Sunday since I was three years old. After almost forty years of hearing that phrase, it finally hit home. His will *will* be done, and there is nothing I can do about it. It was what my faith had always taught me; it was only now that I accepted it was true. That acceptance brought me some peace as I walked through this, just like prayer is supposed to do. *As I walk through the valley of death, I will fear no evil.*

It was about three hours later that the pager went off. I was in the hospital cafeteria trying to eat a late breakfast, but I was really just playing with my food. I raced back up to the assigned waiting area, where we were told that Mona was in recovery, the surgery had gone well, and Dr. Wilson was coming in to speak to us shortly. The surgery "going well" only meant that there had been no major complications. It told us nothing about the cancer or whether Mona would live or die. Did she have pancreatic cancer or not? Did they get it all? Would it come back?

A half-hour never seemed so long. We sat in silence as we waited for the news. Nobody spoke. Nobody even moved.

Finally, there was a knock on the door and we all answered "Come in" in unison. Dr. Wilson entered and sat down without smiling. He began to speak in a very matter-of-fact tone, reiterating that the surgery had gone as expected. With my heart racing and sweat pouring out of me, I asked if the mass was cancer.

He replied, "Yes, it was what I had thought: a pancreatic tumor."

"Do you know the type?" I pursued, knowing that adenocarcinoma would kill Mona in a few months.

"It was a neuroendocrine tumor just like I thought it would be," Dr. Wilson answered. He was not smug or condescending, but he had been right the whole time and he knew it.

I was somewhat relieved since that meant it was not the terribly aggressive type of pancreatic cancer that is almost always deadly. However, it was still cancer. Now, life or death would be determined by whether it had spread.

Dr. Wilson continued, "It was in one lymph node." My heart sank as I learned it was not confined to the pancreas. "But we took out over forty lymph nodes, and it was only in one. I normally do not take this many nodes out, but Mona is young and I wanted to get as many as possible, just in case."

"So it has spread already," I said, my voice cracking. I knew that average life expectancy with a neuroendocrine tumor that had spread was just five years. Five years would put Alexa in the second or third year of high school, Victoria in middle school, and Chase in about fifth grade when their mother died.

Dr. Wilson continued: "Well, it was only in one node and we usually only check ten or so. We are going to have to recheck her every six months for the next five years. If it doesn't resurface after five years, it probably won't."

"And if it does?" I asked, knowing the answer.

"If it does, I go in and take it out."

"But it will just come back again."

"Yes, if we did not get it all, it will be back, but these are slow growers and we will delay it as long as possible."

"There is no other treatment she needs?"

"No, as we talked about earlier, there is no chemo or radiation that works. These grow too slowly for any of that to be effective. We just have to monitor and see if anything pops up."

Dr. Wilson sounded nonchalant about it, but I knew he wasn't. If something "popped up" in the next five years, it would mean the cancer was back. Taking out the spread would be a temporary fix until it popped up again. Eventually, it would be nonresectable and would kill Mona. If Mona was cancer-free after five years, then we could relax and say she had beaten it—though it could still come back at any time. Five years was the benchmark when it was unlikely that Mona would die from it in the next twenty years. We would not know for that long.

I really wasn't prepared for this outcome. I had prepared myself for the aggressive carcinoma and losing her quickly. I had prepared, and prayed, for this being benign and the surgery curing it. I had even prepared myself for this being the neuroendocrine tumor Dr. Wilson had expected, finding a major spread inside, and losing her in four or five years. I hadn't prepared myself for not knowing the outcome. I didn't know if I should be happy or sad. It would take years to find out, and the whole time Mona would be waiting for the ax to fall. She would have to live with the fact that her next checkup could start the clock ticking again toward her death. She would have to learn to live with the fear.

At that point, I knew our lives had changed. We'd always expected to live until well past retirement. Now we didn't know how many years we had left together, and there was a real chance Mona would die early. We had already cheated death once when Jacobs's Jeep hit ours. Could Mona do it again? Nobody could be sure.

Yet I now knew that Mona and I did not get to determine the outcome. Even with all our schooling and enough money to pay for proper medical care, we could not control this ending. We had to worry about the cancer returning, yet it might not be the cancer that determines our fate—a drunk driver heading the wrong way on an interstate could just as easily end our lives. Our fate is in God's hands, according to His plan. This realization brought me peace.

That, of course, was much easier for me to say than Mona. Our lack of control over our fate might be the truth, but the thought of cancer coming back would be Mona's cross to bear, not mine.

"You can go up to recovery. She is waking up," Dr. Wilson announced.

"Dr. Wilson, I can't thank you enough for what you did. We owe you her life."

"You were fortunate. Now she has to get through the recovery."

I noticed he used the word *fortunate*, not *lucky*. He also knew there was no such thing as luck. Dr. Wilson's faith in God led him to take Mona back in for surgery but also told him there was only so much he could do. He understood God's plan also.

Mona's mother, Anne, her sister Carla, and I left for the room. Mona's dad, Joe, wanted to wait so there were not too many visitors, something we had learned from the crash. He also couldn't face seeing his daughter in this condition yet. Joe, like the rest of us, was still struggling with the fact that Mona had cancer.

We walked in to find her heavily sedated though her breathing tube was out. We waited there for about five minutes, not wanting to wake her. We also had learned from the crash to let people sleep as long as possible after surgery because they will be in pain once they wake up. Every minute spent sleeping is one less minute in pain. It was another way the crash had prepared us for this.

Mona slowly opened her eyes and turned her head. The first thing she asked was, "Did they get it all?"

I had not prepared myself for that question, though I should have. I looked at her and could see she was in pain already. At that point, I made a stupid mistake. I did not want to stress her any further, so I lied that they were still waiting on the final lab results. Technically, this was the truth, since the pathologist needed to confirm the findings from surgery and I wanted to do some research into the prognosis of this tumor if it was in a lymph node. I justified my lie with my need to find out more before I told her that they had found it outside the pancreas. I wasn't ready to tell her the truth even though she deserved to know. I chickened out just when she needed me to be strong, just when she needed me to be honest. I failed her miserably.

Mona asked for more pain meds and Anne went to get a nurse while I held Mona's hand and told her how well she had done. The nurse quickly arrived to administer more morphine in the IV, and soon after, Mona drifted off to sleep.

Anne and I left the room. Since this was a teaching hospital with a medical library on site, I decided to go there to research the prognosis. I searched the literature and found very little information. It was almost unheard of to find this cancer before it had spread to the liver. Mona's had spread to a lymph node and was not in the liver, so the information was incomplete. This cancer was deadly in five years once in the liver and curable if removed when just in the pancreas. I just could not find anything about it being in a single node. There was no data I could find that matched Mona's situation.

I wanted to give Mona a firm set of facts, and I had none. I left the library not knowing what to tell her. I did not know what being in a lymph node really meant, though I knew the cancer had spread outside the pancreas, which meant a) it was probably elsewhere, and b) Mona was not cured. If I knew it, she would know it too. Still, I searched diligently for a way to make it not so—no matter how futile the attempt. I wanted to find something that said Mona was fully cured of cancer, including the spread to the one node, even though I knew it had escaped.

I also wondered if the delay we had imposed on this surgery in the vain hope of finding an aneurism and not a tumor had allowed the cancer just enough time to escape. What if we would have had this done a month earlier when Dr. Wilson had suggested it? We had not been ready to believe that cancer could happen in our lives; we were too healthy to contract cancer. Truly, we were too arrogant to believe that this could happen to us. We were good people, so good things should happen to us. Bad things should happen to bad people. We already had learned just how wrong we were. Being good doesn't insulate you from undergoing difficult trials. Living an honorable life doesn't save you from hardship; it just provides the support and prayers of others so you don't have to go through it alone. That support had been invaluable to us, but it hadn't changed the fact that bad things were happening in our lives.

These thoughts swirled around in my head as I went back to Mona's room, knowing she'd wake up about every hour as the morphine wore off. As expected, the pain was intense. It would increase exponentially as she waited for her next allotted dose of pain meds. Watching her obvious agony as the minutes went by and counting down to the time her pump would allow me to press the button on the morphine drip to give her some relief was heartbreaking. The drip was calculated to prevent a patient from receiving more than was allotted by the doctor, but it was not enough. By the time I could administer more, Mona would be moaning and crying from the pain. This was not right. I would never let an animal endure such torture; surely my wife deserved the same treatment. Since she needed better pain control, I rang for the nurse.

An operating nurse named Jaime entered the room, and I explained the problem. I'd soon discover Jaime was yet another angel. At that point, Mona had just received another dose and was sleeping soundly; however, knowing the intensity of the pain involved, Jaime called for the anesthesiologist. Unfortunately, he was not so quick to arrive, taking over thirty minutes. By then, Mona had been through the cycle three more times. The morphine would wear off after about five minutes, but administration was restricted to every ten minutes. Therefore, Mona would cope with pain for two minutes, followed by pure agony during the last three.

For most of us, three minutes does not seem like a long time, but in Mona's case the pain was so intense she wanted to die. Three minutes felt like a lifetime. We would count down and watch the clock until more morphine could be given, then push the magic button. Mona then would drift off to sleep for five minutes before waking up in agony again. When the anesthesiologist finally arrived, he appeared to be about sixteen years old. Just before he'd walked into the room, Mona had received a dose and drifted off again. He looked at her for two seconds and announced to Jaime she did not need anything more. Even after we explained that the morphine schedule wasn't adequate for Mona, the anesthesiologist brusquely dismissed our concerns and turned to leave.

Now Jaime and I were both pissed. I tried to grab my crutches and take off after the anesthesiologist, but Jaime beat me to it.

"I need to speak to you in the hallway," she stated. Her tone of voice left no doubt she was about to tear into this arrogant prick.

Although she shut the door, I could hear every word: "I am invoking my patient's right to adequate pain relief. Her pain is not being controlled for the ten minutes between allocated morphine doses, and it is clear that she requires more. Either give her something else or up the dose of morphine, and do it before she wakes up again!"

"She appears adequately controlled so she gets nothing more," the doctor replied coldly.

I was at the door ready to burst into the hallway when I heard our angel's voice.

"You have not evaluated this patient properly in order to see the pain she is in when the morphine wears off. You can either stay in here until then or take my word for it, but either way, she will need more. If you don't do your job here, I will be calling Dr. Wilson."

"Dr. Wilson is already in surgery."

"I will go in the surgery room myself and tell him his patient's pain is not being managed by you, and I either need him to scrub out or I need someone else to do your job. You decide."

We both knew Dr. Wilson would be on fire if this happened. He would be mad for getting interrupted during surgery, even angrier that an extra person was coming into his operating room and increasing the patient's risk of infection, and really pissed that his patient, another doctor whom he respected and regarded as a colleague, was not being treated properly. Dr. Wilson would not accept inadequate pain control, and the anesthesiologist knew it. Dr. Wilson was also much more respected in the hospital and held great power as a senior surgeon; this young doctor did not want to ignite his ire.

"Fine, I will add some ketamine and lidocaine to her drip with the morphine. She will sleep for the day."

With that, I heard him quickly turn and stomp down the hall. His pride had obviously taken a beating from Jaime, who came back in the room to update me.

"Don't worry. I heard it all," I said. "Thanks for standing up for her; she really needed someone right now."

"I have been here for twelve years—about eleven and a half longer than him—and have given birth to three kids. I know what pain is. My patients don't go through recoveries like this. We have drugs to stop it; there is just no reason not to use them."

"Thank you again. You are an angel."

Because of Jaime, two additional drugs were added to Mona's "cocktail" and she slept for the next six hours. I left to get some sleep also, while Anne stayed in the room with her daughter. The pain would come back every now and then, but Mona would push the button and drift off to sleep again.

However, every time she woke up, she would inquire about the lab results. Because she didn't want to be the bearer of bad news, Anne played dumb. I had placed my mother-in-law in a terrible position: I knew Mona wanted the truth—in fact, *deserved* the truth—but seeing her in so much pain, I just didn't have the heart to tell her. Fact was, I was avoiding it because I was too weak. God would teach me to do better.

This continued for the rest of the day as Anne and I took shifts in the room with Mona. Her dad made it up to see her briefly but had to leave. He was a tough man, but seeing his daughter in this terrible condition was incredibly hard on him. It would not help her if he started to sob. After all, he was still her dad and the rock that had always anchored her family.

The next day I awoke to my phone ringing. It was Mona. I had slept the night in a guest room that the hospital provides one floor below. I answered and asked how she was feeling. She replied flatly, "I need to talk to you."

I knew immediately she had found out; someone else had told her about the cancer spreading to a node. Immediately, I headed upstairs to her room, and as I crutched in, she refused to even look at me; she was much too hurt.

"Why did you lie to me about them finding the cancer in a lymph node?"

"You were in so much pain coming out of surgery I didn't want to tell you. I needed to find out what it meant before I did."

"Scot, we both know what it means. It has spread."

"All the literature talks about is spread to the liver, not a single lymph node. Spread to the liver is much more advanced. I could not find a case like yours. Dr. Wilson said he took out four times as many nodes as he usually does and so did not know what to make of it being in a single one. He said we just have to monitor it."

"Look, whatever happens, I need you to be completely honest with me at all times. I need to trust what you say no matter what. I can't be wondering if you are holding something back when I am going through this. I can understand you not wanting me to be stressed after surgery, but not being able to trust you is much worse. I need you now more than ever."

"I understand. It won't happen again. I promise, I will tell you the truth no matter what."

Mona had received the news of her tumor spreading from a first-year resident who had come to in to her room to check on her. I was pissed at this young student for telling her but knew that I should have never allowed it to happen. It was my fault for not being honest with Mona in the first place. Again, I had learned.

My wife began to cry. The fact that the cancer had spread was sinking in. Initially, her anger at me had distracted her; now that she knew the truth, she was forced to deal with it. I tried in vain to console her, but because she was still very angry at me, I simply held her hand as we both cried.

Finally, I spoke. "Mona, I still believe that this was the reason for the crash. I think God wanted you to find the cancer and get it out. I think He has other plans for us and that is why we didn't die that day. He is with you in this and wants you to live."

Mona nodded but wasn't convinced. She was still in a ton of pain, and the stress had worn her out emotionally. She would need some time to deal with this, and my withholding of the truth had just added to her problems. Unintentionally, I'd made things worse and had learned a valuable lesson. I vowed it would not happen again.

At this point, there was really nothing more I could do or say. Words couldn't change the fact that Mona now had to cope with cancer in her life. She was terrified.

Once again, Mona had to face the fact that life had not worked out like we'd planned.

FOR REFLECTION

Yet you do not know what tomorrow will bring. What is your life? For you are a mist that appears for a little time and then vanishes. (James 4:14)

1. How do you feel when you think about your own mortality? How do you cope with the thought of dying?

2. How can we accept God's plan when it means that we or someone we love will die?

3. There was no clear outcome with Mona's cancer surgery. Before that, Mona was always a planner and a worrier. How did this result force her to change? Do you think that was one of God's intentions?

CHAPTER 35

A Lesson in Humility

Mona spent the next two days drifting in and out of consciousness on the morphine, not really saying much. She was still in a lot of pain and nauseated from the surgery. She was not allowed to eat for another two days while her intestinal tract healed. The cancer was on her mind with every thought.

Joe and I drove home that night to check in with the kids; Mona's sister Denise was staying with them, ensuring they were going to school.

Having received a wake-up call, I decided it was time to get off the OxyContin. I'd been taking up to eighty milligrams during the day and another eighty milligrams at night "for pain" but knew that my current level of pain didn't justify such a high dosage. Oxy just made me feel good. I was using it more than I needed. I was addicted.

Like most addicts, I was functioning pretty well on that huge dose. I had even started to drive with it in my system, though not the full eighty milligrams. We had all been almost killed by an impaired driver, yet I was getting behind the wheel after taking OxyContin. I was no better than Jacobs.

It was another lesson. I could now understand how Jacobs had arrived at such a low point in his life: He had been self-medicating, too, in an attempt to kill his pain. It would be revealed at his trial that he had been sexually abused by his own brother as a small boy. This horrific crime understandably had made him terribly angry. I had struggled with hating him as a grown adult, but he'd had to deal with hating his own big brother as a child. It was no surprise his life had spiraled out of control.

He had lied to his parents and withheld the truth just like I had withheld the truth from Mona. He had started to self-medicate with drugs and alcohol just like I was self-medicating with OxyContin. We were more similar than I had ever thought. Now he was in jail for the rest of his life and I was on the same path. What if I ran into someone as I drove around on my drug of choice? I would be facing prison just like Jacobs. This had to stop.

I had heard all the stories of vets getting hooked on the pain meds that sat on the shelves of their hospital. For me, it was a slippery slope that was all too easy to slide down, especially with a DEA license that enabled me to order any drug I wanted. Drug abuse as a veterinarian will get your license to practice revoked and can lead to prison time. I could lose everything and take Mona down with me.

I already had experienced a few instances indicative of my burgeoning addiction. Once, I had forgotten my drugs at my parents' house after a visit and immediately called them in a panic because I needed another dose of my Oxy (supposedly for pain). They were two hours away, so we arranged to meet halfway at a restaurant where they handed the drugs to me in a parking lot—just like any other addict.

I had even had an embarrassing episode at my kids' school when I stopped by to drop off a backpack Victoria had forgotten. I was oblivious to the effects the drugs were having on me and believed I was "fine" to drive on the lower dose. An hour later, I got a call from a good friend and teacher at the school to alert me I'd dropped my bottle of OxyContin on the way in. It had been discovered by an elementary student on the sidewalk.

Immediately I was horrified. *What if this kid had taken a pill?* Here I was, a respected member of the community, walking and driving while on OxyContin, one of the most addicting pain meds around. I could almost hear God asking me, "You're so much better than the guy who hit you? Really?"

Now, Mona and the kids needed me. I had been the patient on the receiving end of others' care long enough. In that moment, I decided I would no longer be an addict; I would not disrespect the community that had come to our aid, nor disappoint my family after they'd struggled through so much. I had let Mona down once and she had lost trust in me. She had seen the effects of the higher doses of OxyContin and knew I was taking way too much. I would not make her lose any more respect for me. If we had to deal with cancer, my mind needed to be clear.

I stopped cold turkey and did not take my nightly dose. Within two hours, I was agitated and could not sit still. By the time three hours had passed, my legs began to kick uncontrollably. If you've ever wondered about the origin of the phrase "kicking the habit," this is where it comes from—heroin addicts. Since heroin and Oxy are both in the opioid family, they are really no different. I told myself I could just stop the drug because I was mentally stronger than other addicts who were weak. Wrong again.

The kicking got worse as I became increasingly anxious. I craved my Oxy. My leg started to throb, though I wasn't sure if this was just me *wanting* to feel the pain so I could take my drugs. This was hell. I was finding out exactly why addicts can't stop. I wasn't stronger than them; I wasn't better than them; I needed my drugs just like they did. Another lesson in humility.

Thanks, God, I needed that.

Obviously I could not stop cold turkey; I decided to start the weaning process, beginning with sixty milligrams that day. Soon the kicking stopped and I fell asleep. This would be a long journey. I learned I was not some superhero who could just get off this drug because I decided to; I was human just like everyone else.

The next day, I took only fifty milligrams, though I needed another sixty at night. My hands shook some, I was a bit agitated, and I craved more, but I stuck to it. The craving further confirmed I was an addict. All my knowledge of drugs and my iron will to do whatever was needed in my life had not protected me. I was an addict just like the guy on the street corner needing a heroin fix.

I'd needed a lesson in humility and I sure got one. God had stripped away all my pride, all the things that made me think I was better than everyone else. He had made me immobile for months, forced to urinate and defecate in my sheets like a baby and then call for a pretty twenty-something nurse to clean me up as I lay humiliated in my own mess. He had let my body become broken—wasted away to that of a prepubescent boy. When I could eat anything I wanted, He would not allow me to consume more than half a hamburger or half a slice of pizza while I recovered. He had taken me out of my work, out of the business that Mona and I had seen as ours, and showed me it could function fine without me.

God had taken me from my kids and wife, and they had done fine also. He had made me an addict just like Jacobs so I could relate to the tragic events of his life that had led to his addiction. God had made sure I understood that my "plans" were of no use and only His plan counted. I had strayed from where God wanted me to be, becoming more and more fixated on the American dream of a bigger house, a faster car, bigger and better toys—all the while spending less and less time with those who needed me most. Since I was being stupid, He was not afraid to straighten me out. The crash was His method. It was the tough love a good parent might employ when his kid is screwing up. Although it hurts, it gets the message across.

God had humbled me in every way possible, breaking me down until I'd had no choice but to listen up. He, like any good father, had done it through love and given me exactly what I needed to become the man He wanted me to be. Only now was I ready for Him to build me up again.

FOR REFLECTION

Blessed is the man who remains steadfast under trial, for when he has stood the test he will receive the crown of life, which God has promised to those who love him. Let no one say when he is tempted, "I am being tempted by God," for God cannot be tempted with evil, and he himself tempts no one. But each person is tempted when he is lured and enticed by his own desire. Then desire when it has conceived gives birth to sin, and sin when it is fully grown brings forth death. (James 1:12–15)

1. Have you or a loved one been addicted to something? How has addiction affected your life?

2. What are some addictions we face that don't involve drugs or alcohol?

3. How does faith help someone recover from addiction?

4. Though we tend to think of positive examples that inspire us, discuss some negative examples you've encountered that made you *not* want to be a certain way.

5. How does tough love make people change? Do you believe in practicing tough love?

He leads the humble in what is right, and teaches the humble his way. (Psalms 25:9)

6. Have you ever been humbled only to be rebuilt differently? Describe that experience.

CHAPTER 36

Finding Heaven

I often hear people say they were "washed in the blood of Christ." In my case, I was washed literally and figuratively. As I lay there pinned in a smashed minivan, my blood, my values, my goals, my priorities, and life as I knew it began to slip away. As I rode in the helicopter and doctors fought to save me at the hospital, my old life drained out of me. My angels replaced that blood with the blood of unknown people; countless angels who took the time to donate their blood to ultimately be given to me. Those people performed a selfless act to save someone they would never know. I have no idea who these people were but have no doubt that they were believers in a greater good, that life was not about what they could get for themselves but what they could do for others. As their blood entered my body, Jesus entered also; it was the open door through which He had been waiting to pass. I was literally being washed in His blood and would be forever changed. He was now a part of me I could not remove. I was transformed.

After completely breaking me down, He rebuilt me, bit by bit. On one level, he was rebuilding me physically: I was getting stronger and putting weight back on. My bones were healing and the pain was lessening significantly, enabling me to stop the pain meds. Even though my physical therapists had pushed me so hard I thought I'd break from the ensuing agony, I had persevered. For the first time in my life, I had proven to myself I was not the coward I had been on the playground as a child; no longer would I shrink and run away when the going got tough. I'd tested and proven my mettle—just not to anyone else. Since none of my family or friends had seen my therapy sessions, I couldn't impress them with my toughness. From their perspective, I was still a thin, frail shell of a man who relied on crutches for mobility. They did not need to know about my remarkable progress, and I made a point to avoid bragging about it (a lesson I'd learned when I wound up back in the hospital after having to be the center of attention at church). At this juncture, I knew I could handle pain. I had demonstrated to myself that I was a man.

God was also teaching me about addiction and struggle after experiencing my "perfect" Midwestern childhood, far removed from the abuse, alcoholism, drugs, and dysfunction Jacobs had endured. I would no longer dismiss those struggling with their own addictions as weak and inferior people, because I was no better. I had spent a lot of time hating Jacobs, a man whose childhood had been the polar opposite of mine, characterized by a broken home, emotional suffering, and sexual abuse. I thanked God again for another lesson. One more step in my rebuilding process.

Spiritually, I had grown immensely. I had heard His voice time and time again and now saw His works all around me. What I used to regard as fortunate coincidences, I now saw as "God moments," little events He set in motion out of His love for me. I began to notice them more and more, everywhere I went, and each time I did, it made me smile: the parking spot left open at Walmart when I was on crutches; the X-ray revealing my bone had finally healed; and the sun pouring through my bedroom window, warming my face on a cold winter day. I saw God everywhere.

Of course, it was also God who had placed us in Jacobs's path that day so we could ultimately find Mona's tumor.

The third day after her surgery, while I was still at home with the kids, Mona called with a special request.

"They are letting me eat soup today, but the soup they have here is awful. Could you bring me some when you get here? Nothing with any chunks; it has to be just soup."

This was the first step in getting her system to accept food again.

"Sure, I will be there as quick as I can."

Mona's dad and I immediately left for the hospital, stopping at the local grocery store on the way to honor my wife's request. I grabbed about twenty different varieties, along with a strainer in case of chunks. When we arrived, I got out while Joe parked the car. The nurses laughed as I made my way down the hall with the three bags of soup clanging and banging against my crutches.

"I could hear you coming all the way!" Mona exclaimed as I entered her room.

"I wasn't sure which kind you would like so I brought everything they had without chunks," I explained.

"Thank you. That was very nice."

I saw her smile for the first time in what seemed like forever.

She looked much better that day. The post-op pain had lessened, and she'd developed an appetite. Although restricted to about one and a half cans of soup a day, at least it was something. If all went well, she would be forbidden to eat anything "with chunks" for a week after surgery. In the end, she lost a total of about twenty pounds living on watery soup, and she looked emaciated. But if she dared to eat more, she'd become nauseated and want to vomit. Her system just wasn't ready for that yet.

Unlike me when I needed more calories and began eating again, Mona couldn't add ice cream to her food. After any type of pancreatic surgery, a patient cannot ingest a lot of fats. Getting calories into her system would be difficult since she had to eat relatively bland, low-fat foods. Mona would just have to slowly increase the amount and frequency of meals to provide her body with as many calories on a daily basis as possible. Ultimately, it would take her almost two months to regain the weight she had lost, though she would never again be able to eat many fatty foods without getting sick—another reminder of how her life had changed.

We were both still processing the fact that this was cancer. About a week out, as Mona was preparing to leave the hospital, we talked about it. To my surprise, she was starting to come to terms with the fact that we simply did not know how this was going to turn out.

She observed, "I thought about what you said with God wanting us to find the cancer. I think it may be best that we are not sure if it will come back. I have always been the planner and the worrier. Now I won't be able to plan for much. It will remind me of how precious life is and how easily it can be taken away. If the surgery had cured it, I would forget about living for today and just fall back into the daily grind of life. If it was more advanced, then I would just be counting the days until I die and not able to enjoy the ones I have left. I would have that constant thought of cancer in my head every minute. Maybe, for me, it is best to not be sure if it is coming back, not sure if it is cured or not. Maybe God just wants me to remember it, to never forget what He has done for me. I'm okay with that."

"I love you."

"I love you, too."

We were rebuilding the trust and love that had been waning after twelve years of marriage and the responsibilities of three kids and a business. Dealing first with our injuries and then with cancer had made us appreciate each other and our strength as a team. We could not have gotten through any of this alone. We had needed each other, as well as our family and friends. We would never devalue each other or them again.

Another building block of our lives was in place.

Though neither of us knew it at the time, as Mona and I left the hospital that day, we had found heaven—and we could only have found it after our journey through hell. As strange as it was to give up control of our lives, it had removed most of the stress. Problems with work, family, money, bills, cancer, and fear of death were all still there, but now we realized they were just little spiritual workouts put in front of us to make us better people. Though it might not be fun, we could now deal with anything we faced because we knew it was mostly out of our hands. We had been made free of worry.

Family and friends were now a priority. We would attend more family functions and let the petty little arguments and perceived slights pass. We could do this because we had learned to "forgive those who trespass against us."

Forgiving a friend, a brother, or a sister over something that was said or done, possibly decades earlier, was nothing compared to forgiving a man who had nearly killed us. Could we really hold a grudge against something that was said when we had forgiven Jacobs? Those petty little grudges we all carry just seemed stupid now.

Since the crash, we'd been given much from our community, family, and friends. Now it was our turn to start giving back. Six months after receiving a check from the Boy Scouts for a little over one hundred dollars from their pizza sales, we attended a festival in town where the scouts were selling brats and hamburgers for their own fundraiser. I ordered two brats and three burgers with sodas. The bill came to just under twenty dollars, but I handed the kid five hundred dollars and told him to keep the change. He stood there stunned as we turned and walked away; no thank-yous needed or wanted. At about ten years old, he didn't have a clue as to who we were, which was why we'd purposely approached him. We had learned it was best to help others anonymously. I had gone to church once before out of a desire to bask in everyone's attention and wound up back in the hospital for a week. I would not make that mistake again. Humility was needed to find heaven. Anything I had was ultimately given by God, not by me.

Two years later, I found out that Roger, my boss at my first job out of vet school, needed back surgery and would be unable to work for a while. I called his office and announced I would be there to help—just like my friend Mike had done for me. Although Roger's veterinary hospital was over two hours away, I was able to get there multiple times. Following Mike's example, I took no pay; I just wanted to help. Since Roger was the surgeon in his practice, he'd be forced to turn away cases requiring more advanced procedures. I told his staff to schedule as many of the tough surgeries as possible for when I was there, because Roger's patients needed fixing and his practice needed the income. His vets and staff were tired and overworked, much like ours had been in the aftermath of our accident. Having an extra hand allowed them to catch their breath. I knew this because I had been there too. I put in long days but felt great, convinced this was what God had intended: He wanted me to use the gifts He had given me to help. By paying it forward, I was finding heaven.

I also knew I needed to pay God back. While I was aware this was an impossible task, I needed to listen to Him more. Pastor Mary Ann, who had visited us so often in the hospital and had organized the meal drop-off and prayer chains for us, asked me to lead a Bible study at church. I had never even read the Bible much and had never been to a Bible study before, but now I would lead one. She thought that this one would fit me well since the study was titled "Dealing with Adversity." I had certainly done that. We formed a men's group that included five others and met regularly for the eight-week study. We would continue to meet for two more years.

All of us in the group had been through our own private hell. One man, whom I will call Neal, was recently divorced with a child a year younger than Victoria. His wife had left him for another man, and he was angry. He needed to forgive his ex-wife for the sake of his daughter but did not know how. We talked about how forgiveness was the only way to get through this, just like I had to forgive Jacobs. He was carrying the baggage of hate, but it was ultimately just weighing him down and preventing him from finding joy again. God would make him whole and rebuild him, but he needed to forgive his wife and accept her new husband. This would allow him to live without the anger he now felt and teach his daughter to forgive also. Our little group would help him through.

Another man, whom I will call Ron, was a grandfather and had been in a terrible car crash on Christmas Eve of the previous year. He had been driving with his wife during a typical Wisconsin snowstorm when a twenty-year-old woman coming the other way lost control, hitting a snowdrift and sliding sideways into his path. There was nothing he could do. He T-boned her car directly into the driver's-side door, instantly killing her. He later found out she was on her way from one job to another, having volunteered to work someone else's shift so a coworker could spend Christmas Eve with her kids. The guilt of her death had been crushing him.

We talked at length about God's plan and how Ron had not been in control of the events of that night. Only God had been. I shared with him the story of finding Mona's cancer, which demonstrated how we see just a small slice of God's plan. While I could not tell him precisely what good would emerge out of the tragedy, I did know it would make him stronger. Over the course of the two years we met, Ron lost his sales job due to a downturn in the economy. He was nowhere near ready to retire, mentally or financially. Consequently, he went back to work stocking shelves for close to minimum wage at Home Depot—a step down for him, since he'd been a top salesman in his company just a month before.

However, Ron was doing what needed to be done to support himself and his wife. I saw him frequently since I shopped there often and would talk with him briefly. Within a few months, he was put in charge of dealing with contractors, and in a few more months, he was using his sales skills to set up remodeling projects for customers. Two years later, he was offered a job selling water softeners by a company he'd worked with through his job at Home Depot. He was earning nearly the same pay as his previous sales job but without the long days of travel he'd hated. By accepting God's plan, Ron had learned humility and found peace. He had gone through his hell, just like Mona and I had, and like us, he had found his heaven.

Pete (again, not his real name) was another man in our Bible study group, a sensitive, caring man who worked with mentally disabled teens and young adults. God had truly given him a gift, as his patience was endless, yet he was hurting also. One of his students, a boy named Brandon, came from a terribly abusive home, where he'd been beaten and neglected for years. His parents simply couldn't cope with his mental and physical disabilities. Eventually, he was removed from the home and wound up at Pete's school, where they developed a very close relationship. Given his traumatic background, Pete was especially protective of this twelve-year-old.

But the boy had a heart defect that would ultimately claim his young life. He had died just over a year before our Bible group had started to meet. After participating for six months without ever mentioning his grief over Brandon, Pete finally broke down in tears as he recounted holding the boy's hand as he passed away in the hospital, his family nowhere around. He simply could not get past the injustice of this boy's life and kept Brandon's picture on his bathroom mirror, praying for him every day. Pete recounted how he'd tried to bring in some of the boy's drawings to show some of the other students in the class on the one-year anniversary of Brandon's death. However, as he turned into the school, his car slid on some ice and hit a light pole, requiring the fire department and an ambulance to extract him from his vehicle in front of all the parents and students. Peter was terribly hurt and embarrassed; for him, it was just another kick in the gut.

After discussing it for a while, I asked him what had happened to Brandon's drawings. He replied that they were gone and that he suspected they fell out when they extracted him from the car and placed him into the ambulance. He had no idea where they went.

Once I'd given it a sufficient amount of thought, I realized there was a different explanation. I asked him, "What if Brandon had put you into that pole? Maybe Brandon was telling you he was in a much better place, free from all his physical and mental disabilities and away from the abuse he had grown up with. Maybe it was Brandon who had destroyed all those drawings. Maybe he knew these were holding you back and that you had to move on."

I told him about God putting us in a crash in a similar way. I had put the anger of the collision with a drunk driver behind me, much like turning a page in a book. I knew I needed to close that terrible chapter if I wanted to start a new one, and Pete had to do the same. His collision with a pole and loss of Brandon's artwork was a message it was time to do it. Pete was stuck in a rut and refusing to move on; therefore Brandon, now Pete's angel, had sent him a clear message with this accident. Pete needed this crash and the pain of his injury to force him to write the next chapter in his life, with the understanding that the tragedy was all part of a greater plan. Pete would never find his heaven if he kept obsessing over a chapter that God had already penned. After this breakthrough, he took Brandon's picture off his bathroom mirror and left it in the woods where they used to love to walk together—a final step in closing that chapter.

Helping Pete and Bob navigate successfully through their hardships was incredibly rewarding, but I knew I was only in this Bible study because of the accident with Jacobs. Through my pastor, I'd been given the opportunity to share the lessons God had taught me and apply them in my efforts to help others. I was perfectly positioned to get involved—another step toward heaven.

When I had fully recovered, Alexa, fifteen by that time, signed up to go on a mission trip to Kentucky and asked me to accompany her. We spent a week there repairing homes and helping the local population, providing yet another lesson about how blessed I am. Both Alexa and I enjoyed it immensely and have since taken a mission trip each year. I even gave up a Canadian fishing trip to travel to an Indian reservation because Alexa wanted us to go together. How many teenage girls want to spend a week of summer vacation with their dad in New Mexico, laying shingles on roofs in the intense July heat, helping people they don't know and will never see again? I had to go with her.

Since then my second-oldest, Victoria, has joined us on a mission trip to repair hurricane damage, which she also enjoyed immensely. Chase is excited to join us when he is older. I am so proud of them all. Would we be doing this if not for the crash? Of course not. We were too busy with our own lives to bother with spending a week helping others. Another step toward heaven.

Mona gets a yearly reminder of God's will when she meets with Dr. Wilson to get rechecked for cancer. Both of us are tense for a month prior to the appointment, and the day of the test is filled with dread. If the cancer returns, we both know it will be terminal.

But we have come a long way. We have traveled through hell and come out the other side. Our relationship not only survived but emerged from the experience even stronger. Mona knows I learned my lesson and will not hide anything from her again. With that comes complete trust.

This journey shook us to the core. It forced us to become stronger and re-examine our relationships with God and each other. We would never have done that had we not been forced to do so following the crash.

A friend once asked if all the pain and agony I'd endured had really been necessary if it had been solely about finding Mona's tumor. To him, it didn't seem fair that I had to go through it because they would have found Mona's tumor anyway, given her injuries. Why did I have to get so beat up?

My response was simple. First, life isn't fair, so why would I ever expect it to be? I know better than to want "fair." Second, I love my wife and God gave me the chance to save her. It required a terrible crash and life-threatening injuries, but I, like most husbands, would gladly make this type of sacrifice if it meant saving the life of the woman I loved and the mother of my children. It was a gift from God that I could do this for them. The fact that He also allowed me to survive and remain relatively healthy when all was said and done was just another of His gifts. It showed how He acted with love, not vengeance. I thank Him every day for putting us in the path of Jacobs. Third, I needed to change and I wasn't going to do it on my own because I had no idea I needed to change anything. I thought I was doing pretty well. Fact was, I had to become a better person, and this was my path to arriving at that destination. I had to go through the hell of my injuries and convalescence if I was ever to find my heaven.

Mona and I now stand and sing in church with all our hearts, rejoicing in God. Nine times out of ten, we cry during the service. It touches our souls.

Having experienced true pain, I became a better veterinarian. I'd developed my reputation by performing very complicated surgeries, using some basic pain control. After our experience, pain control became a passion for me. My favorite is the same mixture of drugs Mona had been given after her Whipple procedure, the one our angel, Jaime, had fought so hard to make sure Mona got. Now every animal that undergoes a major procedure or is suffering in pain is automatically placed on the pain drip, even if I have to give it for free because the owner can't afford it. I am not going to let an animal lie there in pain the way Mona did.

Since I returned to work, I go back in after hours and through the night to check on animals at the hospital. If they are uncomfortable, they get more pain meds. The thought of a dog or cat sitting there in agony for hours is guaranteed to keep me awake; I might as well drive in to check on them since I will not be able to sleep anyway.

We even built a kennel inside our house so we can take animals home with us to monitor overnight. I would like to say we do this because we are such great people, but I know better than to be that arrogant. Because of my experience, I know all about pain and how it saps your will to live. We call the owners with an update before bedtime so they can go to sleep without wondering if anyone is really checking on their beloved pet. This is all part of my mission to use the gifts God has given me to be the best I can be. Anything less would be an affront to Him.

Presently, money is simply not why I do my job anymore. I know I could lose all the material things I own at any time, so I no longer worry about it. It is true that I still have to make money to support my family and my employees, but money is not my motivation for working. I work because I love it and I know I am doing what God put me here to do. I am pleasing Him by using the gifts He gave me. The fact that I get paid for it just ensures I can keep doing it. I had it backward before: I used God's gifts for me; now I use God's gifts for Him.

I am a better veterinarian, a better husband, a better father, and a better Christian. I was even asked to speak at a few legislative hearings about changing Wisconsin's ridiculously lax drunk driving laws. It will be a slow process, but change is coming. I spoke in favor of a change in the law I had proposed, that those with a suspended or revoked license cannot purchase a vehicle. It would have prevented Jacobs from buying the Jeep that nearly killed our entire family.

Ultimately, the crash saved us in countless ways. The terrible violence of that day created great peace in our lives, and with that peace, we found our heaven. Heaven is described as "a peaceful place free of earthly worries." We ask that those who have died "rest in peace," so doesn't it make sense that we will find our heaven when we find peace? Isn't that what the Buddhist monks are searching for, *nirvana*? By learning to let go of hate and forgiving immediately and unconditionally—even those who don't ask for it—we find peace. By choosing to see our struggles as a spiritual workout needed to gain strength, not an unfair burden of a vengeful God, we find peace. Haven't we then reached heaven?

We used the insurance settlement from the crash to buy a small farm. Now Mona and the kids have a place to raise her miniature horses, as well as chickens, turkeys, pigs, and goats for the fair. For us, it is truly a little slice of heaven on earth where we marvel daily at the beauty of God's creatures. My job on the farm is to manage the wildlife. My son and I spend the summers putting up duck nesting boxes and planting food plots for the deer. Chase has also developed a great love of the outdoors and wildlife, with the ability to explain how and why to manage the woods and ponds to best serve the animals that call our piece of heaven their home. I see it as my way of thanking God for allowing me to see His heaven here on earth; I will make sure his creatures are taken care of.

The crash and the cancer made me realize that heaven wasn't necessarily something you had to attain *after* death. I now believe heaven is something that is here on earth if we just open our eyes. Jesus gave us detailed instructions on how to get there, along with angels all around us to help guide the way. We just have to do all the things he instructed us to do, like "turn the other cheek" and "trust in him."

Jesus also gave us the Lord's Prayer to guide us on the path toward heaven:

Our Father, who art in heaven, hallowed be thy name.
Thy kingdom come, thy will be done
On earth as it is in heaven.
Give us this day our daily bread
And forgive us our trespasses
As we forgive those who trespass against us.
And lead us not into temptation
But deliver us from evil.

For thine is the kingdom and the power
And the glory, now and forever.
Amen.

I had repeated this prayer every week in church since I could talk but never really *got it*, never really thought about what it said. It took a trip through hell to make it clear to me. When I finally *did* understand and put it into practice, I found peace, and with peace I found heaven.

To get through it, we first had to reach out to God (hallowed be thy name).

We had to let "God's will be done on earth as it is in heaven" and accept that we did not control our fate. I had no control when a speeding Jeep crossed the median and hit us. I had no control over whether I lived or died, whether or not Dr. Lang would be there to save me, or whether I would be the one-in-one-hundred who responded to the factor VIII shot as I lay there bleeding to death. Later on, when we'd discovered Mona's cancer, even the most state-of-the-art hospitals and medicines would've been powerless to stop its spread. Only God could. His "will" would be done.

Next, we had to forgive Jacobs. When I did that, I could be forgiven for lying to Mona and becoming addicted to drugs. God had "forgiven our trespasses" as we had "forgiven those who had trespassed against us." It didn't matter whose sins were worse, or who was a "better" person—all the sins were bad, requiring forgiveness. My addiction to pain meds was no different that Jacobs's addiction to alcohol. My driving with OxyContin in my system was no better than his driving with a dozen beers. Beating the addiction was God "leading me not into temptation" and "delivering me from evil."

By finally doing what we had repeated every week in church, I had found my slice of heaven on earth. It had always been there; I just wanted to find my own path to it. I could have the career I wanted by studying hard; I could make good money and buy things to make me happy by making myself into a better vet. I had put my faith in *me*. Now I knew that that was not enough. I had to put my faith in God to work *through* me.

With the crash, I had been forced to stop relying on myself and become humble. I found that once we let go of our pride, we could see the path to the peace we'd always been seeking. The path was in the Lord's Prayer, not in my own ideas. I had been too arrogant to accept God's instruction before, so He'd given me the slap upside the head I needed to wake up from my delusion—the delusion that I could find heaven on my own, that I could make my own path. I had tried taking a shortcut to heaven because *I* knew best; *I* could do it without undertaking God's spiritual workout.

God, of course, knew better. The crash and Mona's cancer had forced us to turn off the road we'd been traveling on and forced us to contemplate what was truly important in life. Only by surviving the crash did we find the fortitude to successfully navigate through the hell of her cancer and emerge on the other side stronger than ever. *This* is where we found our heaven. Traveling through hell first had been a prerequisite; there was just no easy path.

The angels who assisted us along the way had discovered this truth also. Robert, the flight nurse, had been through the hell of war and losing a soldier because of his mistake. That day in Afghanistan had transformed him into the flight nurse who would be skilled enough to save me.

Dr. Lang had been forced to learn about dedication to others through his autistic son, and that experience had turned him into the surgeon who refused to let me die. He had also developed the necessary patience to talk calmly with upset family members and convince them of the right course.

The Amish, who had endured the hell of losing their children to a madman in Pennsylvania, had been strengthened in their faith in God and shown others, including me, the power of forgiveness.

All had discovered that there was no easy path.

Now, this all made perfect sense. Even Jesus, after He was crucified, descended into hell for three days before he ascended into heaven. I was in a coma for three days and woke to a new life—my own path to heaven. Why would I think I could find heaven without suffering as Jesus had?

The one who hadn't taken the difficult path was Jacobs, the drunk driver who was now in prison for the next forty-seven years. Rather than confronting his demons of sexual abuse, he tried to take the easy path and drink it away. In the end, it destroyed him. It would not have been easy to admit to what had happened to him, especially as a young boy, and I can't say that I would have handled it any differently, but by not using the experience to become stronger, it had made him weaker. It had broken him to the point where he'd remained a victim instead of becoming a survivor. He had gone through hell but had not come out on the other side to find his heaven. Now he would spend the rest of his life in prison; he would stay in hell.

A few years after the trial, Jacobs sent me a letter outlining how unfair Mona and I had been to him at the trial. He complained about Mona calling him a "monster" for leaving us dying in the car and for having to spend so much time in prison for a "simple drunk-driving" charge. I felt bad for him because he had still not accepted what he had done and his motivation for doing it. He still hadn't dealt with the abuse and was still playing the victim. I knew he would never turn the page on that chapter in his life. He was stuck.

A few years later, we got a letter from the prison saying Jacobs had died in prison. He was forty-five years old. He had never found heaven on earth—only hell. Maybe now he could find it, but only in death.

The growth and strength Mona and I developed is now forged within us permanently. This happens only when the changes come with great effort, when it is a trip through hell. If the path to heaven were easy, the changes we had made in our lives would be only temporary and we eventually would go back to where we were before. We would lose our heaven. God had forced us to take the right path, the long and hard one.

Mona and I recently attended a small Bible study group (something neither of us had ever even thought about doing before the crash), where the question was posed, "Who taught you the most about God in your life?"

As each participant took a turn, their answers were things you'd expect like "my dad" or "my mom" or "my pastor."

My response?

"Mike Jacobs, the drunk driver who hit us." While it may have shocked the other people in the room, it was the truth. By nearly killing my family and me, Jacobs had taught us an important lesson most of us rarely learn: how to forgive. He taught us how precious life was and how quickly it can be taken away. He taught us how to value those things that are truly important, such as family, community, purpose, and faith—not those material things we all work so hard every day to achieve. When I was in the hospital, all I wanted was to get back to my family—not my house or my cars, just my family.

Jacobs also taught me to listen for God's voice, the voice I heard in the cabin before the crash and countless times afterward, guiding me in the direction I needed to go. And he taught me to thank God for the goodness and hardship in my life. The goodness is not of my doing but His; the hardship is just another spiritual workout designed not to punish but to help me grow and become a better person. It is the next ramp I need to conquer. We all need to keep working out to stay strong. God just keeps letting us improve.

Through Jacobs, I learned that hate—like the hate he was holding on to for his brother—would destroy me just as surely as it had destroyed him. Only through forgiveness could we leave the hate behind. Dropping the baggage of hate allows us to keep moving forward to better things. You can prevent even the greatest eagle from soaring by tying a weight to its leg. Similarly, we are prevented from reaching our own soaring heights by carrying the massive weight of hatred and anger. Yet we also have the power to choose to release it through forgiveness. It is our *choice*—yes, *choice*—whether we drop it or not.

Forgiving Jacobs was not up to *him*, it was up to *me*. God gave us free will to enable us to let go of the things that are weighing us down. We just have to do it. Jesus changed the name of his disciple Simon to "Peter" when Peter decided to follow him. Likewise, we have a choice as to whether we remain a "victim" or change our name to "survivor" when we accept His will and follow Him. Peter gave up his earthly things when he decided to follow Jesus. We can also choose to give up our earthly troubles and past hurts when we choose to follow His plan, instead of our own.

Most importantly, Jacobs taught me to give up the control I had craved my entire life. My life was going to follow God's purpose for me, and there was nothing I could do to change that. I needed to stop making plans since only His mattered. I had no idea what His plan even was; therefore, I just needed to shut up and listen. Yes, it is just that simple. God had taught me to find heaven on earth, but I was just so full of myself he had to send me through hell first.

As we got into the car after the Bible study, I turned on the radio. We were still contemplating what we had discussed in our group when a country song by Montgomery Gentry started playing. I always said you could find all the philosophical enlightenment you need from the lyrics of a country song, and this one proved me right. The simple verse I heard streaming through the radio became my motto.

"If you want to hear God laugh, just tell Him your plan."
Well said.

FOR REFLECTION

Now there was a man of the Pharisees named Nicodemus, a ruler of the Jews. This man came to Jesus by night and said to him, "Rabbi, we know that you are a teacher come from God, for no one can do these signs that you do unless God is with him." Jesus answered him, "Truly, truly, I say to you, unless one is born again he cannot see the kingdom of God." Nicodemus said to him, "How can a man be born when he is old? Can he enter a second time into his mother's womb and be born?" Jesus answered, "Truly, truly, I say to you, unless one is born of water and the Spirit, he cannot enter the kingdom of God...." (John 3:1–5)

1. Think about God's works all around us. Identify the ones you appreciate, but also identify those that you perhaps overlook. How can you be more aware in daily life?

2. What does "heaven" mean to you? Is it present on earth, or can it be found only after death?

3. The Apostles' Creed says Jesus descended into hell before he rose into heaven. Is it possible for us to find heaven without going through hell?

ACKNOWLEDGMENTS

There were two people who were instrumental in getting this story told. The first was Monica Martin. Monica is an author, client, and friend. She writes a series of children's books detailing the adventures of a dog named Cheech Mageech who travels to different states teaching kids about each one. Her excitement for my story was the final push I needed to get my book out there. She was an angel placed in my office at just the right time having "just heard about" my second angel, Daria DiGiovanni.

Daria was yet another angel who became my editor and collaborator. The founder of the Writestream Radio Network, she was invaluable in putting my story into a form such that it could be told. Her editing and publishing expertise took this book from a rough draft sitting stagnant on my computer for the last few years and, in just a few months, got it ready to be shared with others. I hope there are readers out there who can see themselves in my book and take some comfort in its pages. This is possible only because Monica came into my office on that particular day and because of Daria's hard work and dedication.

Lastly, I want to thank KiCam Projects. This group is dedicated to finding stories that inspire and to making a difference in people's lives. Their dedication to their mission and their faith in my story allowed me to bring it to so many more people. Working together, we are truly changing lives. They are angels.

About the Author

Dr. Scot Hodkiewicz was a successful veterinarian living the American dream in Lake Geneva, Wisconsin, with his wife and three kids. He was king of *his* world with a thriving business, the respect of his community, and a beautiful young family. God had smiled on him.

That is, until the day they were all nearly killed by a drunk driver.

So began his journey through the hell of near death, complete with a mangled body and broken spirit. God had humbled him in order to rebuild him into the man He wanted him to be.

Today, Dr. Scot and his wife, Mona, are still practicing veterinarians who live on a three-hundred-acre farm in Wisconsin—their piece of heaven—with their three children, Alexa, Victoria, and Chase. Together, they raise miniature horses and a menagerie of other animals. When not working, Dr. Scot devotes his time as a volunteer for high school mission trips and at a local wildlife rehabilitation hospital. He also serves as a church leader. Mona volunteers at the local humane society, treating animals free of charge and finding them homes.

Dr. Scot's book, *Going Through Hell to Get to Heaven*, chronicles the family's journey from the top of the mountain to the depths of hell—one that ultimately led them to discover heaven here on earth.